Technology in Rail Transport Management

Technology in Rail Transport Management

Edited by

Prabha Shastri Ranade

2010

Icfai Books
The Icfai University Press

TECHNOLOGY IN RAIL TRANSPORT MANAGEMENT

Editor: Prabha Shastri Ranade

First Edition: 2010
Printed in India

Published by

The Icfai University Press
52, Nagarjuna Hills, Punjagutta
Hyderabad, India – 500 082
Phone: (+91) (040) 23430–368, 369, 370, 372, 373, 374
Fax: (+91) (040) 23352521, 23435386
E-mail: info@icfaibooks.com, icfaibooks@icfai.org, ssd@icfai.org

ISBN: 9788131407851

Editorial Team: Ajab Gandhi, Pooja Dave and Meenakshi Raju Ponnada
Quality Support: V Sandhya Srikanth and S Sirisha

Contents

Section II

Indian Scenario

Section III

Metro Rails in Indian Cities

Overview

Advancement in technology has made our lives more comfortable than in the past. With the increase in use of modern and novel technology, transit systems have improved. New technologies have been developed due to certain requirements of the transportation sector. A need was felt to develop mass rapid transit systems in metro cities of India to reduce the burden on normal railways as well as road transport service providers. Cities like Delhi and Kolkata were facing a situation of rising population and increasing vehicles which had led to problems like congestion and pollution. Indian Railways took an initiative towards development of urban mass transit system by starting metro rail. Countries like China, Germany, Japan, the US, the UK etc., have developed many new technologies in rail transit systems. This book "Technology in Rail Transport Management" aims to present an overview of technology used in rail transport systems all over the world.

The book is divided into three sections. Section I gives a global scenario about the use of modern technology in rail transport system. It is a collection of accounts of technology used in rail transport in countries namely, Japan, Korea, China, the UK with respect to the railways. Section II gives a picture of developments in Indian Rail Transport System. It gives an overview of the technologies used and modernization plan of Indian Railways. Section III deals with the metro rails in India. With the increasing demand of an efficient and developed urban mass transit system, metro rails have been constructed in cities like Delhi and Kolkata. New metro rails will be launched soon in Mumbai and Bangalore.

Section I: Global Overview

In the opening article titled **"Japan Celebrates the Birth of High-Speed Rail: Forty Years ago this Month, Japan Opened the World's First Dedicated High-Speed Railway, Signalling a New Start for Railways Worldwide (Shinkansen Anniversary)"**, the author *Mike Knutton* talks about the 'Tokaido Shinkansen' high speed rail in Japan. Japan has been a pioneer in rail technology. The high speed rail, started between Tokyo and Osaka in 1964, celebrated its 40th anniversary. It proved to be successful as it carried its first 100 million passengers in less than 3 years. Its speed has been increased to more than 300 km/h while the entire network covers the distance of about 2000 km. The article has been enhanced with a value addition titled **"Technology in Maglev Train"**.

The subsequent article **"Recent Experience of and Prospects for High-Speed Rail in Korea: Implications of a Transport System and Regional Development from a Global Perspective"** written by *Dong-Chun Shin,* gives an idea of high speed rail in Korea. The article describes the operations, management, maintenance, and benefits of Korea Train Express (KTX). A detailed discussion is provided on various impacts on the transportation system, such as capacity increase, cargo transport system, etc. The article highlights the lessons learned from Korean and other countries operating high speed rail.

The third article **"Fire Safety Design for Rapid Transit Systems"** written by *Siew Yee Cheong,* discusses the technology used in designing the fire safety features for the rapid transit underground stations and rail tunnels. With the increasing number of rapid transit systems being constructed, ensuring safety to the commuters and firefighters has become a matter of concern and, therefore, fire engineers are facing challenges of providing a fire safe rapid transit system design. The article deals with various fire safety requirements at stations and talks about the fire protection and fire detection systems provided in Singapore rapid transit system.

The fourth article "**On-Line High-Speed Rail Defect Detection – Phase III**" based on a study, deals with the current rail defect detection systems based on ultrasonic testing. A study was conducted by Federal Railroad Administration with the help of *Francesco Lanza di Scalea, Piervincenzo Rizzo, Stefano Coccia, Ivan Bartoli* and *Mahmood Fateh* to develop and test a rail defect detection system based on ultrasonic guided waves. The rail defect detection technique involves new concepts like using of ultrasonic waves that will travel along the train running direction, generating and detecting the ultrasonic waves in the rail using non contact means and modern signal processing algorithms. The article has been enhanced with a value addition titled "**On-Line High-Speed Rail Defect Detection – Phase I**" and "**On-Line High-Speed Rail Defect Detection – Phase II**".

The fifth article "**Protecting Passenger Transport Systems from the Threat of Terrorism**" gives a view of the response of London Tube to the attacks on 7th of July. The author *Geoff Dunmore* discusses the measures that can be taken for protection of passengers and employees of rapid transit system. Technologies can be of great help for providing safety to passengers with the help of devices such as Closed Circuit Television (CCTV) which captures the image of the by-passer. After the horrendous attacks on 7th July, London Underground authorities have taken many steps to ensure passenger safety, like increasing the number of CCTV to 12000 by 2010. These steps would, at least, help reduce casualties and trace criminals.

The sixth article "**Railroaded to Death: The China-Tibet Train**" introduces a train considered to be an engineering marvel which has created a new beginning in the world railroad history. The author *Vinay Lal* has described the China-Tibet train as well as the difficult route through which it passes. The article mentions that the train runs on a very tough terrain with 550 kms of track running on frozen earth. It is called an engineering marvel, as it runs at a very high altitude, having a destination which is the highest railway station in the world. The author concludes by raising certain questions with respect to this step initiated towards the development of Tibet. The article has been enhanced with a value addition titled "**Qinghai-Tibet Railway - An Engineering Marvel**".

Section II: Indian Scenario

The seventh article "**Railway India**" gives the profile of Indian Railways, their perspective plan and thrust areas and public-private partnership in rail projects. Indian Railways has taken an initiative towards improving the technology. IR has also formulated a plan to improve safety measures for the passengers aiming to reduce the number of accidents and chances of casualty. Indian Railways are aimed at being transformed into a modern system as per the global standards, according to the Integrated Modernization Plan (2005-10).

The next article "**Integrated Railways Modernisation Plan**" discusses the requirement of modernizing the Indian Railways. The author *R K Singh* talks about the Integrated Modernization Plan (2005-10) and other initiatives like modernizing the track structure, modern disaster management system and the bridge management system. As per the author, modernization can be done in the form of creating new assets or by using modern technologies in place of the existing ones. Financial strategy required to finance the modernization plan is also discussed in the article.

The ninth one "**Indian Railways: IT Innovations in Passenger Services**" is a case study by *Chinmoy Kumar*. It gives an idea of the various innovations implemented by Indian Railways to improve their passenger services. IR implemented computerization on a large scale all over India, which led IT to be a driving force towards better reaction to the increasing demands of passengers. Various IT projects were implemented and expanded with the active involvement of CRIS (Centre for Railway Information System). Over the years, Indian Railways have built a communication infrastructure that has helped to meet the rising requirements of passengers and opened a new opportunity for revenue generation.

The tenth article "**Safety as Key Business Theme! – Indian Railways Perspective**" is authored by *P C Sharma* and *Amitabh*. The authors highlight the efforts to improve Railways' safety performance. Indian railways have laid more stress on improving the infrastructure and rolling stock wherein new rolling stocks are being manufactured with efficient air brake system. To minimize accidents, modern technology has been implemented into the system and signaling and interlocking aids have been installed. The article has been enhanced with a value addition titled "**Railways to Modernize and Upgrade Technology**".

The eleventh article "**Radio Frequency ID in Railways (A Feasibility Study)**" is about the feasibility of the Radio Frequency Identification technology (RFID). In this article, the authors *R Senthil Kumar, I Jeyakumar, J S Bindra, D Sunil, Siddharth Kati* and *Rajesh Kumar* have presented the recent system of coach/wagon number taking and various report generation methods. The authors have studied the introduction of RFID in MG system of TPJ division of Southern Railway.

The twelfth article is "**Technology in Construction and Management of Konkan Railway**" by *Prabha Shastri Ranade*. It discusses the technologies involved in the construction of the lines of Konkan Railway. The article also discusses the safety measures employed by Konkan Railways, which include installation of inclinometers, anti collision devices and high strength steel nets. Frontline technologies were employed in the construction of bridges and tunnels. Konkan Railways has the longest tunnel and the tallest viaduct in Asia.

Section III: Metro Rails in Indian Cities

The thirteenth article "**Urban Mass Rapid Transit System: Current Status**" highlights the Mass Rapid Transit System (MRTS) which is a very important requirement in today's era of urbanization. The article explains the reason behind the need for MRTS and discusses the modern MRTS projects proposed in the cities such as Delhi, Mumbai, Kochi, Hyderabad, Goa, Chennai, Bangalore, Visakhapatnam and Kolkata. The article briefly mentions the developments in Mumbai Metro Rail Project (Phase I-A) and Delhi Metro Rail Project (Phase II).

The next article "**Interview with M D/Delhi Metro Rail Corporation**" presents the excerpts of an interview with *E Sreedharan*, Managing Director of Delhi Metro Rail Corporation (DMRC). It gives an idea of the challenges faced by the DMRC in the construction of metro rail in Delhi. The article presents Sreedharan's experiences shared in the interview. The article highlights the safety measures taken and the use of technology in Delhi Metro Rail. It is concluded with Sreedharan's views on the future of integration of Indian Railway system with Delhi Metro. The article includes a value addition titled "**Delhi Metro Moves Ahead**".

The fifteenth article "**Understanding the Metro Rail Demand**" written by *Mukti Advani* and *Geetam Tiwari*, discusses the investments made by Kolkata, Chennai and Delhi in MRTS/LRT systems. The authors in their paper, have analyzed the methodology and arguments in order to validate these systems. The paper shows the evaluation of Delhi Metro with respect to capacity, travel time and accessibility to the system. The article also explains the user's perspective of mode choice.

The sixteenth article "**Mumbai Urban Transport Project: Development and Challenges**" written by *P Nair* and *Deepak Kumar*, discusses the development and challenges of the Mumbai Railway Vikas Corporation (MRVC). MRVC, started as a separate corporation jointly by the Ministry of Railways and the Government of Maharashtra, has made considerable development in the Mumbai sub-urban railway system. The article also presents a brief picture of suburban systems of diverse metro cities of India.

The seventeenth article **"Technology in Indian Metro Rail – A Boon to Commuters"**, by *Ajab Gandhi,* gives an idea of the metros in India and the modern technologies used. The article highlights the benefits to the commuters on the adoption of new technologies. It also gives a brief account of the role of various companies in providing resources and technological innovations in successful completion of Delhi Metro Project. Technological aspects of Kolkata Metro, the first metro in India, are also covered in the article.

The last article "Sky Bus: A Technological Innovation of India" written by *Ajab Gandhi* introduces 'Sky Bus' which is an excellent mode inter connecting urban areas and the benefits that can be availed by the commuters. It also highlights various alternatives to Sky Bus. During the trial run of Sky Bus due to occurrence of an accident the project got delayed. The article describes the cause of the accident and the various steps that need to be adhered. There is a brief account on recent updates on the Goa project as well as other proposed projects of Sky Bus.

Section I

Global Overview

1

Japan Celebrates the Birth of High-Speed Rail

Forty Years ago this Month, Japan Opened the World's First Dedicated High-Speed Railway, Signalling a New Start for Railways Worldwide (Shinkansen Anniversary)

Mike Knutton

This article summarizes the events of Tokaido Shinkansen, which is a high-speed railway in Japan since 40 years, discussing the future prospects. Comparing today's standards forty years on, speed had increased from the Tokaido's initial 200 km/h to more than 300 km/h, where the Shinkansen network has reached to total of 2000 km now, which includes cities like France, Germany, Spain, Belgium, Italy, Britain, Korea, Taiwan – followed with Netherlands this year. It focuses on Tokaido Shinkansen, how it became the considerable alternative under the government's major decisions for signaling a new start for railways worldwide.

Source: International Railway Journal, October 2004.

Japan did much more than encourage the growth of its own economy when it opened the 515 km standard-gauge Tokaido Shinkansen high-speed railway between Tokyo and Osaka just prior to the 18th Olympic Games in Tokyo in October 1964.

It opened a completely new era in transport with a radically different railway, and in so doing, performed an invaluable service to the entire railway world by triggering a global boom in high-speed rail and injecting new life and restoring self-respect to an industry in decline. And all, in the money of the day, at a cost of about $US1 billion or 377 (pounds sterling) million!

Forty years on, speeds have increased from the Tokaido's initial 200 km/h to more than 300 km/h, the Shinkansen network now totals about 2000 km, and the high-speed rail map of the world now also includes France, Germany, Spain, Belgium, Italy, Britain, and Korea, with Taiwan to follow in 2005 and the Netherlands in 2007.

"The new line was a response to serious and accelerating limitations in transport capacity along the main arterial corridor between Tokyo and Osaka. The situation arose as a consequence of the fact that the Tokaido corridor was home to about 40% of Japan's population, nearly 70% of its industrial output, and 60% of national income.

Three possibilities existed: adding two tracks to the existing Tokaido line, building a new but compatible line that could connect with existing tracks at major stations, or building a totally-separate and independent line. Perhaps the most significant decision of all was the choice of standard gauge instead of the 1067 mm gauge of the rest of the 20,500 km Japanese National Railway (JNR) network.

The choice freed engineers from the shackles of compatibility with existing equipment and allowed them, with free rein in designing track, cars, power supply, communications and control systems, to develop what was at the time a radically different kind of railway. Oddly enough, high speeds were not essential to solve the saturation problems on the existing line but the added costs of high-speed design were so small once the concept of an independent line had been selected that it was decided to take the extra step. The Japanese government approved the project in 1958 and construction began the following year. The line was designed for emu operation and electrified at 25 kV ac. It was originally intended to operate passenger trains during the day and 130 km/h container freight trains at night, but the freight aspect never materialized, probably because track maintenance had to be conducted at night. Freight train journey time would have been 5 h 30 min between Tokyo and Osaka, compared with 3 h for a passenger train making two stops, and 4 h for a train stopping at all 10 intermediate stations.

Built to avoid level crossings, the double-track Tokaido Shinkansen has 93 km of concrete and steel elevated structures, 19 km of bridges, and 65 km of tunnels, the longest being 7.8 km. Raised embankments were also used liberally to obviate the need for level crossings. The maximum gradient is 1.5% except for some short sections of less than 1 km at 2%. Minimum curve radius away from station areas is 2500 m. The track was laid with long-welded, high-carbon 53 kg/m rail, for the most part on pre-stressed concrete sleepers, and fastened with double elastic clips bolted to the sleepers. A rubber pad provided insulation between rail and sleeper.

Insulated expansion joints, consisting of four parts for each rail were specially designed for the line. JNR also designed a movable-nose turnout for use on the frog portion of switches, permitting high-speed operation with little or no impact on the train.

Tunnel cross-sections are semi-circular above the line of maximum width 2.3 m above rail level, and the radius of the semicircle is 4.8 m. This provides 4.2 m between track centres. A 700 mm concrete lining is standard while tunnel tracks rest on concrete sleepers and ballast.

JNR selected 25 kV 60 Hz power for the new line instead of the 1.5 kV de supply on the existing line. JNR first experimented with ac power at 20 kV in 1956-57 and subsequently used it at both 50 and 60 Hz. The new line served areas of both 50 and 60 Hz commercial power with the dividing line at the Fuji river, site of the longest Tokaido bridge.

Dual frequency equipment was considered but rejected in favour of 60 Hz throughout, with rotary frequency converters installed at Yokohama and Odawara.

The 25 substations along the line are controlled from Tokyo using transistorized control equipment developed by the Japanese Railway Technical Research Institute. Scott-connection transformers rated at 30,000 kVA reduce the voltage from 70 kV to the 25 kV of the Tokaido catenary.

Various types of catenaries – normal compound, continuous mesh, modified Y-type, and composite – were tested at speed up to 175 km/h and the composite compound catenary, with composite wire adjusters between the messenger wire and the auxiliary messenger wire was adopted, as the tests showed significantly smaller discontact ratios for this type.

The contact wire is at a standard height of 5 m with a 2% tolerance. Since the line was designed for electric operation from the start and has no level crossings, the variable wire height between 4.5 m and 5.4 m on the old line could be avoided. This allowed a smaller pantograph to be used.

The cab signal-based – Automatic Train Control (ATC) system incorporated automatic braking in response to coded signal indications. The driver was responsible only for bringing the train to a final stop at stations, maintaining speeds where restrictions did not correspond to ATC steps, and for response to hazards against which the signal system did not afford protection.

Acceleration was automatic with the driver simply operating the handle of the master controller. When the train reached the desired speed, the driver changed the setting from powered operation to coasting and alternated between these to maintain speed.

The ATC system provided six speed steps – 210, 160, 110, 70, and 30 km/h, and full stop. The dynamic brake was programmed to decelerate trains at 1.65 km/h/s above 160 km/h, 1.79 km/h/s between 160 and 110 km/h, and 2.23 km/h/s at lower speeds. Air brakes took over normal braking action at speeds below 50 km/h. Under normal braking, a train could decelerate from 210 to 160 km/h within 1600 m and another 1800 m for it to come to a halt.

Shinkansen services started on October 1, 1964 at a frequency of two trains each hour. The first-class fare between Tokyo and Osaka was $US6.03 and the second-class fare $US3.28. Services were provided by a fleet of 360 Japanese-built Series 0 railcars, dubbed bullet trains because the noses of the driving cars resembled bullets and were reportedly based on the DC-8 airliner, which represented the state-of-the-art of international air travel at the time.

All cars were powered with 185 kW traction motors driving each axle and operated in 12-car sets of six permanently-coupled pairs. During pre-service tests, the trains were successfully run at speeds up to 257.5 km/h. The only discomfort to passengers occurred with pressure problems on entering and leaving tunnels, which was ultimately solved by air-sealing the cars. Inside doors are airtight and air-conditioning intakes and exhausts are shut when trains pass an electronic coil at the entrance to each tunnel.

Thanks to the choice of standard gauge for the high-speed line, the 25 m-long car bodies could be built 400 mm wider than conventional trains operating on the 1067 mm-gauge network. The gauge was considered necessary for stability at high speed and it also permitted complete modernization without any limitations to fit existing equipment.

Tests in 1961 indicated that a significant weight saving would result without affecting strength if the cars were built without full-length centre sills. This was adopted. Another idea using X-form side posts for added strength and thinner outer plates and floor plates was not adopted because the weight savings did not justify the added complexity and cost.

Each car is 3.38 m wide and 3.975 m high. The 2.5 m wheelbase bogies had rolled monoblock wheels, disc brakes, and air springs with leveling valves for bolster springs. One car of each two-car pair carried a 1810 kVA main transformer and a 1500 kW bridge-connection silicon rectifier. These provided current for eight 415 V permanently connected traction motors. The eight motors of each two-car pair were in parallel groups, each with four motors in series.

A standard consist comprised two first-class cars with two-abreast reclining seats on each side of a centre aisle for 132 passengers, and eight second-class cars in a 3+2 configuration seating 855 passengers. Two cars had buffet sections. Five companies each built 72 cars. They were: Hitachi, Kawasaki, Kinki Sharyo, Kisha Seizo, and Nippon Sharyo.

Network Development

Boosted by the Tokyo Olympics, the Tokaido Shinkansen was an immediate success and notched up its first 100 million passengers in less than three years by July 13, 1967. As the network expanded, the one-billionth passenger was carried in 1976.

Train speeds on the Tokaido line have risen from an initial 200 km/h to 270 km/h today and are probably stuck at that level because of infrastructure constraints, while newer lines operate at up to 300 km/h. Many further models of train, each with its own individual appearance (Series 100, 200, 300, 300X, 400, 500, 700, 700T, 800, E1, E2, E3, and E4), have been developed. Technical advances have been legion and the newest version, the 300 km/h N700, will be the first Shinkansen train with active tilting and an aero double-wing nose shape when it starts commercial operation in 2007 after two years of testing from next year (IRJ September p70).

Technological improvements in traction systems have seen gradual increases in the top speed of trains, while factors such as power consumption and noise and vibration suppression have improved markedly in response to increasing environmental concerns in recent years.

Body construction has evolved from steel to double-skin aluminium alloy hollow extrusions, and traction from de series motors to three-phase ac cage asynchronous motors with three-level PWM converters and IGBT semiconductors.

Brake control has advanced from a power-generating brake on the Series 0 and 100 trains to ac regenerative brakes on the Series 700. The earliest bogies were bolster type, which gave way to bolsterless bogies on the Series 300 and the addition of semi-active suspension on the Series 700.

Train weights have come down from 925 tonnes for Series 0 and 100 trains to 711 tonnes, including 74 tonnes for electrical equipment, for Series 300 trains, and 708 tonnes, including 62 tonnes for electrical equipment, for Series 700 trains.

The first line extension from Osaka to Fuknoka – the Sanyo Shinkansen – on the island of Kyushu was completed in 1975. There is also an isolated Shinkansen line section on the island between Yatsushiro and Kagoshima that opened in March 2004, though a connection between the two is now under construction.

The main high-speed line in the east of the country is the Tohoku Shinkansen which now runs from Tokyo to Hachinohe and opened as far as Morioka in 1981. From this line, the Joetsu line branches to Niigata (opened in 1982) and the Hokuriku line to Nagano, which opened in 1998. Two further lines, known as mini-Shinkansen, to Akita and Shinjo, have been created by upgrading existing sections of line and converting them to standard gauge. The Shinjo line opened to Yamagata in 1992 and Shinjo in 1999, while the Akita line opened in 1997.

An extension of the Tohoku line from Hachinohe to Shin-Aomori is under construction as a precursor to a line serving Sapporo on the northern island of Hokkaido via the Seikan undersea tunnel. The Hokuriku line is being extended towards Kanazawa.

JNR operated 60 trains a day on the Tokaido Shinkansen when it opened in 1964. This has increased almost fivefold to nearly 290 trains a day today. The line now carries more than 120 million passengers a year – with legendary safety and punctuality.

Just as the Tokaido Shinkansen marked a step change in the quality of public transport as a response to capacity and lifestyle challenges – so, tomorrow, the Chuo Shinkansen could present the next advance. This 500 km line would also link Tokyo, Nagoya, and Osaka with magnetically-levitated trains operating at speeds in excess of 500 km/h. It would provide an alternative to the Tokaido line in case of accidents or natural disasters and is also seen as a tool to correct the overcentralisation of people, power, and resources in Tokyo, and to encourage more balanced national land development.

A test section, on which maglev trains have exceeded 500 km/h, may become part of the new line. It is a national project in which the government will take the major decisions about – if and when the line will be built. Meanwhile, the Tokaido Shinkansen will continue to be the mode of choice for travel in the Tokyo-Osaka corridor.

Commemorative Conference

Two Japanese railways, JR Central and JR West, will host an international high-speed railway conference to commemorate the 40th anniversary of the Tokaido Shinkansen at Tokyo's Imperial Hotel on November 9.

Held under the auspices of Japan's ministries of Foreign Affairs and Land, Infrastructure and Transport, it is the fourth in a series of high-speed rail conferences. Under the theme: "For The Future of the Earth – What can be Accomplished by High-Speed Railways?", it will concentrate on environmental issues and further development of the mode.

Keynote speaker at the environmental session will be Mr. Lester Brown, president of the Earth Policy Institute, the United States, who will also participate in the special session that follows. A panel discussion will also be held on environmental and energy issues.

A second panel discussion involving top executives from railways in France, Germany, Britain, and the United States as well as JR Central and JR West will examine the future role of high-speed railways in global environmental issues. The mission of high-speed railways will be explored through debate on its environmental and energy superiority, railway operators' initiatives for better utilization, and the need for transport policies.

On the following day, delegates will have the opportunity to make a technical visit either to the JR Central research and development complex, which opened in Nagoya in 2002, or JR West's Shin-Osaka General Control Centre, which controls the railway's conventional lines including commuter and limited express services.

(Mike Knutton is a Senior Editorial Consultant with the International Railway Journal and can be reached at mk@railjournal.com).

Technology in Maglev Train

Few Countries developed high-speed trains using electromagnets, which came to be known as Maglev Trains. Maglev is short form of Magnetic Levitation, a technology used to run these trains wherein powerful magnets are used that allow the train to float along its guide way without touching it, which reduces friction and increases speed. Thus it is a replacement of old steel wheel and track trains. The idea of magnetic levitation was conceived and worked on for 20 years by a French-born American, Emile Bachelet in the 1890s.

There are two types of Maglev technology namely Electromagnetic Suspension (EMS) and Electrodynamic Suspension (EDS). The difference between Maglev trains and the conventional trains is that engines are not those typically used in the conventional trains. Engines of Maglev train do not use fossil fuels as used in the conventional trains. The electrified coils in the guide way walls form a magnetic field which jointly with the track helps to drive the engine of the Maglev train. The track known as guide way consist of magnetized coil which repels the large guidance magnets attached underneath the train, enabling the train to float on air between 1 and 10 cms above the track. As the train rises up, electric current is supplied to the electrified coils within the walls of the guide way thereby creating an exceptional system of magnetic fields that pull and push the train. Also to change the polarity of the magnetized coils, power supplied to the electrified coils is continuously fluctuated. As the Maglev trains glide over the track, it eliminates friction and thus allows these trains to travel at a pace of above 310 mph, which is double the speed of the Amtrak's fastest train. As Maglev trains have no wheels, it is almost impossible for these trains to derail. In case of Electrodynamic Suspension, the train is driven by the repulsive force between the magnetic fields exerted by the rail as well as the train.

Shanghai Maglev train is the first commercial Maglev line in the world. The train can cover 220 mph in 2 minutes. Also countries like Germany and Japan have developed Maglev train technology. In case of Japanese Maglev trains, superconducting electromagnets are used that can conduct electricity even when the power supply is not present. Thus Japanese system helps them save energy by freezing the coils. Also in the EDS system the train has to roll on rubber tyres until it reaches a speed of 62 mph when it starts floating. But these rubber tyres are an advantage in case of power failure. In Germany, a monorail system uses the Maglev technology known as Transrapid. The Transrapid system does not roll on wheels and has an emergency backup of battery power supply in case of power supply failure. Thus Maglev has been one of the innovative technologies used in rail transport.

(Compiled by Pooja Dave, Research Associate, Icfai Business School Research Centre, Ahmedabad.)

2

Recent Experience of and Prospects for High-Speed Rail in Korea: Implications of a Transport System and Regional Development from a Global Perspective[1]

Dong-Chun Shin

This paper summarizes the comparison of high-speed rail experiences with that of other states in relation with the future of the rail transport system in Korea as Korean trains express (KTX) dependent on foreign aids, where new technological changes in the transport system had revised the railways transport system. But its implementation is a major hurdle for them as it provides congestion in the technique until it is completed. It improves the scenario of accessibility and connectivity with high-speed. Moreover, this article also focuses on conflicts of interest and differences of opinion between central and local governments on projects of surface station and underground station.

Source: http://www-iurd.ced.berkeley.edu, IURD Working Paper 2005-02. Berkeley: Institute of Urban and Regional Development, University of California.

I. Introduction

Korea[2] inaugurated KTX (Korea Train Express) services on the Seoul-Busan and Seoul-Mokpo lines on April 1, 2004, becoming the fifth country to run high-speed rail (HSR), following Japan, France, Germany and Spain.

I.1. Background and History

The concept of KTX grew from the recognition that chronic bottlenecks on the country's highways and railways, particularly on the Seoul-Busan corridor, not only caused traffic congestion but weakened the nation competitively. The Korean Government also hoped that HSR would contribute to a balanced regional development by somewhat mitigating the over-concentration of the nation's functions in the Metropolitan Capital Seoul Region (MCSR).

Preliminary feasibility studies, sponsored by the International Bank for Reconstruction and Development (IBRD), were undertaken in 1973-74 and continued with follow-up feasibility studies from 1978-1981. The basic business plan and route design for the Seoul-Busan line was unveiled in 1990. According to the business plan, the new line would be exclusively used for passenger services and the conventional lines mainly for cargo transport. In the early 1990s, a special task force was established in the Ministry of Construction and Transport (MOCT) to advance this national infrastructure project in cooperation and coordination with other Government ministries. In addition, the Korean High-Speed Rail Construction Corporation was formed under MOCT to construct new lines and obtain vehicles.

A modification to the basic business plan was made in 1998, reflecting changing economic and social environments, including escalating construction costs during a financially difficult period[3] and a regional conflict between the southeast and southwest regions. In accordance with the modified plan, a new KTX line from Seoul to Daegu would be completed, and the Daegu-Busan sector would be electrified by 2004 (the first phase). KTX would also operate on the electrified Seoul-Mokpo line by 2004. The remaining work on the new Daegu-Busan line would be finished by 2010 (the second phase).

I.2. Costs and Finance

Costs were estimated to be 12 trillion Won (US$11 billion)[4] by the time the first phase was completed in 2004, and 20 trillion Won (US$18.2 billion) by completion of the second phase (2010). Actual costs greatly exceeded the original estimate.

Korea mobilized diverse financial resources to build its HSR system: 35% of funds came from the government budget, 10% from loans guaranteed by the government, and 55% from loans from domestic and foreign financial institutions. The loans would be repaid by KTX operating revenues in the coming years.

I.3. High-Speed Rail Overview

I.3.1. Benefits of High-Speed Rail

HSR is typically defined as heavy rail public transit (or transport) with speeds between 200 kmh (125 mph) and 300 kmh (187 mph).[5] It is widely accepted that high-speed rail confers many benefits. Figures shown below are drawn from the actual experiences of France and Japan. First and foremost, high-speed rail provides large transport capacity with high-speed. In Korea's case, HSR is nearly four times more efficient than highway travel. Comparing the three principal alternatives for increasing transit capacity on the Seoul-Busan corridor, HSR was deemed best in terms of transport efficiency.

Comparison of Alternatives for Capacity Increase on the Seoul-Busan Corridor (Ministry of Construction and Transport, Korea)

	High-Speed Rail (A)	Highway (B)	Double-Track Rail (C)	A/B	A/C
Construction costs	0.382 bil. Won	262	250	1.46	1.53
Transport capacity	520,000 passengers per day	25	27.5	2.08	1.89
Travel time	1 hour 56 min.	5 hours 20 min.	3 hours 50 min.	△ 27	△ 1.98
*Transport efficiency	3.93	1	1.60	-	-

*Transport Efficiency: Transport Capacity/Travel Time x Construction Costs.

HSR usually connects one city center to another, providing more convenience for travelers compared to airports, which are normally located on the outskirts of a city. The system, which relies on electricity, consumes less energy than the other alternatives (only 19% of the energy used by cars and aircraft). It also requires less land (29% of the land needed for a four-lane highway). It emits fewer pollutants like CO_2 and SO_2 (16%–18% of that from cars and aircraft). Moreover, HSR has an excellent record for safety and punctuality. It provides comfortable rides with less fatigue for passengers compared to other transportation modes. Finally, the introduction of HSR into a country, facilitates the development of related technologies and industries, such as civil engineering, vehicle manufacture, industrial materials, and design. According to a survey, Japanese travelers take the Shinkansen mainly because of high-speed, comfort, and punctuality of operation.[6]

I.3.2. Global High-Speed Rail Systems in Service and in Progress

With the advent of high-speed rail systems across the world during the last four decades, we seem to be witnessing a renaissance of the railway era that began in the late 19th and early 20th centuries. Among the most distinguished high-speed rail systems presently in service is Japan's Shinkansen (sometimes called a 'bullet train,' its literal translation means 'new trunk line'), which was completed just before the Tokyo Summer Olympics in 1964. It currently maintains an extensive network of about 2,000 kilometers in a country with a population of 130 million. The Shinkansen has three classes of compartments: Nozomi (speed of hope), Hikari (speed of light), and Kotama (speed of sound). France's TGV (Train à Grand Vitesse) was launched between Paris and Lyon in 1981. It now has four lines (Northeast, North, Atlantic, and Alps) covering 1,500 kilometers. Germany's ICE (Inter City Express) began operation in 1988. It now has a network of 427 kilometers, linking Hanover and Würtzburg, and Manheim and Stuttgart. Spain's AVE was put into service in 1992 before the Barcelona Summer Olympics took place and now runs 417 kilometers between Madrid and Seville. Apart from the traditional high-speed rail systems mentioned above, there is a maglev (magnetic levitation) system that runs a short distance of 30 kilometers between downtown Shanghai and Pudong Airport in eight minutes. The system has been in service since 2003. In the United States, several states have been preparing for the construction of high-speed rail. The state of California has already set up business plans to build a 700-mile network between San Diego and Sacramento that could transport up to 68 million passengers per year by 2020, and involves an investment of US$35 billion.[7] The proposed system stretches from San Francisco, Oakland, and Sacramento in the north to Los Angeles and San Diego in the south. With high-speed trains operating at speeds up to 220 mph, the express travel time from downtown San Francisco to Los Angeles would be just under 2½ hours. The system's design would enable intercity travelers (taking trips between metropolitan regions) and long-distance commuters to connect with existing rail,

Japan's Shinkansen

France's TGV

air, and highway systems.[8] A bond measure to mobilize financial resources necessary for construction will be decided by a state referendum in 2006.

Along the Washington, DC–New York corridor, the Acela Project introduced a faster form of rail transit. The state of Florida, too, has concrete plans to build high-speed rail between Orlando and Miami.[9] Many recent studies conclude that US cities will see multiple economic, social, and environmental benefits from rail transit (including conventional heavy rail, light rail, metro, and high-speed rail).[10]

II. KTX Operation

II.1. KTX Vehicles

The vehicles used for Korea's high-speed rail system were imported by Alstom (the French company that manufactured TGV vehicles) or manufactured in Korea under license by Alstom. In all, 12 vehicles were imported from the French manufacturer, and 46 vehicles were produced in Korean plants. The train's length measures 388 meters, with 20 fixed compartments and a total of 935 seats—127 first-class seats configured three to a row, and 808 economy-class seats configured four to a row. The train has a traction power of 13,560 kw (18,200 HP) and reaches its maximum cruising speed of 300 kmh (185 mph) in 6 minutes, 8 seconds.

II.2. KTX Lines

Because Korean topography is mountainous, many KTX routes pass through tunnels (46%) or over bridges (26%). The Seoul-Busan line stretches 412 kilometers and passes through 9 stations: Seoul, Yongsan, Gwangmyung, Choanasan, Daejon, Dongdaegu, Milyang, Gupo, and Busan. Three of the stations are located in the Seoul metropolitan area—Seoul, Yongsan, and Gwangmyung. The average distance between stations is 58.9 kilometers.

The Seoul-Mokpo line runs 407 kilometers and also has 9 stations—the same stations on the Seoul-Busan line from Seoul to Daejon, plus Seodaejon, Iksan, Songjongri, Gwangju, and Mokpo. The average distance between stations on this line is 58.1 kilometers.

KTX Network

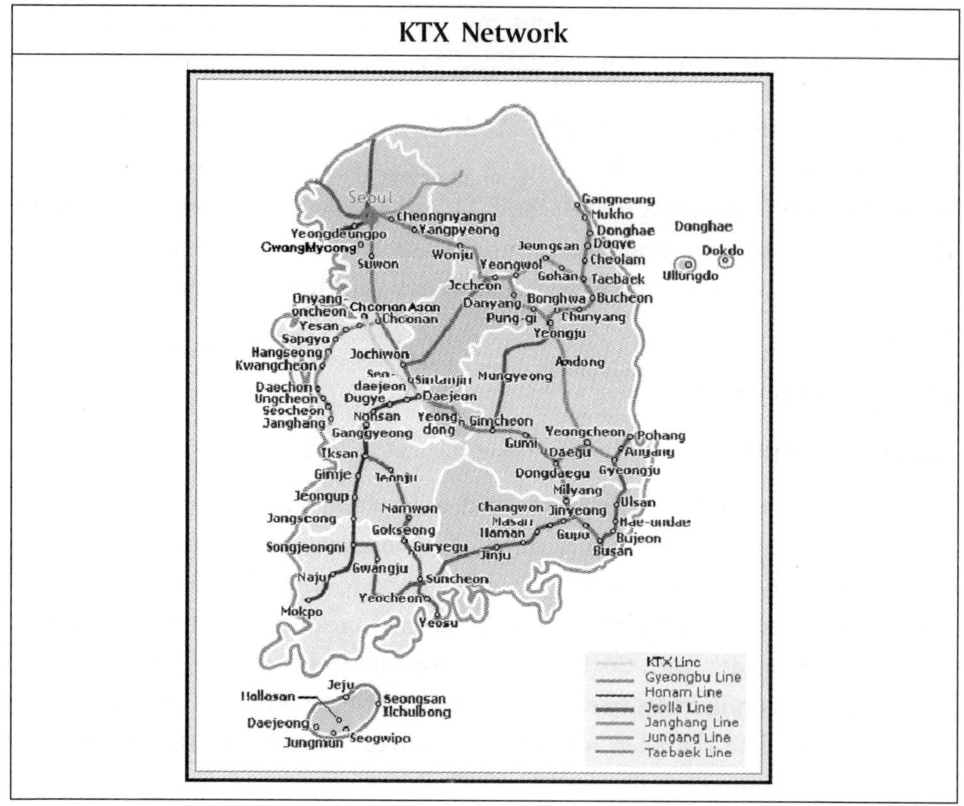

II.3. Operation

II.3.1. Running Times, Fares, and Schedules

On the Seoul-Busan line, going from Seoul to Dongdaegu (222 kilometers) takes 1 hour and 40 minutes (down from 3h:3min) and costs 34,900 Won (US $31.70). Traveling from Seoul to Busan (412 kilometers) takes 2 hours and 40 minutes (down from 4h:10min) at a cost of 45,000 Won (US $40.90). On the Seoul-Mokpo line, the trip from Seoul to Gwangju (352 kilometers) takes 2 hours and 38 minutes (down from 3h:52min) and costs 36,000 Won; the trip from Seoul to Mokpo (407 kilometers) takes 2 hours and 58 minutes (down from 4h:40min) at a cost of 41,400 Won. The average KTX fare is 1.3 times that of conventional express trains. Ninety-six KTX trains depart from and arrive at Seoul Station. Due to lesser travel demand elsewhere, fewer trains stop at the other stations—87 at Daejon, 80 at Dongdaegu, 64 at Busan, 16 at Gwangju, and 14 at Mokpo.

KTX: Distance and Time

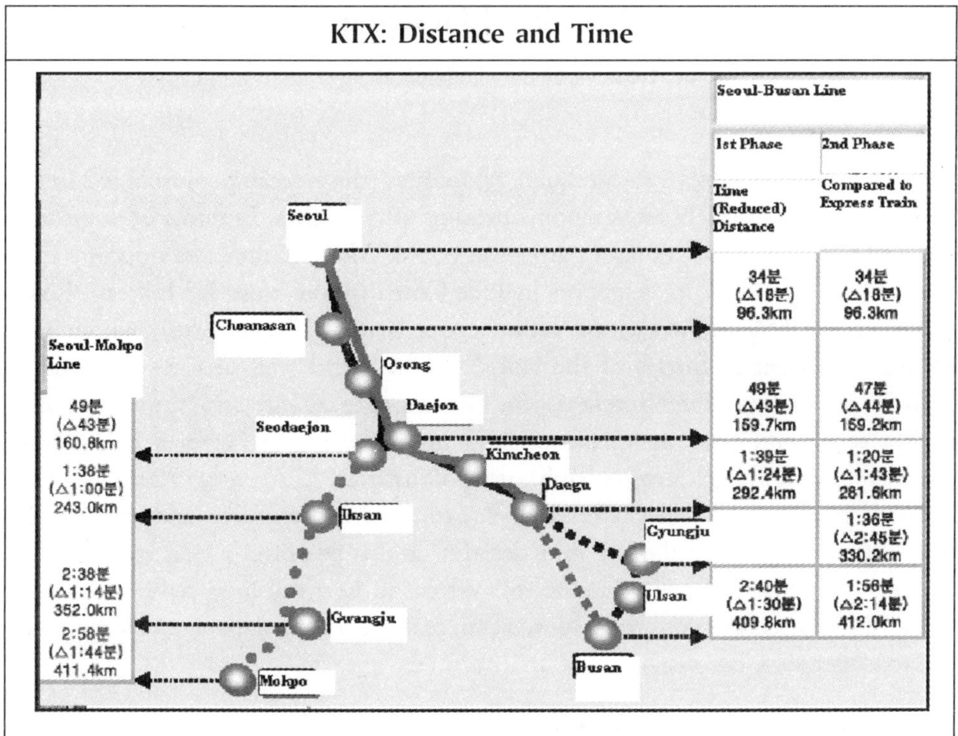

II.3.2. Management and Maintenance of KTX

In 2003, the National Assembly passed a law, as part of the railway reform package that had been pushed by the government since the early 1990s. Following the example set by most other rail-running countries of the world,[11] the law aimed to separate operation and maintenance of Korea's railways, as well as increase efficiency and secure accountability in management. The construction of KTX lines was undertaken by the Korea High-Speed Rail Construction Corporation, and conventional railways were managed and maintained by the Korea National Railway Administration.

Under the new law, KORAIL—a government agency slated for semi-privatization in 2005 in accordance with the legislature mentioned above—became responsible for the management and operation of KTX and conventional railways, while KR (Korea Rail Network Authority), which is also a semi-privatized entity, undertook the construction and maintenance of KTX and conventional rail facilities.

III. Transportation and Regional Development in Korea

III.1. Transport Condition

III.1.1. General

The nation encompasses 98,480 square kilometers (the Korean peninsula is 219,020 sq. km.), and in 2003, boasted a population of 48.5 million. In terms of population density, Korea currently ranks 11th in the world. Mountainous areas occupy more than 70% of the land. Its neighbors include China (population: 1.3 billion), Russia (population: 150 million), and Japan (population: 130 million), which rank among the larger countries of the world. Korea could well become a center for logistics, connecting huge markets, if it can improve its infrastructure—including higher-capacity ports and airports—and management to better accommodate passengers and freight from neighboring countries. Currently, Korea's railway network extends 3,125 kilometers and, due to rapid motorization and urbanization across the country over the last four decades, it also possesses a relatively extensive highway network of 86,900 kilometers. While no new rail lines have been added since 1945 (when the country achieved independence from Japanese colonial rule), the road network has expanded at an enormous rate.[12]

III.1.2. Two Main Corridors

Korea has two main transport corridors and much of the country's development has occurred along them. The Seoul-Busan corridor runs southeast from Seoul. Over 70% of the population resides along the corridor, and over 70% of the nation's GDP is produced along it. In addition, about two-thirds of passenger trips and 70% of all cargo trips originate there, since most of the nation's industrialization and urbanization has been concentrated along this axis. The other corridor, Seoul-Mokpo, runs southwest from Seoul. More farming areas lie along this route and, hence, lighter travel-demand.

III.1.3. Road-Oriented Transport System

In terms of total passenger transport, roads accommodate 55.9%, railway 20.6%, subway 17.4%, air 5.6%, and maritime 0.4%. As a percentage of total cargo transport (in tons), roads carry 70.7% of cargo transport, maritime 21.8%, railway 7.4%, and air 0.1%. The road-oriented transport system of the country has brought about some negative effects. For example, chronic roadway congestion has resulted in high logistics costs (16% of GDP compared to 10.7% in the US),[13] a high ratio of traffic accidents (250,000 fatalities of persons per year, or 0.52%

of the total population), and higher energy consumption (77.6% of total transport sector energy use), in addition to air pollution, noise, and other costs. In addition, a US report has suggested that urban pollution causing ozone-layer depletion is closely linked to higher death rates in cities and metropolitan areas.[14]

III.2. Regional Development

III.2.1. Over-Concentration in Metropolitan Capital Seoul Region

The Metropolitan Capital Seoul Region (MCSR)—Seoul, Incheon City, and Gyunggi Province—comprises only 12% of South Korea in terms of its physical size. However, the region's population is about 22 million, or 45.3% of the total population in 2002,[15] making it the third largest metropolitan area in the world, after Tokyo and Mexico City.[16] Moreover, its population density is higher than that of any other metropolitan area in the world, and its degree of population concentration is much higher—compared to 18% in Paris and 32% in Tokyo. During the country's period of industrialization and urbanization, people in rural areas flocked to larger cities—mostly to the MCSR—due to labor surplus in the agricultural sector.

The nation relies heavily on the Metropolitan Capital Seoul Region in every respect. It is a super-hub of administrative, economic, and cultural activities. Located in this region are 84% of the country's public offices, 65% of its universities, and 91% of major corporate headquarters. The region's congestion exacts enormous socio-economic costs in transportation, housing, and pollution.[17] The MCSR, only an hour's drive from the Demilitarized Zone, is also a source of national security concern.

Deconcentration policies attempted by previous administrations over the last three decades—such as special incentives for industrial complexes built in other regions and annual quotas for factories in the capital region—have been neither successful nor effective. The policies were intended to constrain the MCSR's growth through a zoning system and move public agencies, universities, research facilities, and companies to other regions. However, without stronger policies and measures designed to both encourage relocating from the capital region and commuting from the local regions, deconcentration of the region is not likely to be achieved.

Though the government tried various means of implementing more effective policies, the MCSR continued to grow in population, activity, wealth, and power, while local regions saw continuing decline and shrinkage, creating a vicious cycle.

Map of Metropolitan Capital Seoul Region

Vested interests of the region's wealthy and powerful have encouraged staying with the status quo. Despite stronger government policies aimed at dispersing the population across the country, the elite will not be so quickly moved out of the MCSR.

III.2.2. Regional Disparity in Development

From the 1960s to the 1980s, major infrastructure investment and development was concentrated primarily along the Seoul-Busan corridor, resulting in great disparities in regional development. The MCSR, for example, produces 46% of the nation's GDP, the southeast region 23%, the southwest region 11%, and other regions 20%.[18] Recently, the government embraced a firmer approach to achieve balanced regional development. Among the measures are plans to relocate government and public agencies to outlying regions, and even to transfer powers enjoyed by the Central Government to them.

IV. Actual Traffic and Services

IV.1. Traffic After Start of KTX Service

IV.1.1. Traffic Data[19]

A total of 6,415,000 passengers, an average of 70,000 passengers per day, rode the KTX since its inception April 1, 2004, through June 30, 2004—46.4% of the ridership forecasted by the Korea Transport Institute in 2003. This result, much less than expected, was attributed to the recent economic slowdown, inconvenience of getting to KTX stations, and only partial completion of the entire project. Because only the first phase was complete—a new line serving the Seoul-Daegu sector—KTX experienced some difficulty attracting passengers along the Daegu-Busan sector. Passenger load analysis might be premature at this stage, however, as other countries running high-speed rail, experienced similar disappointment during their initial operations.

IV.1.2. Travel Patterns of KTX Passengers

The characteristics of Korea's high-speed rail travelers fall in line with those of other HSR-running countries. KTX riders are predominantly between the ages of 21 and 50 (83.9%); 14.3% are over 50 and a mere 1.8% are younger than 20. Many KTX passengers (36.6%) travel to visit families and relatives, 35.2% travel for business, and 19.5% for tourism. More than half (51.3%) of KTX passengers previously traveled by conventional express train, 18.7% by air, 13.2% by automobile, and 12.9% by intercity express bus. Riders reached KTX stations through various means: 49.6% arrived by subway, 13.9% by bus, 21.1% by taxi, and 12.7% by automobile. Compared to other countries, the share of taxi usage in Korea is larger due to low taxi fares—US$1.50 for basic distance by standard taxi—the ready availability of taxis, and the many different classes of taxis accommodating customers' needs.[20]

IV.1.3. Conversion from Other Modes of Transport to KTX

As other HSR-operating countries have experienced, Korea anticipates that the launch of KTX service will convert trips presently made by other modes of transport—conventional railway, intercity bus, automobile and airplane—to high-speed rail.

IV.1.3.1. From Conventional Railway to KTX

In the Seoul-Chonanasan sector, 3.4% of rail travel switched to KTX; on the Seoul-Daejon line, 14.1%; on the Seoul-Daegu line, 26.9%; and on the Seoul-Busan line, 36.2%. The percentage of total travel converted from conventional railway was higher for longer trips than shorter ones. After the inauguration of KTX service, average travel distance per passenger also changed: 282 kilometers by KTX and 120 kilometers by conventional rail, down from 182–210 kilometers.

IV.1.3.2. From Other Modes to KTX Plus Conventional Rail

30.4 % of travel on the Seoul-Busan corridor switched from other modes of transport to KTX and conventional rail, which means that newly introduced KTX services resulted in an overall increase in rail travel in Korea. On the other hand, there was a relatively small increase in travel by rail on the Seoul-Mokpo corridor.

Change of Transport Share by Rail
(Lee Chang-Woon, Research Report, 2004)

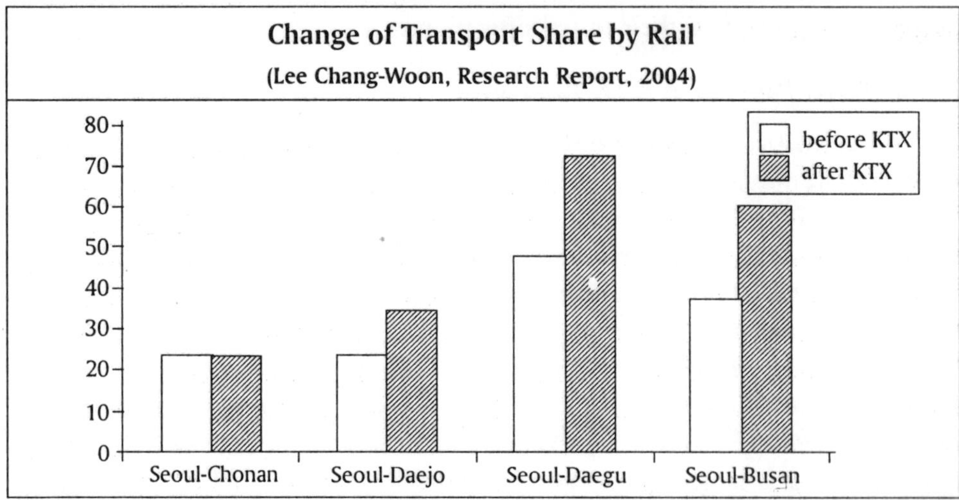

IV.1.3.3. From Inter-city Bus to KTX

Of all travel in the Seoul-Daegu sector, 21.5% switched from inter-city bus to KTX; in the Seoul-Gwangju sector, 7.7% switched; and in the Seoul-Mokpo sector, 14.5% switched to KTX. However, for short trips to the Chonanasan area, travel switched from rail to inter-city bus, probably because conventional rail service was curtailed with the introduction of KTX, and there are still relatively few KTX stations at present.

IV.1.3.4. From Automobile to KTX

Travelers also switched from automobiles to KTX in the Seoul-Daegu sector (15%) and in the Seoul-Busan sector (20%), which primarily reduced highway traffic.

IV.1.3.5. From Air to KTX

The most dramatic change after the inauguration of KTX was the mode switch from domestic air services, mostly on longer hauls. In the Seoul-Daegu sector, 71.5% of air travel switched to high-speed rail; in Seoul-Busan, 29.5%; in Seoul-

Gwangju, 22.9%; and in Seoul-Mokpo, 56.1%. Flight times of less than one hour are not economically viable, even in such a small country as Korea. Except for services to and from Jeju Island, which is located about 200 kilometers from the peninsula, domestic air services will likely yield to KTX after the second phase is completed in 2010.

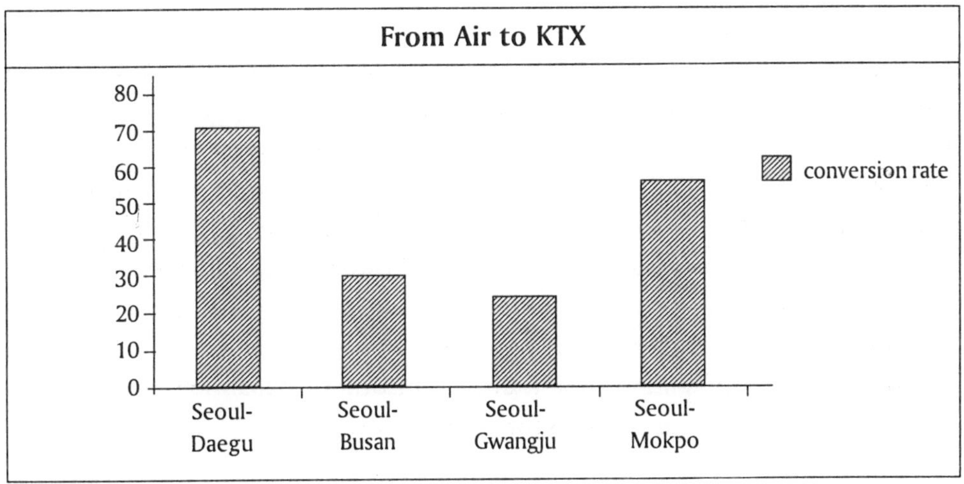

IV.2. Services

KTX has a reputation for good service, in general, although it encountered some minor delays and technical difficulties during its initial period of operation. Passenger dissatisfaction included reverse-direction seating, insufficient leg-room in economy class, malfunctioning audio systems inside compartments, and higher fares compared to other forms of transit.[21] About half of the seats in compartments are positioned in reverse direction, just as the French manufacturer places them in trains used in European and other countries. Though riders in other countries rarely complain about the positioning, many Korean passengers dislike the reverse-direction seating, allegedly due to cultural differences. Because of low demand for those seats, KORAIL is planning to reposition them to face forward to accommodate customer preference.

Another issue among riders is the difficulty of accessing KTX stations and the inconvenience of connections between KTX stations and other transport terminals such as bus, subway, and taxi. KTX stations currently lack bus terminals, and taxis are limited because of a licensing system that permits taxis to operate only in areas and stations for which they are licensed. In addition, the number of taxis is regulated by the annual quota system, which is administered by regional transportation authorities.

V. Impact on Transport System

V.1. Capacity Increase

The capacity of Korea's railway transport system (KTX and conventional railway) will be dramatically increased when the second phase of the project is completed in 2010. Passenger transport capacity is expected to increase 3.4 times, from 180,000 per day in 2003 to 620,000 in 2010. Cargo capacity is anticipated to increase by 7.7 times when a new line on the Daegu-Busan sector is put into service in 2010. In addition, conventional wisdom asserts that many socio-economic benefits will result from mitigating congestion and saving travel time—amounting to an estimated $1,850 billion Won per year (US$1.68 billion) according to a study by the Korea Transport Institute, "Expansion of 'Daily-Life Zone' and Change in 'Equal Transport Time Zone.'"

Much as all roads lead to Rome, in Korea all roads lead to Seoul, its capital city. Since the introduction of KTX services, 60% of the country's total population now lives within a Daily-Life Zone, defined as the zone or area where one can commute up to three hours, round-trip, work for 6–8 hours, and return home the same day.[22]

KTX service also increased the size of the "Equal Transport Time Zone," defined as a zone one can reach in a given time from Seoul, regardless of transport mode. The zone mapped below, which can be traversed from Seoul in 3–4 hours, expanded from 72.4% to encompass 88.5% of the country. Subsequently, the size of the zone requiring more than four hours of travel from Seoul decreased from 27.6% to 11.5% after the introduction of high-speed rail services in Korea.

Another change included the expansion of commute areas to and from the MCSR. According to a survey,[23] about 11% of the workers in Chonanasan region—96.3 kilometers from Seoul—who are now living separated from their families in Seoul, are likely to move to Seoul now that commuting has become possible. (Door-to-door travel now takes only 1.5 hours, including 34 minutes for the

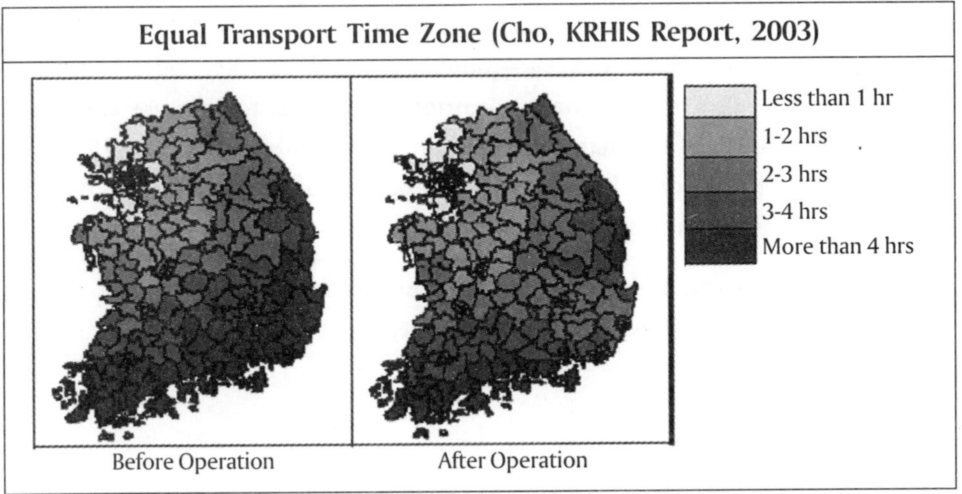

KTX ride.) However, commuting from Daejon—159.7 kilometers from Seoul—is less likely due to a good two-hour travel time and high fares.

V.2. Cargo Transport System

Because KTX presently serves only passengers and the Seoul-Busan line is only partially completed, cargo transport capacity by rail will not substantially increase until the second phase is completed in 2010. After that, conventional rail lines will be able to transport cargo solely, particularly along the Seoul-Busan corridor. More than 90% of cargo transport along the Seoul-Busan corridor currently moves by truck. A cargo trip on conventional railway lines in that sector takes about 10 hours; by highway, the same trip takes roughly 7 hours. Cargo transported by railway along the Seoul-Busan corridor is transferred from containers to trains at Busan Port, the world's third largest container port, unloaded at Euiwang ICD (Inland Container Depot), located in a suburb of the MCSR, and then delivered by truck to individual destinations.

V.3. Lessons from Other Countries Operating High-Speed Rail[24]

Soon after TGV services were launched in France, travel on the Paris-Lyon line increased 2.6 times between 1981 and 1985. A third of that growth came from the mode switch from air to high-speed rail, 18% came from former road travel, and 49% was attributable to newly generated travel demand. When Eurostar commenced service between Paris and London in 1995, transport mode shares changed dramatically: high-speed rail went from 0% to 33%, air from 70% to 41%, and others from 30% to 27%—indicating travel was diverted mostly from air service. TGV also operates on conventional rail lines to increase speed and expand service area. In Germany, travel more than doubled between 1988 and 1993, the initial period of ICE service. Twenty percent of this increase was diverted from road and air to high-speed rail.

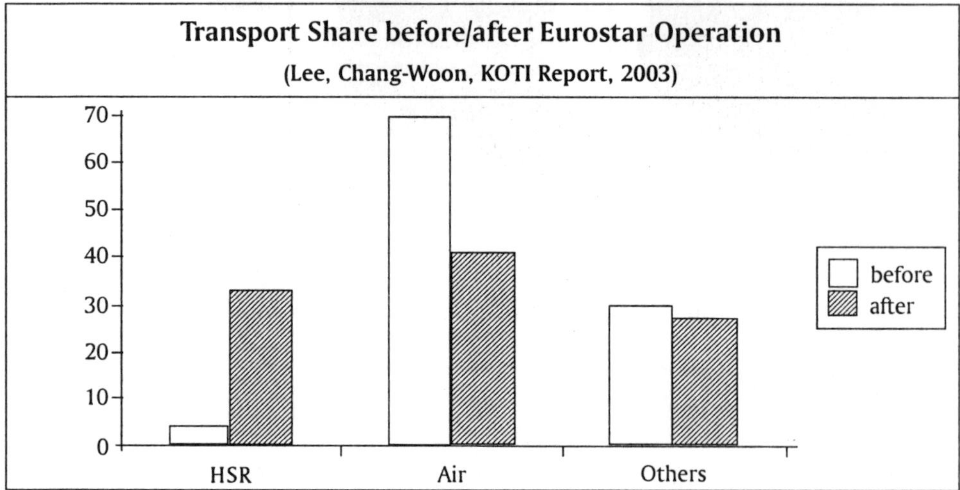

In Japan, the Shinkansen brought about revolutionary changes in people's lives—in particular, a much-reduced travel time and the enlargement of the daily life zone, which in turn generated new travel demand. The conversion to high-speed rail from other transport modes was much greater for trips less than 800 kilometers than for longer trips, and as a consequence, air service between Tokyo and Nagoya was greatly reduced. The Shinkansen's operation resulted in increased investment in high-speed rail, encouraged by its great efficiency and rapidly growing travel demand. Indeed, the entire rail sector saw a large investment increase. The ratio of highway to high-speed rail investment tilted greatly in favor of high-speed rail: 260 times greater in 1966, 1.27 times in 1970, and 1.14 times in 1975.[25]

In sum, most high-speed systems in the world have been built along densely populated main corridors simply because they must meet high traffic demand to be economically and commercially viable. High-speed rail is more competitive than air travel on trips of up to three hours, or about 750–800 kilometers.[26] High-speed rail services have also changed people's travel patterns, particularly when using inter-modal connections between high-speed rail and air. For example, when traveling between Brussels and Rome, passengers now take the TGV between Brussells and Paris (a short haul), and then choose air services between Paris and Rome (a longer haul).

VI. Impact on Regional Development

VI.1. Deconcentration of the Capital Region

The KTX itself is not a cure for the concentration problem in the capital region. Without a more cohesive policy aimed at boosting regional development, reducing the region's concentration will be difficult, as commute zones are growing and much of Korea has virtually become a daily-life zone, thanks to KTX services.

VI.2. Stimulus for Development near KTX Stations

By facilitating nearby development, KTX stations could become foundations for new city development or revitalization. For example, before the arrival of KTX, the Yongsan district was sluggish and in decline. Now, in addition to the Yongsan KTX Station, the district boasts a complex with an electronic and computer center, cultural facilities, a shopping and fashion arcade, restaurants, and a parking lot. It has become a model for district development in Seoul. Moreover, development of cities and regions where high-speed rail stations are located will occur more quickly, with KTX stations becoming new multi-development centres of regional growth. New town development plans in the vicinity of the Chonanasan (70,000 acres) and Gwangmyung KTX stations (486 acres) are prime examples. Though high-speed rail may spur local regional development, it does not necessarily ensure balanced growth.

VI.3. Other Effects on Regional Development

Tourism and service industries along KTX corridors are expected to grow, just as they have in other countries operating high-speed rail. Land prices, however, will also rise in the areas along KTX corridors, particularly in areas close to the stations. KTX service will likely entice some people to move from remote rural regions (such as Gangwon and Chonbuk) to areas near KTX stations, mostly located in larger cities.

Yongsan KTX Station

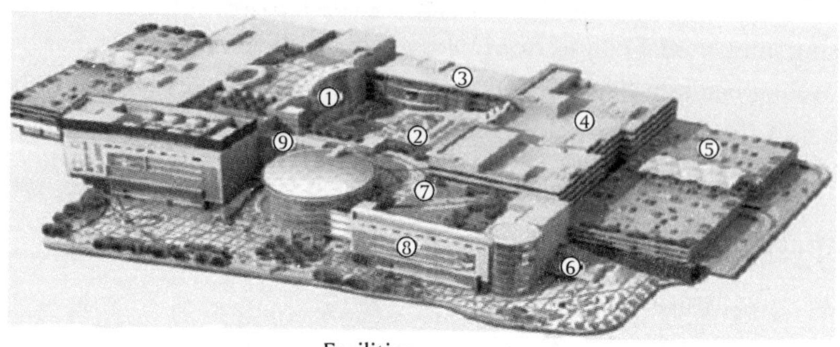

Facilities

① Digital Space ② Cultural Space ③ Restaurants
④ Movie Theaters ⑤ Parking Lot ⑥ Shopping
⑦ Park on the Roof ⑧ Fashion Mall ⑨ Station Facilities

VI.4. Korea's New Policy for Balanced Regional Development

After the present government took office in 2003, it advanced a number of firmer policies intended to bring about balanced regional development. Among them was a government plan to move public agencies and private companies to nearby cities—especially to areas where KTX stations are located. As a result, a total of 268 agencies are slated to move to local regions by 2012.

The government also has been trying to establish regional innovative clusters—a complex task requiring industry, academia, and local government to cooperate closely to succeed. In addition, it has employed 'company city,'[27] 'compact city,' and 'new self-sufficient city' (e.g., with high-tech industrial complex) concepts in many projects to disperse functions from the capital region and achieve the balanced regional development objective. Nevertheless, the government must proactively work to help less-developed areas grow. In order to reform the culture of governance in substantive ways, it must delegate authority from the central government to local governments and provide regions with additional manpower and financial resources.

VI.5. Experiences of Other Countries Operating High-Speed Rail

In Japan, most high-speed rail stations became city centers with transit terminals, hotels, offices, department stores, cultural facilities, restaurants, shopping arcades and parking, while also contributing to redevelopment of surrounding areas.[28] Osaka, Japan's second largest city, became a new regional center of growth as the Shinkansen's network expanded. Tourism and the service industry grew rapidly in cities, like Hiroshima and Fukuoka, where high-speed rail stations were located.

The Shinkansen also has influenced business activity; many companies have moved their branch offices to cities with high-speed rail stations. Among cities with high-speed rail stations, those that grew were better able to absorb the new growth and received a greater level of support from the central government. The Shinkansen seems to have alleviated overcrowding in the Tokyo metropolitan region, contributing to more balanced regional development in the country. In France, large cities with populations over 500,000 experienced growth. Le Mans, for example, successfully shifted to a high-tech industry base, and Lille became a transport hub. However, conflicting views have arisen about the deconcentration of the Paris metropolitan region after the introduction of TGV service. Many claim that a pull effect, a kind of centripetal force towards the Paris metropolitan region, has been working for short-distance areas, whereas a push effect—outward from the capital region—has been working for long-distance areas. In short, high-speed rail service has worked as a catalyst to stimulate city growth, promoting development of areas adjacent to high-speed rail stations, additional high-speed rail stations along the corridor, increased commuting, and the development of service industries and tourism along high-speed rail corridors.[29]

VII. Lessons and Future Prospects

VII.1. Lessons from the Korean Experience

The decision-making process for the route along the Daegu-Gyungju–Ulsan–Busan sector was very complex. Strong opposition mounted against a proposed route through the outskirts of Gyungju, out of concern for environmental and cultural preservation of this UNESCO-designated cultural heritage. Civic groups, environmental and cultural heritage experts, government organizations, and lawmakers took part in this debate, which lasted nearly three years. In the end, a route around Gyungju City was adopted. Another debate revolved around whether the route should take a shortcut to Busan or go through Gyungju and Ulsan, an area known as the Southeast Coast Industry Base with heavy industry and a population of three million. The government finally settled for an economically viable alternative to the shortcut. The construction of that route is now underway as part of the second phase of the project.

Concern and criticism grew over the escalating construction costs of this huge national infrastructure project. During the first phase, costs ballooned from 585 billion Won to 1,074 billion Won, and finally to 1,274 billion Won, allegedly due to increasing costs of purchasing land from private owners and to inflation of overall prices because construction was delayed longer than originally anticipated.

The original plans had to be modified during construction when closed mines were discovered underneath the planned route. Concern about the KTX's safe operation prompted the National Audit Board and other professional safety agencies to conduct thorough safety inspections and monitor construction.

Another conflict erupted over whether the Daejon and Dongdaegu stations should be built above or below ground next to present railway stations. The construction plans for these two stations have flip-flopped repeatedly over nearly a decade, from underground to surface and vice versa. Those who favor an underground station assert that it would mitigate a deepening city divide, whereas proponents of a surface station cite lower construction costs and increased safety. Conflicts of interest and differences of opinion still persist between central and local governments, local governments and district residents, and professional experts and politicians. Until construction of the two new stations is complete, however, the KTX must slow to less than 30 kmh as it enters the two downtown stations on conventional track.

Naming a KTX station at the border of two cities (Choan and Asan) also became a long and difficult process. After several years of regional rivalry and disagreement over the name, an advisory committee was established in 2003 under the Ministry of Construction and Transport to select names for some KTX stations. In this particular case, the committee deliberated for some months before deciding that the station's name would be Choan-Asan.

Also of note is a Buddhist nun who staged several hunger strikes in recent years to protest the construction of a tunnel under Mount Cheonsung, some

30-40 kilometers from Busan. She demanded an extensive and thorough environmental impact assessment around that area, to be made by a joint committee consisting of government-appointed experts and environmental NGOs. The environmental impact study, however, had been undertaken from 1992–1994, before the construction of the high-speed rail line was launched, and was followed by an official government promulgation of the decision to start construction.[30] Many tunnels have been constructed—underground, in the mountains, in waterways, and within cities, even during the first phase of the project. The High Appellate Court in the Busan district upheld a decision by a local court which gave the go-ahead for construction of the tunnel as planned. The protester ignored the court ruling and staged a second, longer hunger strike. Construction was once more stopped by this incident, de facto nullifying the court decision, and consequently incurring large cost overruns and further delaying the second phase of the national project.

VII.2. Current Limitations and Difficulties

Partially opening the Seoul-Busan Line will not accommodate the transport demand along that corridor, especially for cargo. Electrifying the Daegu-Busan sector, where KTX and conventional rail run on the same track, will not reduce congestion there until the second phase of the project is completed in 2010. Although cargo will enjoy exclusive use of conventional railway lines when a new line has been completed on the Seoul-Busan corridor, it will suffer in the interim from shortage of travel time-slots. Another problem lies in the fixed number of compartments per train, which make accommodating fluctuating travel demand difficult. When Korea signed a contract for vehicle manufacture, it expected that travel demand would justify the design. However, during the week many seats remain empty.

VII.3. Future Tasks

VII.3.1. Completion of the Second Phase

Since cargo transport will use the conventional railway line when the new line has been constructed, on-time completion of the second phase is very critical for addressing capacity shortage. In 2010, cargo transport by rail is expected to dramatically increase by 7.7 times.

Many difficult issues remain to be solved during the second phase. As mentioned above, the first action is to decide as soon as possible whether Daejon and Daegu stations will be built above or below ground.

Also in the second phase, new stations will be added to existing KTX corridors. Additional stations will bring better accessibility, expanded KTX service, and regional development. However, the addition of more stations means the KTX must run at a slower speed, increasing passengers' travel time. As other countries with high-speed rail[31] have learned, though, trains do not necessarily have to stop at all stations; they can stop, for example, at odd-numbered stations or limit stops at stations with lower travel demand. Competition for new stations is stiff among cities along the KTX corridor; some even exert political pressure on decision-making bodies like the Ministry of Construction and Transportation. At present, 4–5 additional KTX stations are under consideration for the second phase of construction.

The development of a prototype Korean high-speed rail vehicle is nearing completion. When Korea began efforts to introduce high-speed rail service in the early 1990s, it also began to undertake the G-7 project, a collaboration of government, research institutes, academia, and industry to develop a Korean prototype high-speed rail vehicle. Overcoming many development obstacles, the consortium has tested the prototype successfully in recent years and has achieved a vehicle speed of more than 300 kilometers per hour. A few more years of work are anticipated before the system is fully stabilized and can be put into commercial operation. In contrast to current KTX vehicles, the Korean prototype has a unique design, which allows the number of compartments to be adjusted according to demand.

Improving the accessibility and connectivity of high-speed rail stations is another pressing need—to provide travel convenience, attract more passengers and, ultimately, make the KTX economically viable. Good connections between KTX stations and international airports are important because they can drive more traffic to both airlines and KTX. Currently, railway connection work, scheduled for completion by 2008, is underway between Seoul and Yongsan KTX stations, at one end, and Incheon International Airport[32] at the other. Once

Korean Prototype High-Speed Rail (Korea Railway Research Institute)

completed, KORAIL and the airlines will likely draw up a mode-sharing agreement to their mutual benefit. In addition, inter-modal KTX stations—through which all transport modes (such as KTX, inter-city express bus, subway, and taxi) could be linked to each other—need to be expanded.

VII.3.2. Construction of New Lines

KTX service is in place on the existing electrified line along the Seoul-Mokpo corridor, but is hampered by serious limitations on capacity and speed. (Top speed is only 160–170 kmh.) For this reason, the Korean government is planning to build a new line to meet future travel demand. In addition to this was a plan in the mid-1990s to build high-speed rail with private capital along an east-west corridor, linking Seoul to the east coast—a major tourist destination for city dwellers. This project, however, has yet to materialize because private investors who can develop the areas along the proposed line cannot be found. When all planned lines are completed, Korea's high-speed rail network will extend nearly 1,000 kilometers.

VII.3.3. A Rationalized Future Transport System in Korea

Comparing its high-speed rail experience with that of other countries, Korea should rationalize its transit system in the following ways: emphasize urban rail and bus in metropolitan areas; conventional rail, KTX, and intercity express bus for distances between 100 and 200 kilometers; KTX for distances between 200 and 400 kilometers; and KTX and air services beyond 400 kilometers. France and Japan demonstrate similar emphasis in their transport systems.

VII.3.4. Reconnecting the Missing Link between South and North Korea

A grand railway network linking Korea from Japan[33] to Europe via China and Russia—the so-called Eurasian Railway—has long been envisioned. By completing the 12-kilometer link between South and North Korea, cargo could be transported through either the Trans-Siberian or Trans-China Railway once it is shipped from Japan or Korea to Russia or China. A container freight train running from the Far East to Europe on the Eurasian Railway would make shipments less expensive and encourage competition between railway and maritime modes. Because many countries would benefit substantially from the link's completion, many attempts have been made to bridge the gap at both the international and the regional level. However, this issue likely will not be resolved without a genuine reconciliation or rapprochement between the two Koreas.

Eurasian Railway

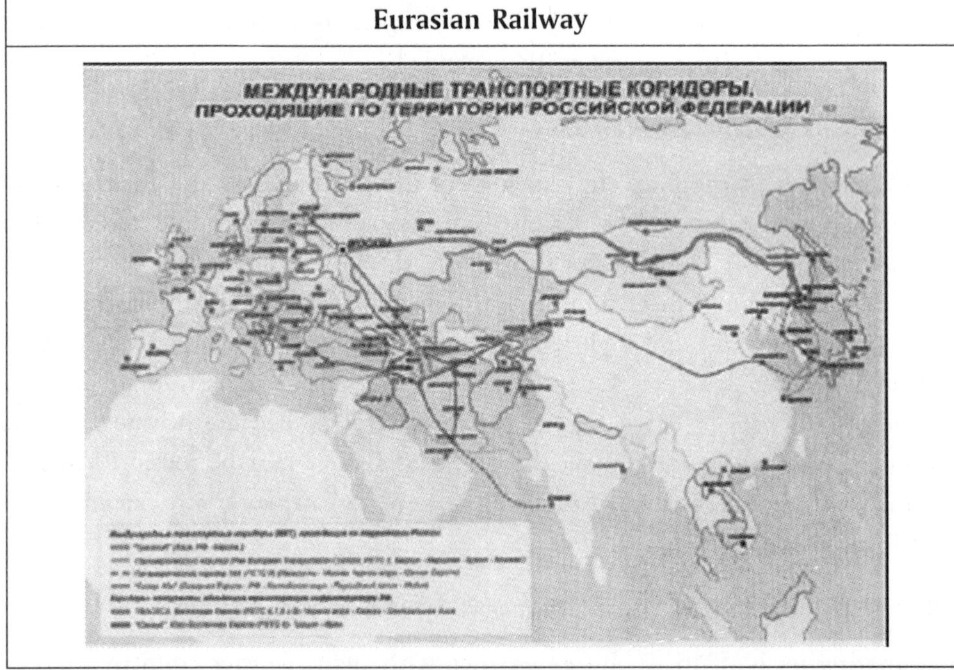

VII.4. Rethinking Sustainable Transportation and Regional Development

High-speed rail is an energy-saving and environmentally friendly mode of transit. Despite new investment by transportation authorities, highways and roads in dense metropolitan areas are becoming more congested. According to recent statistics, global oil demand amounted to 82.4 million barrels per day in 2004.

The US consumes 20 million barrels per day (about 25% of world demand), importing 56% of its total demand—20% of it from the Persian Gulf.[34] In addition, oil prices fluctuate wildly, partly due to the volatile situation in the Middle East. Unless oil consumption is reduced, energy independence cannot be accomplished. The development of alternative energies (e.g., hydrogen) is important in the event oil prices rise to unaffordable levels or world oil reserves are reduced or ultimately depleted.

The concepts of transit-oriented development (TOD)[35] and smart growth,[36] which encourage greater use of public transit as a means of achieving sustainable development, would go a long way toward solving the problems faced today. Integrating work with residential areas and city functions with business activity will reduce travel demand substantially. Korea would very likely follow such a trend in transport and regional development.

(Dong-Chun Shin is Director General, Ministry of Transport, Seoul, Korea and a visiting scholar, Institute of Urban and Regional Development, University of California, Berkeley.)

References

Books

Chen, Don, Transportation Reform and Smart Growth: A Nation at the Tipping Point, Collins Center for Public Policy, Miami, 2001.

KRHIS, Land for 50 years: Retrospect and Prospect towards the 21st Century, Seoul Press, 1996.

Lee, Jeong-Sik, Kim, Young-Woong (ed.), Globalization and Regional Development, Hanwool Academy, 2001.

Litman, Todd, Evaluating Public Transit Benefits and Cots: Best Practices Guidebook, Victoria Transport Policy Institute, October 2004.

O'Donohue, Evelyn Mary, Transit Oriented Development in a Small Town, Manuscript, 2003.

Research Reports and Materials

Cervero, Robert, High-Speed Rail and Development of California's Central Valley: Comparative Lessons and Public Policy Considerations/Robert Cervero and Michael Bernick; report prepared for California Intercity High-Speed Rail Commission, Working paper (University of California, Berkeley. Institute of Urban & Regional Development); no. 675, July 1996.

Cho, Nam-Geon, Surveys on the Regional Economic Impacts from the High-speed Rail, Korea Research Institute for Human Settlement (KRHIS), July 2003.

———, The Spatial Impact of High-Speed Rail and its Countermeasures, KRHIS, 2003.

Leavitt, Dan, Revenue and Ridership Potential for a High-Speed Rail Service in the San Francisco/Sacramento-Los Angeles Corridor/Working paper (University of California, Berkeley. Institute of Urban & Regional Development); no. 609, 1994.

Kim, Je-Chul, Aviation Policy Direction in a Changing Air Transport Environment in the 21st Century, December 2004, KOTI.

KRHIS and The Nomura Research Institute, New Paradigm for National and Regional Development after Opening High-Speed Rail in Korea, July 2004.

KRHIS and the Netherlands Institute for Spatial Research, Utrecht University, proceedings (edited by Won-Bae Kim), International Conference on Urban Networks and infrastructure Planning in the Metropolitan Region (September 2002), December 2003.

KRHIS, International Seminar on Impacts on National Spatial Structure by High-Speed Rail in Korea, October 2003.

Korea Railway Research Institute, Basic Planning on Inter-modal Transportation System on Seoul-Busan HSR Line, 2003.

Lee, Chang-Woon, A Study on the National Transportation System in High-Speed Rail Era, Korea Transport Institute (KOTI), December 2004.

Mo, Chang-Whan, Forecasting Traffic Demand on Roads and Railways Connecting South and North Korea, November 2003, KOTI.

OECD, Territorial Reviews: Korea, 2001.

Samet, Jonathan M, Dominici, Francesca, Curriero, Fransk C, Coursac, Ivan, Zeger, Scott L, Fine Particulate Air Pollution and Mortality in 20 US Cities, 1987-1994, *The New England Journal of Medicine*, December 14, 2000, Vol. 343, No. 24.

Sands, Brian D, The Development Effects of High-Speed Rail Stations and Implications for California/Working paper (University of California, Berkeley. Institute of Urban & Regional Development); no. 566, 1993.

Smart Growth Strategy/Regional Livability Footprint Project, Shaping the Future of the Nine-County Bay Area, Alternative Report for Round Two Public Workshop Participants and Other Bay Area Residents, April 2002.

Vaca, Erin. Intercity Rail Ridership Forecasting and the Implementation of High-Speed Rail in California/Working paper (University of California, Berkeley. Institute of Urban & Regional Development); no. 568, 1993.

Websites

California High-speed Rail Authority: *http://cahighspeedrail.ca.gov*

Florida High-speed Rail Authority: *http://www.floridahighspeedrail.org*

French TGV: *http://tgv.com/EN*

International Energy Agency (IEA): *http://www.iea.org*

Japanese Shinkansen: *http://www.Japan-guide.com*

Korea Rail Network Authority: *http://www/krnetwork.or KORAIL: http://korail.go.kr*

Railway Technology: *http://www.railway-technology.com*

Smart Growth Strategy/Regional Livability Footprint Project: *www.abag.ca.gov/planning/smartgrowth*

Notes

1 This paper is based on a presentation given by the author at a Visiting Scholars Roundtable on November 17, 2004, under the auspices of the Institute of Urban and Regional Development at the University of California, Berkeley. The presentation of this subject matter is grounded in the author's professional experience as Director General in the Ministry of Construction and Transport in Korea, directing the nation's high-speed rail project during 2002–2003. The opinions expressed in this article are those of the author and do not necessarily represent those of the Ministry of Construction and Transport.

2 The Republic of Korea (South Korea) is located geographically in the southern part of the Korean peninsula, as distinguished from North Korea.

3 Korea experienced a financial crisis caused by the shortage of foreign exchange reserve in 1997.

4 1 USD was equivalent to 1,100 Korean Won as of November 2004.

5 The International Union of Railway's high-speed task force provides definitions of high-speed travel, however, there is no single definition of the term, but rather a combination of elements—new or upgraded track, rolling stock, operating practices— that lead to high-speed rail operations. *http://www.uic.asso.fr/d_gv/toutsavoir/definitions_en.html*

6 Lee, Chang-Woon, 2003.

7 During 1992–1993, the Institute of Urban and Regional Development at the University of California, Berkeley, undertook a research project on high-speed rail in California, which produced many workings papers; see references.

8 California High-Speed Rail Authority: *http://cahighspeedrail.ca.gov*

9 Railway Technology: *http://www.railway-technology.com*

10 For example, Litman, Todd, Evaluating Public Transit Benefits and Costs: Best Practices Guidebook, Victoria Transport Policy Institute, Oct. 2004.

11 In Japan, construction and maintenance are run by a state-sponsored organization, while the management of the lines is handled by many different companies, privatized many years ago as part of railway reform.

12 In Korea, many contend that political figures representing the interests of particular regions have pushed for the expansion of road networks, whereas the railway network has suffered because it is not linked to parochial interests or benefits.

13 Ministry of Construction and Transport, Korea, dealing with national, regional city development and planning, housing, construction and technology, water resources management, infrastructure and transportation issues.

14 Samet, Jonathan M, *Fine Particulate Air Pollution and Mortality in 20 US Cities*, 1987-1994, *The New England Journal of Medicine*, December 14, 2000, Vol. 343, No. 24.

15 KRHIS and the Netherlands Institute for Spatial Research, Utrecht University, proceedings (edited by Kim, Won-Bae), International Conference on Uıban Networks and Infrastructure Planning in the Metropolitan Region (Sep. 2002), Dec. 2003.

16 Wikipedia, metropolitan areas by population.

17 A two-million-unit housing construction project was pushed by the government from the late 1980s to the early 1990s in order to address worsening housing shortages and skyrocketing home prices in five satellite cities adjacent to Seoul City in the MCSR. However, it brought forth a tremendous increase in traffic, resulting in severe congestion, since the five new cities were only bedroom communities from which most people commuted to Seoul for work.

18 OECD, Territorial Reviews: Korea, 2001.

19 Lee, Chang-Woon, *A Study on the National Transportation System in High-Speed Rail Era,* December 2004, Korea Transport Institute (KOTI)

20 Therefore, taxi is regarded as a type of paratransit in Korea.

21 The fare level of transit is generally much lower than in most advanced countries—for example, the subway costs \$0.60–\$0.70, the taxi \$1.50, and the bus \$0.50–\$0.60.

22 Cho, Nam-Gun, KRHIS Research Report on *The Spatial Impact of High-Speed Rail and its Countermeasures*, 2003.

23 Cho, Nam-Geon, *Surveys on the Regional Economic Impacts of High-Speed Rail*, Korea Research Institute for Human Settlement (KRHIS), July 2003.

24 Cho, Nam-Gun, KRHIS Research Report on *The Spatial Impact of High-Speed Rail and its Countermeasures,* 2003.

25 Lee, Chang-Woon, 2003

26 In the Paris–Lyon sector, 90% of travelers use the TGV and 10% use air transport; Lee, Chang-Woon, 2003.

27 In the course of developing a new city under a company's or companies' initiative, attractive incentives such as making land purchases easier and corporate tax exemptions are normally granted to companies. A 'company city' would combine business activities and city functions, and provide a business-friendly environment.

28 The station is managed by a development company charged with securing public space such as cultural facilities and botanical gardens.

29 Cho, Nam-Geon, *The Spatial Impact of High-Speed Rail and its Countermeasures*, KRHIS, 2003.

30 Generally, people are given the opportunity to express views on proposed routes in terms of environmental concerns and other aspects affecting them. The government publishes proposed routes, together with their environmental impact assessment, in an official Gazette. In addition, the ministries responsible for such matters—for example, the Ministry of Environment and the Ministry of Construction and Transport—participate in the Cabinet's decision-making process.

31 For example, there are many kinds of Shinkansen services: Nozomi, stopping only at very large cities like Tokyo, Nagoya, Kyoto and Osaka; Hikari, stopping at more stations than Nozomi; and Kotama, stopping at nearly every station.

32 It ranked 9th in passenger traffic volume and 5th in cargo handling in 2002 (Airport Council International).

33 The construction of a Korea–Japan Channel tunnel is required.

34 International Energy Agency (IEA): *http://www.iea.org*

35 "Transit Oriented Development (TOD) refers to residential and commercial areas designed to maximize access by transit and non-motorized transportation, and with other features to encourage transit ridership. A TOD neighborhood has a center with a rail or bus station, surrounded by relatively high-density development, with progressively lower density spreading outwards. For example, the neighborhood center may have a transit station and a few multi-story commercial and residential buildings surrounded by several blocks of townhouses and small-lot single-family residential, and larger-lot single-family housing farther away." TDM Encyclopedia, Victoria Transport Policy Institute.

36 "'Smart growth' means different things to different people. There is no single definition of smart growth; its meaning depends on context, perspective and timeframe. The common thread among different views of smart growth is development that revitalizes central cities and older suburbs, supports and enhances public transit, promotes walking and bicycling, and preserves open spaces and agricultural lands. Smart growth is not no growth; rather, it seeks to revitalize the already-built environment and, to the extent necessary, to foster efficient development at the edges of the region, in the process creating more livable communities." The website on Smart Growth Strategy/ Regional Livability Footprint Project.

3

Fire Safety Design for Rapid Transit Systems*

Siew Yee Cheong

Manufacturing technique proves to be a new risk management tool, which provides a cost-effective means to evaluate fire safety systems. Worldwide MTRS projects were embarked with a target to build and operate an efficient and effective transport network, which provided integrating cost-effective and sustainable needs for urban population. This article also studies the urban needs for cost and benefit analysis of fire safety intervention methods and an improved means of comparing the effectiveness of fire safety measures used by different transit systems and explains how various types of engineering methods have proved effective in the fire safety design, which can be highly beneficial for fire safety analysis and design of rail mass transit systems.

1. Introduction

Many new Rapid Transit Systems are being planned, designed and constructed in major cities in the world. Generally, nations are launching these projects with

- This paper was originally published in the Conference Proceedings of Fire India 2004.

the aim of building and operating an efficient and effective land transport network that is integrated, efficient, costeffective and sustainable to meet the needs of their urban population.

With the above aim in mind, Builder / Owner / Operator of such rapid transit systems (RTS) not only has to ensure the safety of the railway but also that of the safety of commuters who use the system. Therefore, it is necessary to adopt a vigilant fire safety design that would meet the international standard as well as to incorporate comprehensive fire safety strategy to protect the life safety of transit's commuters, minimise loss of property and to facilitate evacuation, fire fighting and rescue operation in the event of an emergency.

2. The Singapore Mass Rapid Transit (MRT) System

The implementation of the Singapore's MRT system started in 1983. Prior to this, there were no transit's facilities in Singapore, other than a surface railway operated by the Malayan Railway Authority that had been operating between Singapore and the West Malaysia for many decades.

The Singapore Government has established a Statutory Board (previously known as the Mass Rapid Transit Corporation (MRTC) and now known as Land Transport Authority (LTA) and entrusted it with the responsibility to build these MRT & LRT systems as part of the overall land transportation planning for the nation. Upon completion, the systems are to be handed over to operate and maintain through a License Agreement with the LTA.

Within 20 years, Singapore has already built and is currently operating 2 major MRT lines with 66 stations and 110 km of MRT guideways and 3 independent Light Rapid Transit (LRT) systems in the suburban areas.

Presently, projects to build a new MRT Circle line in 5 stages are underway. This new line, which cross-links existing MRT lines, comprises 33.3 km of trainways with 29 stations. When fully completed in 2010, traveling time will be reduced for commuters due to its convenient connectivity to numerous existing stations on the EW, NS and NE lines.

During the initial stage, as Singapore has no experience in designing the rapid transit system, references were made available to overseas railway engineering design standards for guidance to develop the station conceptual layout. Challenges were encountered in designing the stations to concurrently comply with the prevailing Singapore's building and fire regulations because the functionality and occupancy nature of a station are uniquely different from than of a conventional commercial building.

Finally, it was decided to adopt NFPA 130 as a base design guide. The Standard was first issued in May 1983 by the National Fire Protection Association Inc. USA and it is specially prepared to cover fire protection and life safety from fire in fixed guideway transit systems.

NFPA 130 is under constant reviewed by a technical committee to incorporate changes arising from advancement of technology or evolvement of new concept and thinking in relation to fire science, human behaviour and safe practices. Subsequent revisions were published in 1986, 1990, 1997 and 2000. The latest 2003 edition was recently published.

A Standard on Fire Safety for Rapid Transit System was released by LTA in 2001 and revised in 2003 to be applied as a local design code for the Rapid Transit System. This local Standard amalgamates the fire safety requirements in NFPA 130 with local regulations and practices in one single document for ease of reference and application.

3. Typical Layout of an Underground Station

A typical underground station consists of concourse level at the first basement and a platform level at second basement. The central portion of the concourse level is designed as a ticketing hall where ticket machines, automatic fare gates, station control room are located. Equipment Rooms serving the operations of the station are located on both sides of the ticketing hall.

Where possible, some small shops, automatic teller machines, public telephones, etc are provided along the corridors leading from the various entrances to the ticketing hall. The platform is approximately the length of the rolling stock used in the system and separated from the tracks by the platform screen doors. The platform level, directly beneath the concourse level is basically an open central area to facilitate passengers' waiting and boarding/alighting onto/ from trains. Equipment rooms will also be located on both sides of this central area or beside the trainway.

The concourse and platform levels are linked by open staircases and escalators at the public areas. Lifts are currently being provided for the newer stations, or otherwise being retrofitted into the existing stations. Enclosed staircases are also provided at both ends of the station to cater for quick egress from the station platform in the event of any emergency.

4. Fire Safety Requirements for Station

4.1 Station Construction and Fire Compartmentation

The underground stations are of non-combustible construction with the elements of structure built to a fire resistance period of at least 4 hours. The architectural finishing materials in stations are also of non-combustible types. Electrical cables are of low smoke, halogen free and either fire retardant or fire resistant type.

Station design follows the NFPA 130 fire compartmentation requirements. All non-public areas are separated from public areas by at least 2 hours fire resistant construction. The nontransit occupancies such as commercial spaces have at least 3 hours fire separation from the transit area. Different occupancies within a non-public area are further compartmentalized from one another. For example, electrical substations are provided with minimum 3 hours fire compartmentation; generator rooms are provided with minimum 4 hours fire compartmentation and other plant rooms, stores and refuse storerooms are provided with minimum of 2 hours fire compartmentation. Enclosed staircases and electrical code shafts are individually compartmentalized by at least 2 hours fire rated construction.

4.2 Mcans of Egress

MRT stations are elongated in design with centralized exiting facilities composed of open stairs and escalators to serve normal traffic. NFPA 130 allows open stairs and escalators which passengers normally use for ingress and egress to be used as means of egress in the event of an evacuation. In addition to these open stairs and escalators, enclosed emergency stairs are provided at each end of the platform as a secondary means of egress. Generally, these emergency stairs discharge directly to the concourse transit area. However, at least one of them which is designated as the fireman staircase emerges at the ground level.

The fare gates installed at the concourse level will fully open in the event of a loss of power or upon activation of a control switch in the Station Control Room (SCR) for speedy evacuation. Emergency swing gate is provided adjacent to the fare gates to increase the exit capacity. This gate is held in closed position by a simple latch and may be released manually during emergency.

Movement of escalators can be controlled either locally or remotely from the Station Control Room. Escalators running in the reverse direction of egress will be stopped before the evacuation commences.

The maximum travel distance to an exit from any point on the platform doesn't exceed 91.4 m (NFPA 130). This requirement is not applicable to the concourse level.

The commercial spaces such as shops along the transit route are limited to one big shop not exceeding 100 m^2. The exit routes from these commercial spaces are similar to that of the station. These commercial spaces have minimum 3 hours fire separation from the transit public area.

In stations which are incorporated with an additional shopping level, the large commercial spaces on the shopping level are compartmentalized with minimum of 3 hours fire barrier from the transit public area.

Linking the station with adjacent commercial building at basement level is permitted, provided the commercial development is separated from the station by 1 3-hour fire compartment in accordance with the requirement of NFPA 130. The 3 hours fire shutter installed in the link interface can normally remain open. Through the operation of the smoke detectors installed wither in front or behind the fire shutter or by activation of the fire alarm system in the development, the fire shutter will be automatically shut. For this reason, the link does not form part of the requisite exit routes from either the station or the adjacent development

4.3 Exit Capacity

Time is used as the main criterion in the determination of exit capacity. Escalators, staircases, passageways and fare gates provided in the station are designed not only to handle traffic flow at peak hour but also to ensure that passengers are able to leave the station within a specified time frame.

The time frame set by NFPA 130 is 4 minutes for evacuation of station occupant load from the platform level and 6 minutes for evacuation of station occupant load from the most remote point on the platform to a point of safety entrances at the ground level.

The station occupant load used in the exit time calculation is derived differently. It is not calculated based on the area of the station, but is dependent on the traffic parameters. The detraining and entraining loads are the two components making up the station occupant load. In computing the detraining load, trains carrying the calculated train loads (i.e. converted from the peak 15 minutes traffic load with safety factor to account for missed headway in the peak direction) are assumed to enter the station simultaneously on all tracks in normal traffic direction and discharge all their passengers. The entraining load is calculated from the peak station entry load in similar manner.

Evacuation time from the platform can be calculated by dividing the station occupancy load by the exit capacity available form platform to concourse. Where a station has two platform levels both the evacuation times from lower platform to upper platform and from upper platform to concourse are to be determined.

To calculate the total evacuation time for a station, walking travel time should first be tabulated using the longest exit route and travel speeds given in NFPA 130. Waiting times may occur at various constriction points.

4.4 Station Evacuation

In addition to the open stairs and escalators, enclosed stairs are provided at one or both ends of the station. One of these enclosed stairs which discharges to a point of safety at grade is designed as the firemen's stair and it can double up to provide a safe entry for firemen during fire fighting operation.

For security reasons, doors entering into the enclosed stairs at platform are normally electrically locked. During an evacuation, passengers may leave the platform quickly using the nearest exit (i.e. any of the open stairs, escalators and enclosed stairs). The locking device to the doors of the enclosed stairs will be released remotely to allow usage. As an additional fail-safe feature, the lock can be automatically released upon activation of the station's fire alarm system or upon a loss of power or by breaking a break-glass box located adjacent to the door. Likewise, the fare gates can also assume a fully open emergency exit mode in the event of loss of power to the fare gates or upon actuation of a manual or remote control. Emergency service gates located alongside the fare gates can be opened to increase flow capacity across the fare barrier. Escalators running in the exit direction may be left in the operating mode, whereas those running in the reverse direction are capable of being stopped locally or remotely at the station control room.

4.5 Exit Sign and Emergency Light

Sufficient exit signs and exit directional signs are placed to identify the exit routes within the station. Emergency lighting is installed throughout the station. Both the emergency lights and exit lights are connected to a secondary power supply.

5 Fire Protection and Fire Detection Systems in Stations

The Singapore MRT system is designed to achieve a high standard of fire safety in stations by providing a host of fire protection and fire detection systems surpassing the requirements of NFPA 130. Each Station is fitted with automatic fire sprinkler system, automatic fire alarm system, total flooding gas fire suppression system and for certain plantrooms, fire hose reel system & portable fire extinguisher, voice communication system and dry riser system.

5.1 Automatic Fire Sprinkler System

An automatic fire sprinkler system is provided in areas of transit stations used for commercial spaces, storage, refuse store, mechanical plant rooms and other similar areas with combustible loading. In accordance with NFPA 130, the station public transit areas need not be provided with an automatic fire sprinkler system due to its negligible fire load.

Additionally, all escalator pits in the concourse and platform levels are protected by sprinklers. All electrical or electronic equipment rooms, which are fully compartmentalized with minimum 2 hours fire resistance will not be provided with automatic fire sprinkler system.

5.2 Automatic Fire Alarm System

All plant rooms and station public transit areas, which are not protected by sprinklers, are protected with an automatic detection system. Alarm bells and manual call points need not be provided within the station's public transit area. Instead, emergency voice alarm and emergency telephones are provided to avoid causing panic to passengers and achieve more orderly evacuation. Interfacing between the voice alarm and alarm bells in the non-public plant room areas and shopping level is provided.

Noisy plant rooms are fitted with beacons in addition to alarm bells to further enhance the function of the bells in the event that the noise of the equipment is greater than the sound level of the bell. Field detection devices such as detectors, flow switches and sub-panel are connected to a main alarm panel (MAP) which is installed at a conspicuous location on ground level inside the fireman staircase. In addition a coloured mimic panel complete with LED indicators next to the MAP and repeater panel is installed in the SCR for constant monitoring of the fire alarm.

Summary fire alarm signal and common fault signal generated from each station is transmitted to the Operation Control Centre (OCC). Hot line telephones are provided linking the OCC and SCRs. The OCC, which is manned 24-hrs a day, can communicate with the Singapore Civil Defence Force's Main Operation Centre through a hot-line telephone in the event of emergency.

5.3 Fire Hose Reel System

Hose reels are provided at all levels, except the train platform due to the presence of the 1500 volts dc overhead catenary system or 750 volts 3rd rail system. . Hose reel of 30 m in length are located at prominent and accessible positions adjacent to exists or exit routes. The locations are planned so that the nozzle of a hose reel can be taken into every room, taking into account the various fixtures and furnishings. Water for hose reel system is delivered by duplicate electrically driven pumps.

5.4 Portable Fire Extinguisher

Provision of fire extinguishers is in accordance with local practices in term of types, sizes and distribution. Generally, fire extinguishers will be installed such that the maximum travel distance to reach a fire extinguisher will not exceed 15 m.

5.5 Dry Riser System

Provision of the system conforms to NFPA 130. Independent dry riser systems are provided outside fireman's and emergency staircases at every basement storey, and at the centre of the platform. Breeching inlets are located not more than 18 m from fire engine access way.

5.6 Voice Communication System

Each station is installed with a voice communication system conforming to local code of practice. Alarm bells and fire alarm manual break glass call points are not provided in the station public area to avoid causing panic to passengers. Voice communication is preferred as it could help to achieve more orderly evacuation.

Pre-recorded messages are broadcast either from the Operation Control Centre or the SCR through a public address (PA) system to evacuate passengers from the station in the event of fire emergency. Loudspeakers connected to the PA system are installed throughout the stations including all habitable rooms, basement floor areas, escape staircases, all lobbies forming part of the means of egress, main entrance lobby, corridors leading to exits and ancillary areas at the concourse and platform levels.

Emergency fire phones are provided at the platform and concourse levels such that the travel distance from any point in the public area do not exceed 91.4 m. These emergency fire phones are linked directly with the SCR for reporting of any fire or emergency occurrence on the concourse and platform levels.

Firemen's intercom is also provided to facilitate communication between breeching inlets at the ground level and at the non-public areas located at both ends of the platform. A radio communication network is provided for the Singapore Civil Defence Force (SCDF) to allow two-way radio communication via leaky radio communication system to their Main Operation Centre. The system is suitable for operating in the 470-490 Hz frequency range in accordance with the local requirement. In addition, two-way emergency communication system is provided between the Main alarm Panel located within the Firemen's staircase and the fire fighting lobby, all fire fighting related mechanical equipment rooms, smoke control equipment rooms, and lift motor rooms.

5.7 Passenger Lifts

Passenger lifts will be used for transporting people between platform, concourse and ground level. Power supply for the lifts come from the two electrical feeders drawing power from separate sources.

The lifts are fully automatic, and are provided with safety features such as homing to designated level upon fire alarm or main power failure in accordance with the Singapore's requirements. Intercom system for communication between the lifts, SCR and lift motor rooms is provided.

5.8 Accessibility to Fire Appliances

Underground stations are designed to provide accessibility to fire appliance. The requirements in the local Fire Code are complied with. The fire engine access ways is designed to be not more than 18 m from the breeching inlets serving the stations.

5.9 Smoke Control System

A smoke control system is required in the trackway area of the station (outside the platform screen door) to control smoke generated from a train fire. The heat release rate produced by a train fire was used to design the smoke control system. The design of the smoke control emergency ventilation system achieve the following objectives:

a) to capture and contain smoke generated within the trackway area;

b) provide a stream of non-contaminated air to passengers in the path of egress away from a train fire;

c) limit the air temperature in the path of egress away from a train fire to 60°C.

Under fire condition, the tunnel ventilation fans (TVFs) at both ends of the station and under platform exhaust fans (UPEFs) are activated in exhaust mode. The combined exhaust capacities exceed the smoke generation rate to provide effective smoke extraction. Make-up air is induced through the station entrances.

The station public area at concourse and platform levels and the non-public areas, where the plant rooms are located, are provided with smoke purging system of 9 air changes per hour. This system is operated to purge any smoke generated as a result of a fire occurring in the plant rooms' area or the station's public areas.

5.10 Total Flooding Gas Suppression System

Halon 1301 total flooding systems were installed to protect critical plant rooms in stations constructed in the 80s. Since the ban on usage of new halon system for fire protection, newer stations are now protected by either CO_2 or Inert gas total flooding system.

6. Fire Safety Requirements for Railway Tunnels

6.1 Construction

Trainways in tunnels are divided by a minimum of 2-hour-rated fire walls or constructed in twin bores.

All building materials used in the trainway are of non-combustible type. The fire resistance of the element of structure for the underground trainway will be at least 4 hours. All cable installed within the underground trainways is of low smoke, halogen free and either fire retardant or fire resistant.

6.2 Emergency Exit Stair and Cross-Passageway

To comply with NFPA 130, emergency exit from tunnels are provided via emergency stair or cross passageways, or in the combination of both. The number required depends on the length of the tunnel between the two stations. The exact location of emergency exit stair and crosspassageway is adjusted to overcome problems such as level difference between vertical and horizontal tunnel alignment, geological conditions of site and ease of access at grade.

In general, cross passageways are not further than 244 m apart. The first passageway is located not more than 503 m from the station vertical exit shaft. Openings in cross passageways are protected with fire door assemblies having a fire protection rating of at least 1.5 hours with a self-closing fire door.

6.3 Emergency Lighting

The emergency lighting within the walking surface of the tunnels is provided.

6.4 Fire Protection

All trainways in rail tunnels are provided with a dry riser system. The dry rising main system is installed in compliance with the relevant Singapore Code.

Two independent dry risers shall serve each section of the tunnel with the breeching inlets located at the stations on the ground level. The minimum nominal bore of a dry rising main will be 150 mm. Landing valves in the underground trainway are spaced at a maximum of 60 metres apart. The breeching inlets are located near the vent shafts at ground level and are within 18 m from the nearest fire engine accessway.

6.5 Tunnel Emergency Ventilation System

The tunnel ventilation system shall be designed to comply with the following requirements:

a) Provide a tenable environment along the path of egress from a fire incident in enclosed trainway.

b) Produce airflow rates sufficient to prevent back layering of smoke in the path of egress within enclosed trainways.

c) Be capable of reaching full operational mode within 120 seconds.

The design heat release rate produced by a train fire was used to design the tunnel ventilation system. Tunnel ventilation fans and related components exposed to the ventilation airflow are rated at 250°C for at least two hours. Fire resistant cables are used for all wiring. Power supply for the smoke control fans is from two separate electric feeders.

Operation of the emergency tunnel ventilation system is initiated from the OCC. Local controls is permitted to override OCC in all modes in the event that the OCC becomes inoperative.

6.6 Firemen's Communication System

Firemen intercom is provided between the dry riser inlets at ground level and both ends of the platform non-public area. A radio communication network is provided for the Singapore Civil Defence Force to allow two-way radio communication via leaky radio communication system to their Main Operation Centre using the 470-490 Hz frequency band.

7. Conclusion

In this paper, the fire safety designs for the typical rapid transit underground station and rail tunnels have been briefly discussed. As more rapid transit systems will be built in major cities with significant increase in length, configuration and complexity of operations, fire engineers now face greater challenges to design a fire safe rapid transit system to ensure safety of train commuters and fire fighters.

The tasks ahead for fire engineers are to constantly review and improve the fire safety requirements in the design of rapid transit system in light of impending changes in technologies, materials, operational conditions, arson/terrorist considerations and higher expectation of commuters to enhance the overall safety and efficiency of the system.

(Siew Yee Cheong FIFireE, PE, Vice President, Institution of Fire Engineers, Singapore.)

4

On-Line High-Speed Rail Defect Detection – Phase III

Francesco Lanza di Scalea, Piervincenzo Rizzo, Stefano Coccia, Ivan Bartoli and Mahmood Fateh

The Federal Railroad Administration (FRA) Office of Research and Development's Track and Structures Program sponsored a study for developing and testing a rail defect detection system based on ultrasonic guided waves and non-contact probing. Current rail defect detection systems based on ultrasonic testing have limitations in terms of reliability of defect detection, inspection speed, and other drawbacks associated with the requirement for contact between the ultrasonic probes and the rail surface. More importantly, conventional ultrasonic testing of rails has serious difficulties detecting internal defects in the presence of surface shelling. The rail defect detection technique that is being funded is based on fundamentally new concepts in that 1) uses ultrasonic waves traveling along, rather than across the rail running direction, 2) uses non-contact means of generating and detecting the ultrasonic waves in the rail, and 3) uses advanced signal processing algorithms to de-noise the measurements and extract robust defect-sensitive

Sources: www.fra.dot.gov "On-Line High-Speed Rail Defect Detection - Phase III by Francesco Lanza di Scalea, Piervincenzo Rizzo, Stefano Coccia, Ivan Bartoli and Mahmood Fateh, www.structures.ucsd.edu is reprinted with permission of Federal RailRoad Administration (FRA)"

information. A prototype is being assembled based on this technology and plans are in place to install and test the prototype in the FRA Research Car.

Background

Conventional ultrasonic rail inspection, that is the common approach taken by railroad maintenance personnel for defect detection, uses piezoelectric transducers that are coupled to the top of the rail with ultrasonic wheels or sleds filled with water or other fluids. The transducers are typically operated in a pulse-echo mode with two orientations, namely 0° (normal) incidence for detecting horizontal cracks and 70° incidence for detecting transverse cracks. The most concerning drawback of this method is the fact that horizontal shallow cracks (shelling) can mask the internal transverse defects. This limitation was the most likely cause of a train derailment in Superior, WI in June 1992, where an entire town had to be evacuated as a result of hazardous material spillage. Other limitations of conventional rail defect detection are the limited area of rail inspected at once and the limited inspection speed resulting from the contact requirements.

Figure 1: (a) Transverse Fissure; (b) Detail Fracture; (c) Ultrasonic Guided Wave Detection of Transverse Defects ("Reflection" and "Transmission" Modes)

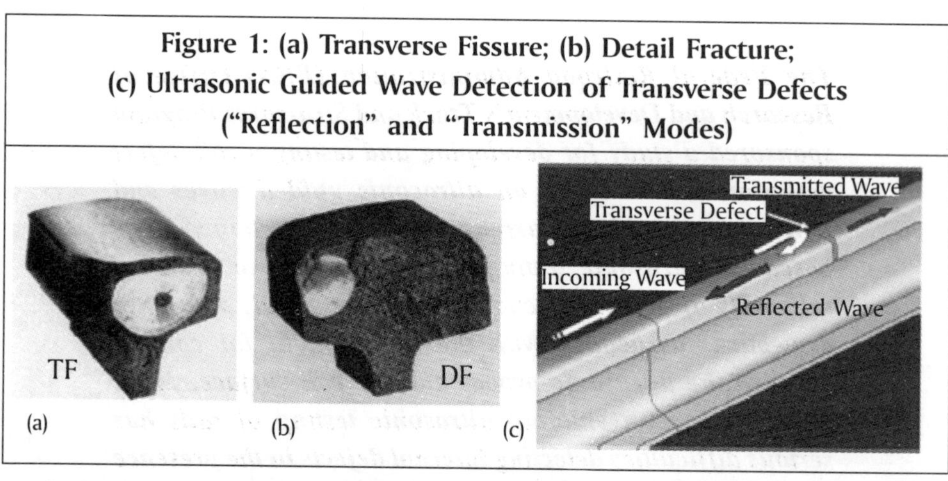

The system under investigation, based on ultrasonic guided waves, non-contact sensors and advanced signal processing algorithms, has the potential to increase the reliability of defect detection in rails and the inspection speed. The technology is particularly suitable for detecting transverse-type defects (TDs). During the decade 1992-2002, TDs were responsible for $162M in associated damage costs in the US and 2,782 derailments according to FRA Safety Statistics Data (FRA 2002). The TDs targeted by the inspection include Transverse Fissures initiating in a location internal to the railhead, and Detail Fractures initiating at the head surface as Rolling Contact Fatigue defects (Figure 1a and 1b). The project is currently in its third year and present activities are being conducted to assemble an inspection prototype and subsequently install and test it in the FRA Research Car.

Elements of the Rail Defect Detection System

The system under development uses an Nd:YAG pulsed laser (1064 nm, 10 nsec pulse duration) focused to an illumination line source on the top of the rail head to generate ultrasonic waves in the DC-2MHz frequency range (Figure 2a). The line source forces the waves to propagate along the rail running direction while insonifying the entire section of the railhead. Hence the waves are "guided" by the geometry of the rail head. This wave propagation direction is particularly suitable to detect TDs, which generate large reflections (Figure 1c). Micro-machined, capacitive air-coupled sensors are used to detect the ultrasonic waves propagating in the rail (Figure 2a).

Figure 2a: The Prototype Non-Contact Rail Defect Detection System: Laser and Air-Coupled Sensors

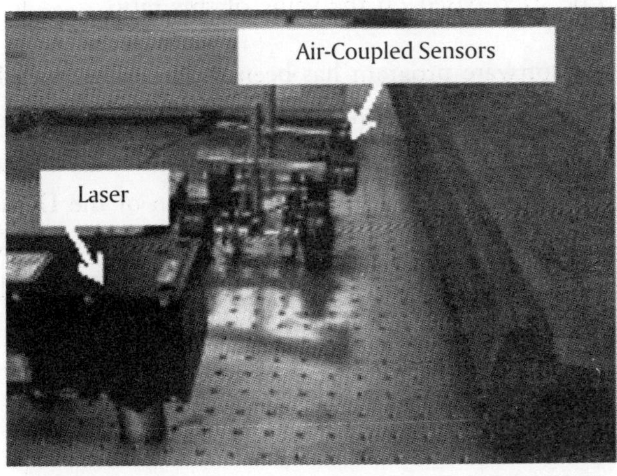

These devices offer a wide response bandwidth (DC-2MHz) with large sensitivities. A 40 kHz high-pass filter is generally used to limit the influence of ambient vibrations and other sources of noise in the field. The air-coupled sensors can be positioned as far away as 3 inches from the top of the rail head thus satisfying the clearance envelope that is generally recommended for rail inspection systems claiming "non-contact" capabilities.

Defects can be detected by monitoring the presence of a reflection or echo of the ultrasonic wave ("reflection" mode) or by monitoring an attenuation of the ultrasonic wave as it travels past the flaw ("transmission" mode). The two modes require different orientation angles of the air-coupled sensors and different positions of these sensors relative to the laser source. Extensive numerical (finite element analyses) and experimental studies have been conducted to examine both of these defect detection modes. As a result of these studies, the "transmission" mode has been selected for configuring the prototype system. A pair of air-coupled sensors is oriented at 6° from the normal to the rail surface towards the laser source. The distance between the two sensors, in combination with the laser repetition rate, controls the achievable inspection speed.

According to the "transmission" mode, defects are detected when the ratio between the ultrasonic measurements of the two sensors decreases from the "no defect" value of unity as a result of the ultrasonic attenuation past the flaw. Defects can also be sized based on the value of this ratio.

A sophisticated software program has been programmed to achieve all of the tasks required by the inspection, including control of the laser firing, synchronization of the sensor measurements with the laser, processing of the measurements by de-noising algorithms, computation of the Damage Index, and display of an indication of a defect and its size. The program is based on National Instruments PXI© technology running under LabView (Figure 2b).

Figure 2b: The Prototype Non-Contact Rail Defect Detection System: Data Control and Display

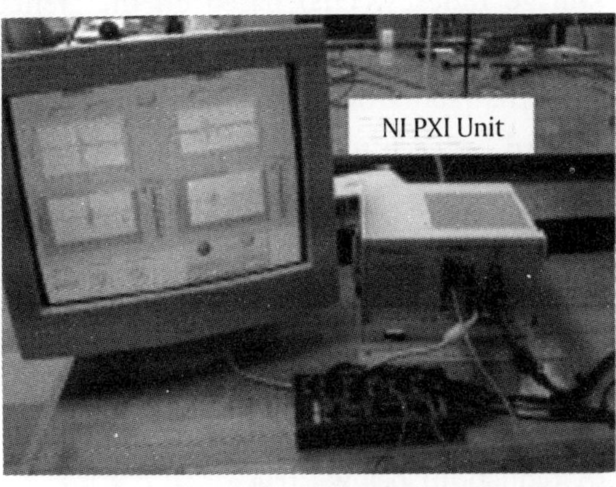

An intermediate version of the user interface for the signal detection part of the program is presented in Figure 3. The traces measured by the two sensors are

Figure 3: User Front Panel for the Signal Detection Portion of the Inspection Software Showing the Detection of a Transverse Head Crack in the "Transmission" Mode

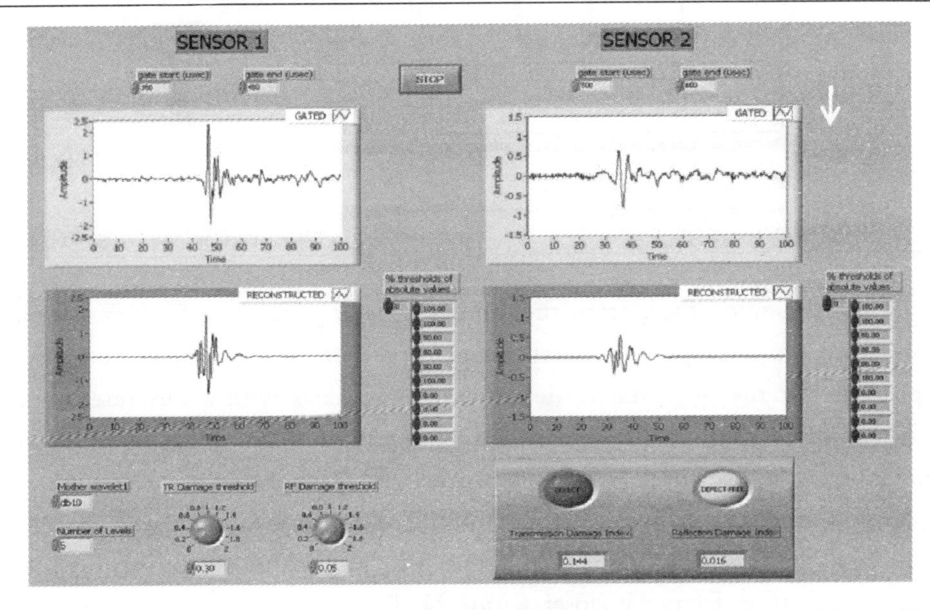

shown, along with their de-noised versions after Discrete Wavelet Transform processing. Two Damage Indexes (DIs) based on the "reflection" and on the "transmission" modes are shown in the lower-right portion of the screen. This measurement, taken in the laboratory, refers to an instance where a transverse head crack was positioned between the two sensors, hence the "transmission" DI correctly alarms of its presence.

Laboratory Tests and Results

Surface-breaking cracks were simulated in a section of rail by narrow notches that were machined at depths (s in Figure 4a) ranging from a minimum of 0.5 mm to a maximum of 8.5 mm, all corresponding to a cross-sectional area reduction of the rail head (% HA reduction) below 20%.

Figure 4a: Schematic of Rail Tested with Crack Defect

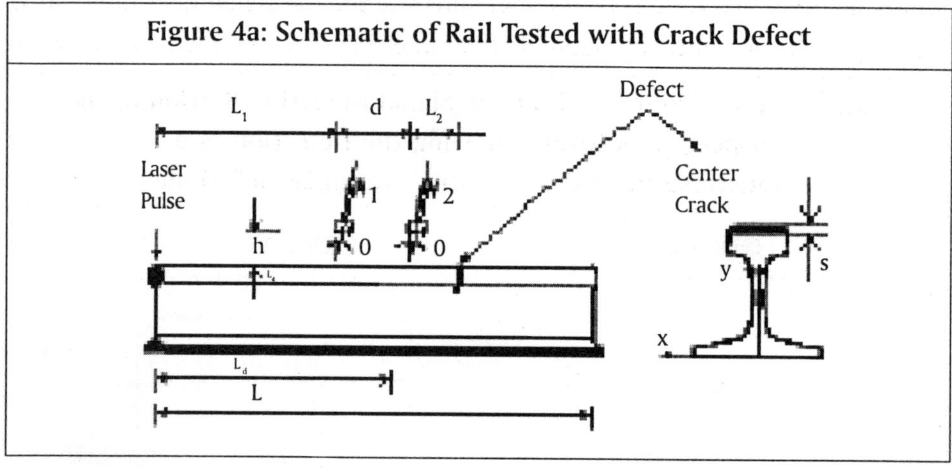

The ultrasonic signals from the sensors were acquired at a 5 MHz sampling rate from ten laser pulse generations at each damage condition. The general approach for the quantitative defect detection starts with a Discrete Wavelet Analysis for de-noising the signals and extracting the damage-sensitive features, followed by an Artificial Neural Network (ANN) algorithm for classifying the damage size (Lanza di Scalea *et al.*, 2005). The DI is then calculated taking the ratio between features of the signal detected by the further sensor #2, F_{sens2}, over the same features from the closer sensor #1, F_{sens1},

$$\text{Damage Index} = \frac{F_{sens2}}{F_{sens1}} \qquad (1)$$

In the "transmission" mode the DI is expected to drop in the presence of a crack due to the reduction in ultrasonic energy transmitted through the discontinuity. The features of variance, RMS, peak amplitude and peak-to-peak amplitude of the threshold wavelet coefficient vectors were computed.

Figure 4b shows the DI from equation (1) using the variance feature. The mean value of ten measurements is plotted as a function of the crack depth and the extension of the vertical line is equal to 2 standard deviations.

Figure 4b: Damage Index vs. Crack Depth

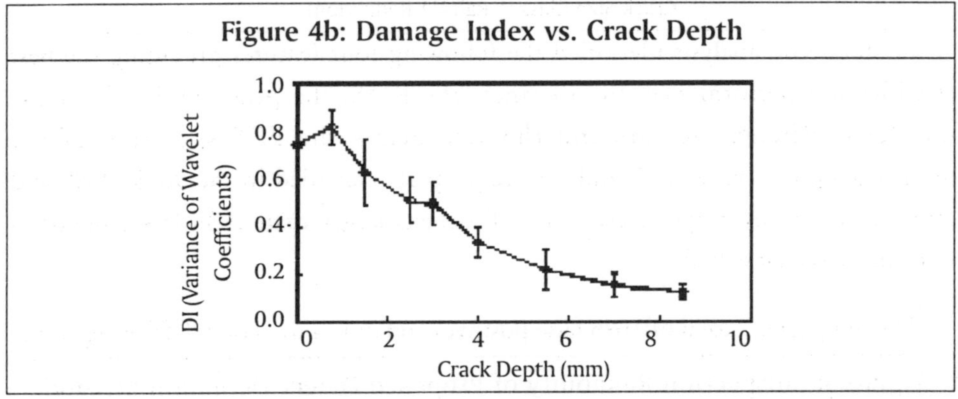

As expected the DI monotonically decreases with increasing defect size. This suggests the potential for sizing the crack. The defect sizes were further subdivided into three classes (Classes 1, 2 and 3), corresponding to % HA reduction in the ranges 0%-1.1% (the pristine condition), 1.5%-9.9%, and 10%-20%. Each class was coded with a 2-digit binary number. A feed-forward, back propagation ANN with three layers was employed. Five of ten acquisitions for each damage condition were used as training data while the remaining data were used as testing data.

Figures 5a and 5b illustrate, respectively, representative classification results of the laboratory tests and a comparison with the AREMA recommendations for rail inspection reliability of transverse defects.

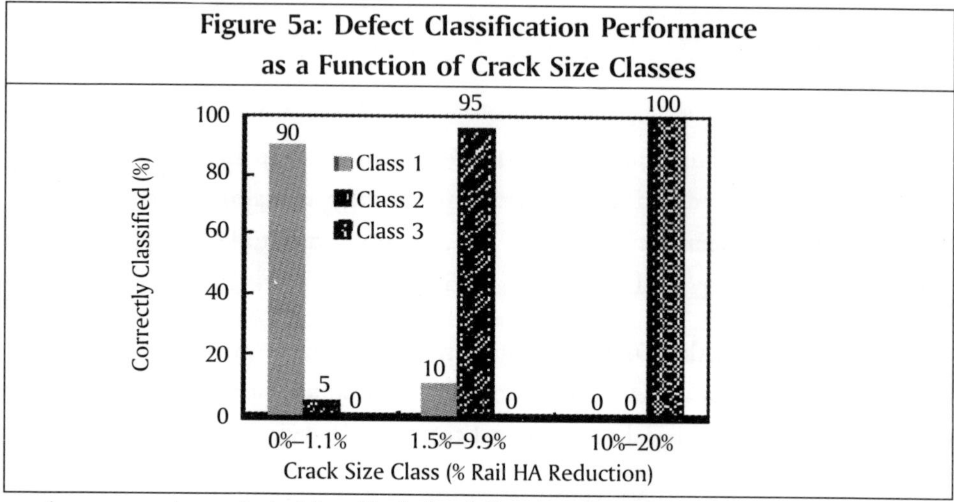

Figure 5a: Defect Classification Performance as a Function of Crack Size Classes

A parametric analysis identified the following four features providing the best classification performance: the variance, the RMS, the peak amplitude of the wavelet coefficient vectors and the area below the FFT spectrum of the reconstructions. Classes 1, 2 and 3 were properly classified in the 90%, 95% and 100% of the cases, respectively. Thus all defects larger than 10% HA reductions were properly classified.

The setup gave a total of 10% false positives and only a total of 5% false negatives.

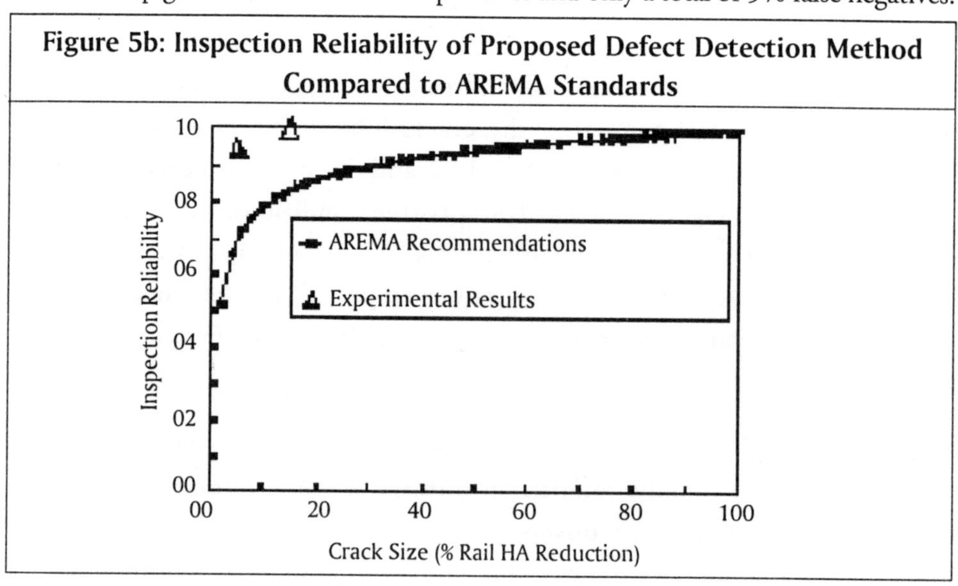

Figure 5b: Inspection Reliability of Proposed Defect Detection Method Compared to AREMA Standards

Conclusions

A rail defect detection system based on ultrasonic guided waves, non-contact probing and advanced signal processing is under development. The system has the potential for detecting transverse defects in spite of the presence of surface shelling thus increasing the reliability of defect detection over conventional rail defect detection systems. In addition, the system can in principle achieve inspection speeds higher than those achievable by conventional rail defect detection systems. Promising results have been obtained in laboratory tests on simulated transverse cracks in the rail head extending below 20% HA Preparations are underway for field testing of the system.

Acknowledgments

Francesco Lanza di Scalea, Associate Professor, Piervincenzo Rizzo, Assistant Project Scientist, and graduate students Stefano Coccia and Ivan Bartoli performed this study at the University of California in San Diego. Mahmood Fateh, FRA Technical Representative, provided essential support through technical discussions and advice. The National Science Foundation funded the initial research efforts.

(Francesco Lanza di Scalea is an Associate Professor at University of California, San Diego. Piervincenzo Rizzo is an Assistant Project Scientist. Stefano Coccia & Ivan Bartoli are graduate students. Mahmood Fateh is a Program Manager and General Engineer, Track Research Division, Federal Railroad Administration, US Department of Transportation and he can be reached at mahmood.fateh@fra.dot.gov).

References

1. Federal Railroad Administration (2002). Safety Statistics Data: 1992-2002, FRA, US Department of Transportation.
2. Lanza di Scalea F, Rizzo P, Coccia S, Bartoli I, Fateh M, Viola E and Pascale G (2005). "Non-contact Ultrasonic Inspection of Rails and Signal Processing for Automatic Defect Detection and Classification," *Insight – NDT and Condition Monitoring, Special Issue on NDT of Rails*, 47(6), pp. 346-353.

On-Line High-Speed Rail Defect Detection – Phase I

According to the Federal Railroad Administration defects in the US rail account for about one-fourth of the 1000 annual track caused train derailments. Federal Railroad administration is the federal agency authorized for enforcing rail safety regulations. Rail defect could be detected with the help of the two techniques like Magnetic Induction testing and Ultrasonic testing. Both these conventional methods have had disadvantages mainly of limited coverage of inspection area and limited testing speed. Also reliability was a concern. Thus, due to the inadequacy of the conventional techniques and increasing number of rail accidents, there was a need to develop a new technique for testing rail defects and lessen the safety concerns. First move with respect to the Strategic 5 Year R&D Plan concerning the rail track safety was made with the help of the University of California, San Diego (UCSD). UCSD performed a research in the area of rail defect detection under grant DTFR53-02-G-00011 with two main aims: To increase the reliability of defect detection and to increase the speed of current rail inspection method in testing the defects.

In Phase I of the grant DTFR53-02-G-00011, two innovative techniques based on ultrasonic stress waves were examined to detect defects. These technologies included Cross Sectional Method and Long Range Method. Cross Sectional Method is a high frequency method which uses ultrasonic transducers to detect and excite the ultrasonic waves which would help to create resonance conditions which in turn make it feasible to investigate the rail in a non-contact mode at the cost of signal detection sensitivity. This method involves inspection of the sensors along the running direction as ultrasonic testing is done across the rail. As per the test conducted in the laboratory on 115-1b American Railway Engineering and Maintenance of Way Association (AREMA) rails, the method was found to be successful to detect the longitudinal internal defects in the head, web and head flange. Nevertheless, it failed to achieve inspection speed range higher than the conventional rail defect detection methods. Also positioning of the sensors on the sides of the rails posed a limit as the rail sides were not always accessible. In the Long Range Method, ultrasonic waves 'guided' by the rail geometry are used traveling in the longitudinal, running direction in the rails. To typify the speed and attenuation of three primary guided wave modes namely longitudinal, lateral and vertical modes, 115-1b AREMA rails were examined in the laboratory as well as field. When these modes interact with the rail defects, it is observed in terms of wave reflection coefficients as a function of the wave frequency. With the help of this technique transverse head defects of different sizes and orientations including transverse surface cracks as shallow as 1 mm from the head surface could be successfully detected. This method proved to have advantages such as increase in reliability, potential on increase in inspection speed, extension in the coverage area and convenience in field deployment.

(Compiled by Pooja Dave, Research Associate, Icfai Business School Research Centre, Ahmedabad.)

On-Line High-Speed Rail Defect Detection – Phase II

Phase I of the research activities conducted by the University of California, San Diego, under grant DTFR53-02-G-00011 included two methods namely Cross Sectional Method and Long Range Method for testing defects. Out of the two, Long-Range Method proved to be the strongest prospective which met the objectives of the research programme. Phase II was a further extension of the study for Long Range Method. In Phase II studies were conducted to display the potentials of guided waves to detect "large" and "small" transverse cracks in the rail head. For this research, Large defects meant transverse cracks larger than 15% of the rail head cross-sectional area (HA) and Small defects included transverse cracks smaller than 15% HA. Tests included use of advanced wavelet transforms-based signal processing and automatic pattern recognition. Also tools such as impact hammers, pulsed lasers and air-coupled sensors were examined as practical methods for performing the filed tests. Two methods were used in this phase for detecting "large" and "small" defects. In the first method impact hammer was used for wave generation and for wave detection air-coupled sensors were used. Through this method "large" transverse cracks at frequencies below 50 kHz were successfully detected. In the second method, pulsed laser was used for wave generation. Through this method "small" transverse surface breaking cracks with shallowness of 1 mm at frequencies between 100 kHz and 600 kHz were successfully detected.

(Compiled by Pooja Dave, Research Associate, Icfai Business School Research Centre, Ahmedabad.)

5

Protecting Passenger Transport Systems from the Threat of Terrorism

Geoff Dunmore

The article explains how the London Tube responded to the attacks on the 7th July and the measures that can practically be taken to protect passengers and employees on public transport systems. The article presents information on the blasts in London, the operational issues thereafter and the vital role of London Underground and the British Transport Police. Technology is seen as the panacea for passenger safety through use of tools like Closed Circuit Television (CCTV) which help in protecting passengers from notorious activities of criminals.

The very nature of mass rapid transit systems requires them to be easily accessible to enable people to travel from A to B as quickly and safely as possible.

The Tube system in London is the backbone of London's transport network with over 3 million passengers per day, serving 275 stations with over 250 miles of track and more than 500 trains during peak periods.

As the oldest underground rail network in the world, London has a long history of threats to its security, predominantly through Irish Republican terrorism. It has developed measures to prevent, deter and ultimately respond to terrorist attacks.

Over 12,000 operating staff drive trains and provide a staff presence on every station, providing a customer service, train dispatch, safety and security and information. At the busier, larger stations – more than 20 staff will be on shift at any one time. Policing is provided by 650 officers from the British Transport Police, who are permanently assigned to London Underground. BTP also provide Special Response Units to provide a rapid response to deal with suspicious items and reduce service delays.

There is extensive coverage of CCTV with over 6000 cameras on the network, this will increase to 12,000 by 2010 as part of the ongoing station modernisation plan under the Public Private Partnership contract. This is being further enhanced to accelerate some of these works and improve recording quality amongst other CCTV initiatives.

This will see the upgrading and expansion of CCTV facilities from analogue to digital and the recording of high quality images to hard drives, rather than magnetic tape. Ultimately, this will mean that no one will be able to enter the Underground Network without their face being recorded by CCTV.

Simple adjustments to station design standards had been devised to provide clear lines of sight with no obstructions on station platforms and route ways, with good levels of lighting, and features such as sloping tops on vending machines and no gaps behind platform furniture – reduces the opportunity to conceal an item without it drawing attention.

The use of litter bins is a simple demonstration of ongoing reviews to balance customer service needs and security. These were removed from the Underground system in the 1970s to prevent them being used to conceal bombs; they were replaced when the threat had receded in the 1980s, to be removed again in the early 1990s. This was an expensive and slow business. Today, the litter bins have been re-designed as simple plasticized rings holding a transparent bin liner, making it easier to check for concealed items and quick and cheap to remove at times of heightened alert.

Response protocols had been developed for multi sited incidents with the British Transport Police and the other emergency services. Deep tunnel rescue plans had also been developed between LU, BTP, the other emergency services and the London Fire Brigade: the lead agency for rescue operations in London.

Since the terrorist attacks in the USA in September 2001, London Underground played a full part in the resilience planning; put in place by the Government in the form of the London Resilience Forum, this has been supported by the Mayor of London who is the deputy chair. LU have had a manager seconded to the London Resilience Team from the outset and this has ensured that the operational realities of a mass transit metro system were properly considered in political and investment decisions.

This team led the work in areas such as evacuation plans for parts of London, and arranged multi agency table top and live emergency exercises. In April 2005, all the London agencies took part in a major command-and-control exercise coinciding with similar exercises in the USA and Canada.

The experiences of these types of exercises proved invaluable and played a vital role for senior London Underground managers and their counterparts in the other organisations on the 7th July.

Events of 7th July

At 08.49, three simultaneous explosions occurred without warning on three separate locations on the Underground network. Two of the explosions happened on trains on the Circle line, one as a train left Edgware Road station in a double track tunnel en route to Paddington. The other bomb exploded on a train in a double track tunnel on its way into Aldgate station from Liverpool Street. The third bomb went off in a tube tunnel between Kings Cross and Russell Square.

Almost an hour later a fourth explosion occurred on a bus in Tavistock Square, close to the Russell square incident.

In total, 52 people were murdered, seven at Edgware road, seven at Aldgate, 24 at Russell Square and 14 on the bus. 700 people were injured.

The indiscriminate murder and maiming of innocent people on the 7th July was unprecedented in the history of London Underground or the UK railways. Following events in recent years in Madrid, Moscow and Paris etc., it has long been recognised that it is extremely difficult to protect against determined terrorists who are willing to sacrifice their own lives to further their cause. Transport systems are not their only targets; anywhere where large numbers of people congregate or can have an economic impact is, as demonstrated in Bali, Sharm El Sheik and Istanbul etc., where the targets were clubs, bars, hotels, financial institutions and embassies.

The phenomenon of the suicide bomber means that traditional methods of detection and interception are unlikely to be effective unless identified at an early stage of planning. With this particular form of attack, effective response to an incident is critical. On the 7th July and subsequently the response from all agencies involved was exceptional. Initially, LU employees were the first on the scene and prevented large scale panic, by calmly leading those who could walk out of the trains and tunnels; they provided comfort and care to the injured and dying.

In 2003, OSIRIS II simulated a CBRN attack on London Underground, involving 55 appliances and 120 officers in tight suits. It allowed emergency and health services to test equipment and rescue procedures in a realistic environment. The exercise and conclusions drawn proved invaluable in July 2005, when 200,000 passengers and 500 trains had to be evacuated as quickly as possible.

It is difficult to prepare people for such events. All the employees involved stood up to be counted upon when needed. Although it is impossible to predict how individuals will react faced with such horrific scenes, the training, drill and practice for general emergency situations has become a standard procedure for LU employees, since the Kings Cross Fire in 1987.

Similarly, contingency plans for a number of different scenarios and emergency plans for each location are now the standard requirements on the Tube.

A RART Trolley used for Evacuating Passengers in the Event of an Emergency

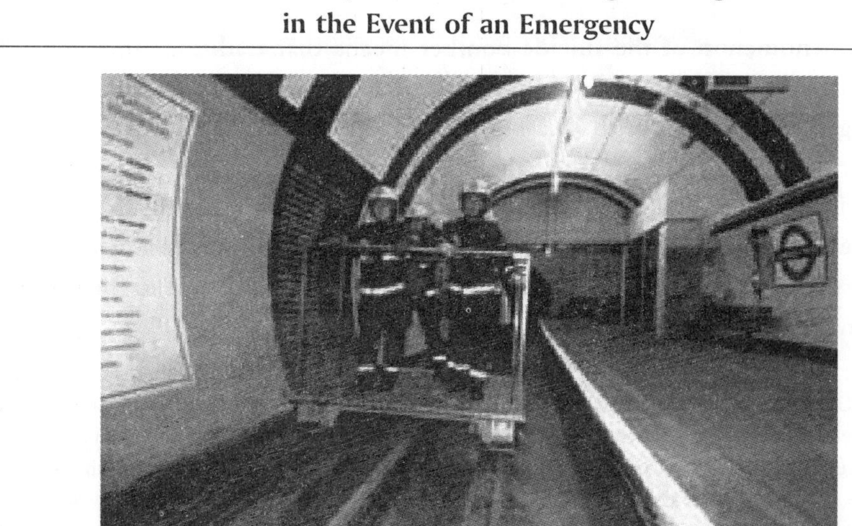

The emergency services were quickly deployed to each site, even though initially it was unclear as to the extent or nature of the incidents. Standard emergency protocols kicked in very early.

It would be wrong to pick out any group or any individual in particular; they were all heroes. All the agencies worked well together and concentrated on their specialised roles when necessary, and worked closely together when and where required.

As it became clear as to the scale and nature of the incidents, a decision was taken to evacuate the entire Underground network. Again this followed a well rehearsed plan for such an eventuality. The whole system was evacuated in just under an hour. It is estimated that over 200,000 people were safely evacuated.

Throughout the rest of the day, the emergency services took control of the four incident sites and the scenes passed from rescue sites to crime scenes for essential forensic investigation. Except for the immediate vicinity of the three incidents on the Underground, all trains were moved to depots to enable essential maintenance overnight to ensure that trains were prepared for service the following morning.

Recovery of Services

On the 8th July, 85% of the Underground service was operating. This was an important show of defiance from employees, and vital to restore public and employee confidence quickly.

As part of the London underground contingency plans, a recovery team was established on the 7th July. A service director was appointed to lead the multi functional teams that would be required at each site to work with the police. These teams would assist with evidence gathering, provide technical expertise and ensure that all the engineering capability was available as soon as each site was handed back by the police.

This organisation of resources of a central Gold team with the corresponding Silver controls at each site led to a speedy recovery of all the three sites, through good local liaison to ensure that the needs of each party was met.

Operational Issues

On the 8th July and subsequent days, managers and other available staff, such as revenue control and office volunteers travelled on the system, wearing high visibility clothing, providing reassurance for staff and customers alike and reminding customers to keep their bags with them and to report unattended items to staff and police.

High profile police presence was achieved through assistance from the Metropolitan Police, City of London and BTP forces across the country. Over the weeks that followed, there were times when over 6,000 police were deployed across the rail and bus networks in London.

Enhanced staff briefings were instigated to ensure that all staff were given rapid access to information as it became known. This proved absolutely important on the 21st July, when in the wake of the failed attempts to bomb three trains and a bus it was decided to keep the network operating and essential to rapidly communicate with staff to counteract some of the misleading media coverage. This positive action enabled the network to keep operating and to recover the latest incident scenes quickly.

As part of the investigation, the police required all CCTV data for the two weeks – prior to and including 7th July. Over 17,000 tapes were handed over with hundreds of digital hard drives. Previously the normal requirement for the vast majority of incidents had involved only a single station or train over a 24 hour period.

The criticality of communications has been highlighted since the bombings. With the exception of the incident trains, the radio system worked during the incidents. Since then it has become clear that there are some weak areas of reception and transmission. The plans to upgrade the radio system across the network have been accelerated, so that this will be in place across the Underground by the end of 2006. During the interim period whilst the system is being upgraded, additional hand held radios have been purchased to supplement the units in each driving cab.

In addition, work is in hand to enable the emergency services to use their radios on the tunnel sections.

Technology

Technology is often seen as the panacea to prevent terrorist attacks. CCTV is a good example of where this has been a useful tool in deterring criminals or those who do not wish to be captured. The images of the bombers on the 7th July clearly show it did not deter them; however it did provide useful intelligence for the police and directly led to the capture of the failed perpetrators on the 21st July. CCTV is also useful in spotting potential hostile surveillance.

Other forms of technology, for example screening equipment used at airports has clear benefits in that kind of environment, which has less throughput of passengers, more time, holding areas etc. Their use in a metro system would be limited due to huge volumes of passengers, lack of holding space etc.

Heathrow Airport is one of the busiest international airports and handles about 67 million passengers a year, while London Underground carries over 1 billion a year.

It is however important to keep abreast of technological solutions to improve security, but they must be fit for purpose within the environment and be extremely reliable, so as not create too many false alarms.

The UK Department for Transport recently announced that it is working with the rail industry and other government departments to find practical solutions that could potentially be introduced in an urban mass transit system. Trials are due to take place early in 2006 on National rail and London Underground.

Conclusion

Customer usage in the Tube has returned to pre-July levels and is exceeding year on year figures. Complacency has started to creep in with people returning to burying their heads in a book or their newspapers. Forgetful customers still leave behind over 300 unattended items every day, which our staff deal with very effectively using the HOT procedure.

The esteem of London Underground employees in the community has never been higher; they received justifiable praise for their vital role on the 7th July and subsequently in the return to normality.

Despite the horrific attacks on the 7th July and the regrettable loss of life and injuries, passenger transport systems remain the safest form of transport compared with private cars, where in the UK there are on an average 3,500 fatalities every year. The public make intelligent risk-based decisions all the time, as pedestrians, car users, on holiday or on public transport, and recognise that none of these activities is without risk. Indeed there are greater risks in the home; in the UK alone 600 people die every year through falls down stairs.

Communication is vital during major incidents and the media play a pivotal role in informing the public, without causing mass hysteria and doing the terrorists bidding by creating an atmosphere of fear or portraying spectacular images of the results of their atrocities. Transport operators, the police and Government have to play their part in ensuring regular up to date and correct information is provided to the media.

There is more public recognition that aviation type security screening is not practical on a mass transit public transport system; by its very nature it needs to be easily accessible and open. Any subsequent security measures implemented must be proportionate and acceptable.

That does not mean that preventative and protection measures should not be implemented; this would be a grave mistake and encourage more terrorist attacks on perceived easier targets. Many of the measures London Underground and the British Transport Police have developed were based on the threat of Irish republican terrorism, but that covered a range of different types of threat, including no-warning attacks. It would also be a mistake to believe that any future attacks will be definitely suicide attacks.

Measures such as attentive staff, who know and understand their environment and give the impression that they are in control, could make a potential terrorist fear that their attack may fail and deter them.

> "Physical security by itself does not prevent terrorism, but good security can displace risk, pushing terrorists towards less lucrative targets where there actions are likely to cause fewer casualties"
>
> – *Mineta Transportation Institute Report, 2001.*

(Geoff Dunmore is the Operational Security Manager for London Underground and has worked for LU for 30 years in a variety of operational and senior management roles. He was seconded to the London Resilience Team in the aftermath of 9/11 to assist with the review of resilience plans for a catastrophic terrorist attack on London. He can be reached at Geoff.Dunmore@tube.tfl.gov.uk).

6

Railroaded to Death: The China-Tibet Train

Vinay Lal

This article relates to one simple word 'development'. According to Henry David Thoreau, one might gather, understand and profound irony of technological blessings only. As world is captivated into the orbit of the world economy, China has assured to bring the fruits of socialist modernization to Tibetans and bring them into the orbit of the civilized world economy through Qinghai-Tibet railroad. This railroad from China to Tibet has created lot of hopes for the Tibetans. This has ended up with a conclusion of the efforts to end Tibet's shelter from the world and bring development to the people who had been forced to live under the burden of a feudal society.

With the Chinese President Hu Jintao's July 1 inauguration of the New Tibet railway, which links Golmud to Lhasa, the assimilation of the "Tibetan Autonomous Region," as Tibet is known in the Orwellian world of Chinese officialese, into the burgeoning Chinese empire may now be described as having reached the ominous point of no return.

Source: Asia Media, August 2006.

No one, except perhaps the most devoted advocates of Tibetan independence, will think of comparing this railway line across "the roof of the world" to the notorious "Death Railway" that most people became aware of through David Lean's film, *The Bridge on the River Kwai.* Yet, as shall perhaps become clear, this may be the most apposite comparison at this triumphal moment for the Chinese.

During World War II, as the Japanese military pushed its way across Southeast Asia and sought entry into India, it commandeered a huge labor force of nearly 275,000 men, comprised largely of conscripted Asian workers and allied POWs, to build a railway line from Bangkok to Burma. Working under the most wretched conditions, nearly 100,000 men succumbed to starvation, malnutrition and fatigue from backbreaking labor, cruel punishment and diseases such as dysentery, cholera and malaria. We have a nearly exact tally of the number of British, Australian, Dutch, and American fatalities – 6,318; 2,815; 2,490; and 131 – but the Japanese, who are scarcely alone in construing European lives as more worthy than those of miserable Indians, Thais, Koreans, and Burmese, didn't even bother to count the dead among Asians, some 80,000 of whom are now estimated to have died in less than a year.

The present China-Tibet railway line appears, at first glance, to present a study in contrast. The Chinese narrative about this accomplishment, at least, is unequivocally clear, and the world seems eager to embrace it. By all accounts, this train line across extraordinarily difficult and beautiful terrain is an "engineering marvel," and the Chinese have been voluble in voicing their opinion that it heralds a new chapter in world railroad history. The latest stretch of the Qinghai-Tibet railroad, from Golmud to Lhasa some 1,142 kilometers away, is largely 4,000 meters or more above sea level, and at 5,072 meters it reaches the highest point of the journey. Oxygen is pumped into cabins to prevent, or alleviate, the distress of altitude sickness; the windows have been equipped with ultra-violet filters to keep out the sun's glare; and a liquid coolant has been added along various stretches to ensure that the permafrost does not melt and thus endanger the structural foundations of the tracks.

The official Chinese news agency released reports which furnish those tidbits that habitually enthrall people interested in world records, and among edifying facts it emerges that a record 550 kilometers of the tracks run on frozen earth and that, at 5,068 meters above sea level, the Tanggula Railway Station is now the highest railway station in the world. Railway buffs who salivate at the prospect of exciting tunnel rides can, at 4,905 meters above sea level, travel through the Fenguoshan, the world's most elevated tunnel on frozen earth, and at 1,668 meters the Kunlun Mountain Tunnel now becomes the world's longest tunnel on frozen earth.

One should not, consequently, be surprised that the Qinghai-Tibet railroad has been described in glowing terms as an object lesson for Western engineers who remained skeptical about the viability of the project and as a stunning instantiation of China's rapid emergence as a world power. Much has been made of the economic rivalry, expected to grow exponentially over the next two decades, between India and China, but at least one Indian newspaper, *Business Standard*, was able to put aside nationalist pride in calling upon Indians to consider that "China's public miracles" – including the China-Tibet railroad and the gargantuan Three Gorges Dam on the Yangtse – suggest "engineering expertise and project management ability on an awesome scale. The Konkan railway and the Sardar Sarovar dam are simply not in the same league." The *Standard* notes that the railway line being laid to Srinagar, which has enjoyed its share of encomiums as a paradise on earth, barely reaches a third of the height scaled by the new train to China.

Before the train's inaugural run, Hu, a trained engineer, who also oversaw with his customary efficiency the administration of a martial law regime in Tibet when pro-democracy demonstrations broke out in 1989, described how the world's highest railway fulfilled a long-cherished dream of the Chinese people and the miraculous enactment of the promise to bring the fruits of socialist modernization to Tibetans and so bring them into the orbit of the civilized world of the global economy. In all these accounts, and countless other similar ones that will continue to emerge in the near future, the story of the China-Tibet railway is writ large in one word: development.

The argument was put rather more elegantly by the historian William Everdell, who has written that we "call 'modern' everything that happened to any other culture after it had built its first railroads." If Hu and the global corps of cheerleaders from the business, media, and political worlds are to be believed, with the arrival of the train into Lhasa from China, Tibet itself has finally arrived into history.

We might expect, of course, Chinese officials and the functionaries who run the state media to celebrate the Qinghai-Tibet railroad as the culmination of attempts to end Tibet's isolation from the world and bring development to a people who had been compelled to live under the yoke of a feudal society. The unimpeachable argument that Chinese repression has wrought untold havoc on the Tibetans – leading to the deaths and imprisonments of hundreds of thousands, exile for just as many more in India where the Dalai Lama has constituted his government in exile, and the deliberate destruction of monasteries and other manifestations of Tibetan culture – evokes little sympathy among those who, whether Chinese or elsewhere in the world, accept that the modernization of a people and its economy are indisputable social goods that we must strive to achieve even if the fulfillment of this ambition entails the sacrifice of a people and the loss of their culture.

Those who speak on behalf of the Tibetans are dismissed as "romantics" or as hypocrites who, while availing themselves of all the comforts and technologies of the modern world, would deny the same privileges to a people held captive to a feudal theocracy. The Chinese are now only prepared to tolerate criticisms that are offered from within the framework of modernity, which explains why, in building the railroad, they have been unusually sensitive to environmental considerations. Official news releases state that the railroad cars have been installed with environmental-friendly toilets, and are equipped with wastewater deposit tanks and garbage disposal facilities. Underpasses have been created to prevent Antelopes and other animals from coming on to the tracks. All of this is reminiscent of the safeguards put into place by the Environmental Protection Bureau, among the most active of state agencies in Tibet. Plastic bags are banned in Lhasa, and the government has shut down industrial units that do not meet environmental guidelines.

The environment is now sacrosanct, but people must remain expendable. Ever so keen to offer Tibet to the world as an illustration of the salubrious effects of the cleansing of feudalism, the Chinese have continued apace with the ethnic cleansing of Tibet. Once a land has been emptied of its people, it must be "repopulated", and among the slightly lesser known consequences of the occupation of Tibet by the Chinese are the immense population transfers that have resulted in the Tibetans becoming a minority in their own country. Han Chinese is now the dominant ethnic group in Tibet, and by 1996 they already outnumbered Tibetans in Lhasa by a 2-1 ratio. It is now 46 years since China invaded and occupied Tibet, and the Chinese have come to understand, bolstered in recent years by their growing economic strength, that they can act with utter impunity.

Alternative to Development?

The ideologues of development, one might say, have embraced a like view. When the blow must be softened, development's hardened advocates will speak of development with "human face," "sustainable" development, "shared" development, "alternative" development, but no one will speak of alternatives to development. We have come to the stage where development's particular contours are hotly disputed, but it is understood that the framework itself must not be abandoned.

Mao's "Great Leap Forward" spelled death for 25-30 million Chinese, victims of ruinous economic policies and grandiose plans of social engineering, and it is prudent to ask what forms death will take in this next phase of China's aggressive march to the tune of modernity.

Chinese actions are calculated to render Tibetans strangers in their own land, but there are many other, equally critical, forms of estrangement. Is it really necessary that every part of the world be absorbed into the orbit of the world economy, and is it necessary that every place be judged against some imagined plateau of modern civilization? Will Tibet's absorption into new tourist circuits be as beneficial to its own people as it will be to tourists? And just what does "beneficial" mean? On whose terms will the Tibetans be brought into the global conversations, perfunctory as they may be, that are presently taking place among those who count themselves as citizens of the world? China and Tibet are now "connected," but what kind of exchanges are likely to take place between the two?

Henry David Thoreau understood the profound irony of technological blessings. As he wrote in Walden (1854): "We are in great haste to construct a magnetic telegraph from Maine to Texas; but Maine and Texas, it may be, have nothing important to communicate." Some conversations and communications cannot take place except under conditions of extreme disparity, and among the most fundamental rights, one that is seldom recognized, is the right of a people to forgo exchanges and conversations that can only render them more vulnerable to dominant worldviews, lifestyles and cultural norms.

There is now a railroad from China to Tibet; and one can only hope against hope that the Tibetans will not be railroaded to their extinction.

(Vinay Lal, AsiaMedia Contributing Writer teaches history at University of Califonia, Los Angeles. He can be reached at vlal@history.ucla.edu).

Qinghai-Tibet Railway – An Engineering Marvel

Qinghai-Tibet Railway is the longest and highest highland railway in the world. Starting of the train has brought with it both appreciations and criticisms. Though the government of China is in high spirits as this will bring an economic revival in a poor and underdeveloped region, critics have found the railways of potentially being destructive for the unique culture and environment of Tibet.

The train is projected to reach the maximum speed of 100 kilometers per hour in the frozen earth areas while on non-frozen earth it is expected to reach 120 kilometers per hour. Tibet being on high altitude, passengers are asked to contact the staff if they feel uncomfortable. The train passes through the Golmud-Lhasa stretch having the highest point which is the 5072-meter Tanggula Pass border between Tibet and Qinghai. Golmud-Lhasa section stretches up to 1142 kilometers and its construction had cost around US$23.68 billion. The pass forming a part of the terrifying Kunlun range of mountains was considered impassable as the northern side of the range is a huge area of permafrost that stretches for hundreds of kilometers across the Tibetan plateau toward the Himalayas.

Constructing railroads through such a region was thought as unfeasible and was a challenging task for China as there is a layer of ice above the permafrost that melts as the sun rises and refreezes with the setting of the sun. Chinese engineers developed a method that would keep the ice on the top level to freeze permanently. To make this possible, coolants are driven into the earth to make sure that the ground near tunnels and pillars stay frozen. Though the Chinese government is self-assured about this technology, questions have been raised on the sustainability of this technology. Also it is predicted that the rail road would collapse within 10 years. Railroad construction was a challenging job for the 100000 workers employed for this project as the altitude was very high and the crew had to be outfitted with oxygen supplies.

The train passes through the Kunlun range which is a natural habitat of the Tibetan Antelope and to protect these rare animals from the probable accidents, 33 wildlife "passageways" have been integrated into the railway's design at the key areas along the route. The government has set aside around $192 million for environmental-protection projects along the route.

The railway will provide golden opportunities for hotels in Lhasa. Also the tourism revenues are expected to be doubled by 2010 according to the government. The railway is also expected to decrease the cost of transporting goods by above half into this region. Thus construction of railroad in this terrain is like a dream come true.

(Compiled by Pooja Dave, Research Associate, Icfai Business School Research Centre, Ahmedabad.)

Section II

Indian Scenario

7

Railway India

One of the largest railways in the world, Indian Railways expanded rapidly since 1853 to become a principal mode of transport. The increased output of basic industries such as power, steel, cement, fertilizers etc., is seen as necessitating facilities for bulk transport in which the Railways have a comparative advantage. To meet the transport demand of future and to ensure safe services to the customers, Indian Railways have laid down ambitious plans for enhancing transport capacity through upgrading technology and introducing improved management systems.

Profile

Indian Railways is one of the largest Railways in the world. Introduced in 1853 the Railway network in India spread and expanded rapidly and has become the principal mode of transport in the country. It has also absorbed advances in railway technology in tune with the requirement of moving large volumes of passenger and freight traffic.

Indian Railway consists of an extensive network spread over 109,221 kms covering 6906 stations. Operating on three gauges – broad gauge (1676 mm), meter gauge (1000 mm) and narrow gauge (762 and 610 mm), trains in India carry about 17.7 million passengers and 1.49 million tonnes of freight every day.

Source: http://siadipp.nic.in/publicat/books/rail.pdf.

Broad gauge although forming 72% of the route, generated 98.5% of freight output and 90.5% of the passenger output during 2002-03. Almost all the double/multiple track sections and electrified routes lie on the broad gauge – 16272 route kms, constituting over 26% of the total network, and 35% of the broad gauge network on Indian Railway is electrified.

Indian Railways has nearly 1,19,984 bridges – of which 9792 are major bridges. In 2002-03, 1151 bridges were rebuilt/rehabilitated. The transport effort is sustained through the use of 7681 locomotives, 214760 wagons and 44756 coaching vehicles. Over two lakh thirty thousand telephone exchange lines, 6809 long haul MW kms 9138 optical fiber communication route kms and over 1686 trunk tele channels kms distinguishes Indian Railway-Telecom network.

Table 1: Network of Railways (as on 1.4.2003)

Gauge	Route kms	Running Track kms	Total Track kms
Broad	45622	64461	87889
Metre	14364	14859	17848
Narrow	3136	3172	3484
Total	**63122**	**82492**	**109221**

Indian Railway system will develop a capacity to carry 624 million tonnes of originating revenue earning traffic, which in terms of transport output is 424

Table 2: Commodity-Wise Tonnage of Revenue Traffic (2002-03)

Commodity	Tonnage
Coal	235.85
Raw material to steel plants	40.99
Pig iron and finished steel from steel plants	13.63
Iron ore for export	16.66
Cement	46.25
Foodgrains	45.60
Fertilizers (chemical manures)	26.46
POL (Mineral Oils)	34.05
Balance other goods	59.25
Total revenue earning traffic	**518.74**

BTKMS, during the final year of the X plan (2006-07). During 2002-03, the revenue earning freight traffic moved by Railways was 518.7 million tonnes. The total passenger traffic in the year was 5048.2 million originating passengers.

Management of Indian Railways

Indian Railway is a department of Government and the Ministry of Railways functions under the guidelines of Minister for Railways assisted by Minister of State for Railways. The policy formation and management of Indian Railway Board comprises Chairman and six functional members. Wide powers are vested in the Board to effectively supervise the running of 16 zonal railways, metro railway (Calcutta), production units, construction organisation and other rail establishments. These are generally headed by the General Manager. Nine subsidiary organizations under the Ministry of Railways viz. IRCON, RITES, CONCOR, RCIL, RVNL, MRVC, IRFC, and KRCL undertake specialized jobs contributing to Indian Railways growth and progress. RITES and IRCON have their business abroad also.

Perspective Plan and Thrust Areas

The growing demand of transport, in general, is directly related to the growth of economy, the mobility of the population and other related factors. The Indian economy in the last few years has seen a robust growth and is expected to grow at the same rate in the next two years of the X plan. Indian Railways has planned to carry the traffic offered by the buoyancy in the economy. The increased output of basic industries such as power, steel, cement, fertilizers etc., is foreseen as necessitating facilities for bulk transport in which the Railways have a comparative advantage. The increasing rate of urbanization was also expected to generate demand for rapid transit system.

The X Five Year Plan had envisaged a growth rate of 4.8% per annum of originating loading and 3.5% per annum of freight output in terms of billion NTKM. As compared to this, the growth of originating loading in the first three years of the X plan is expected to be 5.6% and the freight output in terms of billion NTKM is 5.8%.

On the passenger traffic front however, the growth rate vis-a-vis target has been lower. There was a dip in the number of originating passengers in 2002-03 due to the upward revision of the passenger fares. Further, there has been a shift in the short distance passengers to the road sector with the expansion and growth of road network. Against an envisaged growth rate of 2.6% per annum, the actual rate of growth of originating passengers in the first three years of the X plan is likely to be 1.2%. However the passenger traffic in terms of passenger kms has grown at a rate of 3.9% per annum.

Table 3: Freight Traffic Projections for Final Year of the X plan (2002-07)

	Tonnage (Million)	Average Growth Rate
Originating tonnes	624	4.8%
Net tonne kms	424	4.9%

The thrust areas identified for the X plan period (2002-07) included strengthening of high density network-investment towards building up capacity, technological upgradation of assets for improving efficiency, throughput and increasing average speed of trains, utilizing information technology, improving safety of operations by replacement of over-aged assets through Special Railway Safety Fund, mobilization of additional resources through private-public participation in Railway projects and to increase share of passenger and freight traffic. Large investments in wagons, locomotives and tracks were foreseen and planned for, to augment the transport capacity of Indian Railways. Investment was needed for opening alternative routes to the congested corridors, which included converting meter gauge tracks to broad gauge.

During the X plan it has been planned to wipe out accumulated arrears of asset renewals as well as take care of the fresh accruals. To finance the liquidation of accumulated arrears of such overaged assets, by providing for their replacement, a Special Railway Safety Fund had been created in 2001-02. The replacement of identified assets is being undertaken from this fund with the objective of completing the same by 2006-07. Annual arisings of renewal of overaged assets during the X plan period is being planned simultaneously through Depreciation Reserve Fund (DRF).

To meet the transport demand of future and to ensure safe services to the customers, Indian Railways have laid down ambitious plans for enhancing transport capacity through upgrading technology and introduction of improved management systems. A critical issue to bear in mind is that, Railway infrastructure is capital intensive and has a long gestation period.

Table 4: Passenger Traffic Projections of the X plan

	2002-02	2006-07	Annual Growth Rate
Passengers (millions)	5169.3	5686	1.9%
Pkms (Billions)	494.2	593	3.8%

Indian Railways (IR) has laid thrust on acquiring high-powered diesel and electric locomotives. State of art high capacity 6000 HP Electric locomotives and 4000 HP diesel locomotives have been imported along with Transfer of Technology (TOT). Manufacture of these locomotives is being carried out in Production Units of Indian Railways. Lightweight high-speed coaches from LHB, Germany have also been acquired and commissioned into commercial services, with TOT for manufacture in India. RCF is manufacturing LHB type coaches for the Railways. IR is also in the process of further phasing out inefficient and relatively, operationally risk-prone conventional four wheeler wagon stock, replacing them with high capacity 8 wheeler wagons fitted with air brakes, casnub bogie, CBC and tapered roller bearings having features of zero defects during operation. During the X Plan years, while a policy decision has been taken to procure air-brake wagon stock of an advanced high-speed design with a speed potential of 100 kmph, it has also been decided to convert the existing air-brake wagon to high-speed version by retrofitment. This would considerably reduce the speed differential between freight and passenger trains, increasing line capacity.

Capacity Expansion Plan

i) Target for Additional BG Lines

Traditionally, the Railways have financed the augmentation of line capacity through New Lines, Gauge Conversion and Doubling – from within the funds allocated by the Ministry of Finance towards Capital expenditure. However, considering the large shelf of projects within these three activities, these funds are not found to suffice for completion of the projects within a reasonable time frame. The Railways have explored the possibility of attracting funds from other sources which include State Governments, beneficiary industries, port infrastructure companies etc. A beginning has already been made and execution of some projects within different models of cost sharing with State Governments, Private agencies etc., are already going on. The total BG kms added during the X plan is expected to exceed 5000 kms.

ii) Policy Initiatives taken during the X plan

a) Thrust is to be given for strengthening of Golden Quadrilateral and diagonals connecting the four metros. Active cooperation and participation of several non-Railway agencies in this effort are being sought. This includes – entering into funding arrangements with the State Governments, other Ministries and private parties.

b) Several new initiatives have taken place in augmenting resources with involvement of State Governments.

c) Apart from the State Governments, efforts are being made to develop Rail infrastructure through private partnerships.

d) Railways has recently entered into an MOU with the National Thermal Power Corporation, in order to explore the possibility of setting up captive thermal power plants for the Railways, to reduce expenditure on electric energy bill.

e) With a view to ensure an equitable allocation to railway projects in different states, allotment of funds for the activities of New Lines, Doubling, Gauge Conversion, Electrification have been objectively based on transparent criteria. The 3 major criteria viz. area of the state, the population of the state and the throw forward of projects in the states have been given predetermined weightages, for the purpose of allocation of funds state-wise.

f) Initiatives have been taken to improve line capacity, enhance safety and increase the asset utilisation through the gradual induction of modem signaling and telecommunication system of Electronic Interlocking system, Block proving through Axle Counters, Train Actuated Warning Device at

Level Crossing Gates and Mobile Radio Communication System. In order to prevent drivers from passing a signal at danger and assist him in running trains even under adverse visibility conditions, provision of train position and warning system on about 300 track kms is in progress.

g) Priority is being accorded to the construction of mega bridges as they provide strategic linkages. This includes the Ganga Bridge at Patna and the Bogibeel Bridge over the Brahmaputra. Other sources of funding for these projects are also being explored.

Technological Upgradations

High horsepower Electric Locos, Diesel Locos and Improved technology LHB type coaches have been introduced by the Indian Railways. The technology to produce such locos and coaches has also been adopted by Indian Railways as a step towards technological upgradation. Also high-speed goods wagons are being introduced to upgrade the goods trains for high-speed.

The Indian Railways have completed the first phase of computerized Freight Operation Information System to enable online tracking of cargo. The second phase of the project covering Terminal Management System would be completed in 2004-05 and would improve the quality of services substantially. The increased use of IT by Indian Railways would lead to optimal utilisation of the existing infrastructure, rolling stock and man-power and, in the process, not only increase revenue from freight traffic but also effect substantial reduction in operational cost.

During the X plan period, an endeavour to upgrade technology in all spheres with the objectives of improving reliability, reduce maintenance requirement, increase customer satisfaction and to reduce cost of operation has been made. The technology initiatives include the following:

i) **Track:** Higher axle load and speeds, mechanised maintenance, improvements in welding technology and better methods of detection rail flaws.

ii) **Wagons:** Improvement in axle loads, speeds, pay load to tare ratio and introduction of self-steering bogies.

iii) **Operation of High-Speed Freight Trains on Indian Railways:** Till recently, the Indian railways had been operating freight trains with a maximum speed of 75/80 kmph. A modified design of Casunub bogie fitted to airbrake wagons has enabled wagons to be run at a maximum speed of 100 kmph.

While increasing the maximum speed potential of freight trains leads to improvement in utilisation of wagons and locomotives, it also reduces the speed differential between passenger trains and freight trains. This would augment the section capacities, particularly on those sections working to saturation or near-saturation levels.

iv) **Coaches & EMUs:** Introduction of all stainless steel coaches to reduce maintenance requirements, use of air-springs in EMUs to improve riding comfort, etc.

v) **Computer-Based Centralised Traffic Control System:** Initiative has been taken to introduce Computer-based centralised traffic control system on Ghaziabad-Kanpur section under the modernisation of Signalling and Telecommunication Systems.

Safety

Implementation of Corporate Safety Plan

Railways have formulated a Corporate Safety Plan to enhance safety (2003 to 2013). The main objectives of the Corporate Safety Plan are to reduce the number of accidents and to reduce chances of passenger fatality in consequential train accidents etc.

While clearing of the arrears of replacement of tracks, bridges, signaling gears and rolling stock would be addressed through the SRSF, annual arising for these items will be taken care of by normal provisioning under DRF. In addition, in the plan period, thrust will be given on safety enhancement works as identified and detailed in the Corporate Safety Plan. The total expenditure involved for these safety enhancement works would be Rs.31,835 cr.

Special Railway Safety Fund

A non-lapsable Special Railway Safety Fund of Rs.17,000 crores was set up with the approval of the Government. The funding was to be done by a dividend free grant of Rs.12,000 crores from the General Exchequer and Rs.5,000 crores to be generated by the Ministry of Railways by levy of safety surcharge on passenger fares. The objective was to liquidate the accumulated arrears of renewal of assets up to 1.4.2001 within a time frame of 6 years from 2001-02 to 2006-07.

Out of Rs.17,000 crore of non-lapsable Special Railway Safety Fund (SRSF) set up in 2001-02, to wipe out arrears in renewal and replacement of over-aged assets within a time frame of six years, the expenditure in the first three years is Rs.6504.38 crores. For the year 2004-05, the total allocation (Net) at the time of BE for SRSF is Rs.2933 crores.

Anti-Collision Device: An Anti-Collision Device (ACD) has been developed by Konkan Railway Corporation, designed to prevent collisions like situations e.g. head-on collisions, side and rear-end collisions and those caused due to infringement by derailed vehicles on adjoining tracks. This device also helps in detecting train parting, and provides audible and visual warning at level crossing gates when trains approach.

The system works on satellite-based Global Positioning System (GPS) and Angula Deviation count principle for identification of track layout. The ACD is an intelligent micro-processor-based equipment. It consists of central processing unit, a global positioning system, and a digital modem for communication with other ACDs. When installed on a locomotives, brake vans and at stations and level crossing gates, these ACDs network among themselves to prevent accident like conditions.

The first prototype of ACD was demonstrated by KRCL in December, 1999. After limited trials, the device was put on extended field trials on Jalandhar-Amritsar section of the Northern railway in 2002-03.

To start with, provision of ACD on about 1735 Route kms BG section of Northeast Frontier railway has been taken in hand. The total cost of the work is about 65 crores. This shall be completed in the year 2004-05. Further, sanctioned works of provision of ACD on about 1750 Route kms of sections on Northern, Southern, South Central and South Western railways shall be taken in hand after the successful completion of Northeast Frontier railway pilot project. Additional ACD route survey on about 10,000 route kms has also been sanctioned on important sections of the Indian Railways. On present day prices, its introduction on the entire IR network would cost about Rs.1800 crores.

Crash Worthiness of Coaches: To improve the crash worthiness of coaches, as an immediate measure, coach interiors have been re-designed with improved fittings and features, which would not cause injury. Simultaneously, the coach body is being re-designed to absorb more impact so as to keep passenger-carrying areas intact.

Longer Rails: Indian Railways and Bhilai Steel Plant of Steel Authority of India Limited are also planning together to produce longer rails i.e. 26 metres and 65 or 78 metres, instead of the conventional 13 metres length to reduce number of welds in the track. This would ensure greater safety of the track. The potential for weld fractures on Long Welded Rails (LWR) and Continuous Welded Rails (CWR) would significantly reduce.

Integrated Modernization Plan (2005-2010)

Railways have formulated an Integrated Modernization Plan covering the period 2005-06 to 2009-2010 with the aim towards transforming the Indian Railways into a modern system of global standards. It is hoped that the initiatives outlined will go a long way in bringing about the desired transformation. The total expenditure involved for these identified items would be about Rs.24,000 crores.

Salient Features of the Plan are:

Passenger Business Segment

- Towards high speed travel.
- Shatabdi/Rajdhani trains to run with the latest technology coaches.
- Integrated and Extended National Train Enquiry System.
- Expansion of Computerised Passenger Reservation System.
- Expansion of Computerised Unreserved Ticketing System.
- Computerisation of Parcel Management System.
- Modern and environment-friendly toilets in coaches.
- Mechanised cleaning of stations.
- Mechanised cleaning of coaches.
- Extension of Coaching Operations Information System (COIS) for improved passenger traffic operations.
- Introduction of Public Address Systems on important trains.

- Improved safety features in coaches – Internal and External crash worthiness, anti-climbing features and use of fire retardant material in coaches.

Freight Business Segment

- Running of Freight Trains at 100 kmph on identified sections.
- Completion of 75 Throughput Capacity Enhancement works.
- Development of 50 Modern Freight Terminals.
- Introduction of high axle load operations on selected routes.
- Warehousing facilities near rail terminals through public/private participation.
- Web-based Claims Management System.
- Extension of Freight Operation Information System to cover Terminal, Rake and Crew Management Modules.
- Introduction of Double Stack Containers on identified routes.
- Modernisation of Freight Maintenance.
- Induction of corrosion resistant stainless steel body wagons.
- Induction of light weight aluminium wagons to increase carrying capacity.
- Modernisation of Guard's Brakevan.
- Provision of Bogie Mounted Brake System on freight stock.
- Development of Roll-On-Roll-Off door-to-door service.
- Locotrol for Diesel and Electric locomotives on identified Sections.

Logistic Support for Improving Share in Freight Traffic

A number of steps have been taken during the X plan period to improve Railway's share in freight traffic. Some of these are listed below:

- Rationalisation of freight tariff structure.
- Total number of classes for charging freight reduced from 59 to 27.
- The ratio of the highest and the lowest freight rates reduced from 8.0 to 2.8.
- Reduction in freight rates from 3.7% to 10.7% for certain high-rated commodities.

- Trainload benefit for all block rakes and commodities.
- Higher powers given to General Managers for flexible rating policy for specific pairs of stations.
- Incentives to Premier Customers generating freight earnings of more than 25 crores per annum for traffic originating from the sidings.
- Policy to attract short lead traffic through higher-freight concessions.
- Computerisation of freight movement through Freight Operations Information System.
- Providing warehousing facilities through CWC and private freight terminals. MOU has been signed for providing integrated freight terminals at 22 locations in the country.
- Port connectivity and inter-modal transport.
- Introduction of more and more number of high speed wagons to carry goods faster to the destination.
- Introduction of Refrigerated parcel vans to carry perishables and food stuff across the country on Express Trains.

It was expected that in the X plan about 1500 bridges would have to be strengthened/rebuilt yearly not only on account of the backlog but also larger arising of distressed bridges on account of heavier and more intensive traffic. In 2003-04, 1584 bridges were rehabilitated.

The objective of the X plan was to complete the doubling of the quadrilateral trunk routes, to undertake construction of third and/or fourth lines on certain very busy routes and to undertake doubling on other important routes where the existing single line had reached its saturation limit. In all about 1500 kms of doubling are planned to be completed in the X plan. During the X plan 742 kms of doubling is likely to be completed during the first three years of the plan period.

At present the approaches to all major urban agglomerations are extremely congested with passenger and freight trains competing for available line and berthing capacities. Creation of adequate terminal capacity will remain an area of vital importance to the Railways.

The approaches to major yards, important freight and coaching terminals particularly on the high-density traffic routes had been identified for improvements in the X plan. Facilities would also be created for running of longer passenger trains (26/24 coach lengths) on identified routes. At the same time, the user industries would also have to take effective steps to modernise loading and unloading systems.

Regarding electrification of routes, objective of the X plan was to complete the ongoing works, to take up electrification of the remaining un-electrified sections of the golden quadrilateral as also to cover certain missing links. Conversion of 1500 VDC suburban system in Mumbai area (CR&WR) to 25 KV AC was planned in the IX plan as it is no longer possible to increase the frequency of the suburban services on the DC system as it is not capable of taking any additional electric load is progressing well.

The objective in the X plan was to construct project oriented lines to serve new industries, complete missing links for developing alternative routes, lines required for strategic reasons, lines for establishment of new growth centres and to develop backward areas. About 1310 kms of New Lines were planned for completion in the X plan. However, the achievement on this front is likely to be around 613 kms only during the first three years of the X plan.

One additional project of Udhampur Srinagar-Baramulla has also been taken up as national project at a cost of about Rs.5000 crores, which is to be funded outside the Railway plan.

Signalling is an area where modernization and replacement are urgently needed. In an era of quantum technological advancement resulting in better equipment & providing greater safety through technical aids, e.g. provision of Auxiliary Warning System (AWS) etc., a total of Rs.1600 crores outlay was proposed in the X plan. The provisionally estimated expenditure would exceed the proposed outlay.

Keeping in view the massive transport requirements of the metropolises, the Railways propose to continue investment in projects already on hand and complete all the on-going projects. A joint venture with the Government of Maharashtra under the auspices of MRVC (Maharashtra Rail Vikas Corporation) is already underway for implementing new projects of the Mumbai suburban network.

Similar joint ventures are also on with the Government of West Bengal for extension of the Calcutta metro and with the Government of Tamil Nadu for development of Mass Rapid Transit System at Chennai.

Table 5: Acquisition of Rolling Stock in the X plan

Expected acquisition of Rolling Stock during the X plan is given below:-

	Original Targets Proposed by Railways	Revised Targets Proposed Now
Diesel Locomotives	444	655
Electric Locomotives	343	481
Coaches (conventional)	9,160	9,160
EMUs	1,965	1 745
Wagons (FWUs)	65,000	94,214

Policy and Procedures for Private Participation in Railways

BOLT/BOT Scheme

Projects identified for taking up under BOLT Scheme were Gauge Conversion, Doubling of existing single lines, electrification projects, telecom projects, supply of rolling stock such as wagons and passenger coaches, diesel and electric locos, supply of tracks, machines etc. The scheme had not been successful. The new BOT scheme, with features which are more investor-friendly, is to be put on trial for 2 projects. Meanwhile, a copy of the draft model documents has been sent to some zonal Railways, to facilitate compilation of the requisite technical and other details, which are to form part of the BOT tender for these 2 projects. With the role of financier being recognized and comfort being provided to financier by means of tripartite arrangement between Railway, Concessionare and financier, – a feature which was absent in the earlier BOLT scheme, this scheme is likely to provide substantial investment by private agencies in infrastructural projects, where the BOLT scheme failed.

Luxury Tourist Trains

The Railways run luxury tourist trains in collaboration with the State Tourism Departments e.g. the Palace on Wheels in collaboration with the Rajasthan Tourism Corporation (RTDC), the Royal Orient Express with the Tourism

Corporation of Gujarat Ltd. (TCGL) and the Deccan Odyssey in collaboration with the Maharashtra Tourism Development Corporation (MTDC). An MOO has also been signed with the Karnataka State Tourism Development Corporation (KSTDC) for running such a luxury tourist train. The costs and the revenue in these projects are shared by the Railways and the participating State on a predetermined ratio.

Public-Private Partnership in Rail Projects

Indian Railways is operating in the core sector of the economy and to strengthen, modernise and expand the network, it seeks to attract private capital as also State funding in the following categories of rail projects viz. projects for port connectivity, Gauge Conversion, Connectivity to Remote/Backward areas – New Lines, Doubling, Electrification and Suburban Transportation.

i) A Joint Venture named K-RIDE (Rail Infrastructure Development) Karnataka Limited has been formed jointly with the State Government of Karnataka for early completion of four identified projects in the State of Karnataka. K-RIDE will execute these projects through Project Specific SPVs. First such SPV named HMRDC (Hassan-Mangalore Rail Development Co.) has been formed with equity participation from Ministry of Railways, the Government of Karnataka and K-RIDE. Strategic partners and other financial institutions will also take part in the equity contribution. Besides, the Government of Karnataka has agreed for funding of three rail projects by contributing two-thirds of the cost.

ii) The Government of Tamil Nadu is also continuing to share two-thirds of the cost of Mass Rapid Transport System Project between Thirumayilai and Vellacherry; it has also been agreed to contribute 50 percent of the cost of Salem-Cuddalore Gauge Conversion Project and Chennai Beach – Tambaram-Chengleput Suburban Gauge Conversion project.

iii) Among other significant developments regarding partnership with State Governments for funding of projects, is the signing of a MOU between the Government of Jharkhand and Ministry of Railways, for execution of six projects estimated at Rs.1997 crores. Two-thirds of the project cost will be borne by the State Government and one-third by the Ministry of Railways. These projects will be completed in a time-frame of five years.

iv) Apart from participating in MRVC (Mumbai Rail Vikas Corporation), the Maharashtra Government through CIDCO is contributing two-third of the cost of rail projects being executed in New Mumbai area, viz. Belapur-Panvel Doubling, Thane-Turbhe-Nerul-Vashi line and Belapur/Nerul-Seawood Uran line.

v) The Government of West Bengal has agreed to share one-third of the cost of the extension of Metro Railway from Tolly Ganj to Garia.

vi) An MOU has also been signed with the Government of AP for development of the Multimodal Urban Transport System in the twin cities of Hyderabad and Secundrabad through Joint Venture. Train services have been introduced. An SPV is proposed to be set up for managing the project.

vii) A Special Purpose Vehicle named PRCL (Pipavav Railway Corporation Limited) which was formed with equal equity participation from Ministry of Railways and GPPL (Gujarat Pipavav Port Limited) for construction, Operations and Maintenance of Surendranagar – Pipavav Broad Gauge line, has implemented Surendranagar – Pipavav Gauge conversion/New Line project. The construction of this line has been completed and thrown open for Goods Traffic since March 2003. Earlier, connectivity of Mundra Port on the West Coast to the Broad Gauge network of Indian Railways has already been effected. Gandhidham-Palanpur gauge conversion is being implemented through the involvement of Kandla and Mundra ports. Kutch railway Company, SPV formed with Kandla and Mundra ports, the Government of Gujarat and RVNL are equity holders.

Implementation of certain Port Connectivity works under National Rail Vikas Yojana through Public-Private Partnership is being explored by Rail Vikas Nigam Limited.

Besides non-conventional sources of revenue are also being tapped to supplement the internal generation of funds which are:

- Commercial utilisation of Railway land and its surrounding – this envisages identification of certain station building and wagon loads in prime areas for advertisement as station-cum-commercial complexes.

- Revenue through commercial publicity, including grant of advertising rights on the wagons and selected passenger trains, advertising rights at level crossing gates and additionally advertising at Railway stations.
- Commercial utilisation of the Railways Right of Way proposed to be achieved by completing a nationwide, broadband telecom and multimedia network by laying optical fibre cables.

Glossary

Passenger Kilometre	A passenger transported over one km.
Net Tonne Kilometre	Payload of one tonne carried over one km.
Gross Tonne Kilometre	A tonne, including payload, tare and weight of engine, carried over one km.
Revenue Earning Traffic	Traffic which is paid for by consignor or consignee.
Non-Revenue Traffic	Traffic conveyed free for working the Railways.
Lead	Average haul of a passenger or a tonne of freight.
Net Load	Payload of passengers, luggage or goods carried by a vehicle or a train.
Wagon Turn-around	Interval of time between two successive loadings of a wagon.
Train Kilometre,	Movement of a train over one km.
Engine Kilometre	Movement of an engine under its own power over one km.
Vehicle/Wagon Kilometre	Movement of a vehicle/wagon over one km.
Loaded wagon kilometer	Movement of a wagon, including departmental, loaded with goods over one km.
Route kilometer	The distance between two points on a Railway system treating all lines (double, treble etc.) as a single line.
Running Track Kilometre	The distance of multiple tracks (excluding track in sidings, yards and crossings at stations) i.e. double, treble etc., taken as two, three or more, as the case may be.
Track Kilometre	The distance of running track kilometer and tracks in sidings, yards and crossings at stations.

8

Integrated Railways Modernisation Plan

R K Singh

Modernisation of Railways would enhance its efficiency and enable it to provide a safe and timely transit. A need has arisen for the railways to become customer driven to meet the requirements for business development in both passengers and also freight sector. The article attempts to present the modernisation requirements in passenger and freight segments which includes maintenance of cleanliness at stations, improvement in the design of coaches to enhance safety, employing state-of-the-art features and superior quality of steel in coaches, modernisation of freight terminals etc. To monitor the punctuality of trains, computerized Coaching Information System is being developed and call centres are to be set up to improve enquiry services. The article also covers other modernisation initiatives, which include modern track structure, modern bridge management system and disaster management system.

Modernisation of the Rail Infrastructure is not an end by itself but a means for achieving higher efficiency to provide cost-effective, safe and timely transport of both passengers and goods. Importantly the Railway must become customer oriented if it is to remain the preferred carrier.

"Integrated Railways Modernisation Plan" by, R K Singh is reprinted with the permission of Indian Railways Magazine Unit from September 2005 issue.

Infrastructure

Railways infrastructure consists of the fixed assets like track, bridges, OHE including sub-stations, signaling equipments and buildings and structures. Other assets include locomotives, coaches, wagons, various machines.

Production Units, Workshops and Maintenance depots form the service infrastructure which supports the main transportation infrastructure.

Modernisation of infrastructure would require induction of new technology in areas of track laying and maintenance, bridge construction and strengthening; locomotives both electric and diesel, coaches in both production and maintenance; wagons design and maintenance; signaling and telecommunication works and upkeep: OHE construction and maintenance and design, construction and maintenance of stations, yards, depots, service buildings.

Indian Railways Modernisation Plan (2005-10) attempts to bring out the modernization needs in a manner to focus these towards meeting customer requirements in various segments of business. Infrastructure modernization listed above, will therefore become integral into the planning to meet business development.

Must become customer driven in both passenger and freight sectors.

Passenger Business

Customer needs in passenger segment:

Modernisation Needs at Stations

Cleanliness: The sheer magnitude of the number of passengers dealt with at a large number of railway stations puts a lot of strain on available infrastructure, due to which it is difficult to maintain cleanliness at stations to the expected standards. Enthused by the success of recent experiments at a few stations by induction of mechanical implements and private participation, it is proposed to extend this model of mechanized cleanliness system to 250 A and B category stations by 2007-08.

Passenger Assistance: The Computerized Passenger Reservation System is a success story with a coverage of 97 percent of the reservation workload of which

Indian Railways can legitimately be proud of. It will be the Ministry's endeavour to connect all the district headquarters (rail-head and non rail-head) and places of tourist importance with traffic potential as per extant policy. It is expected that at the end of this period, the PRS network will cover almost the entire reserved segment. 200 locations will be added during the Plan period.

Modernisation Needs on Trains

Coaches: It is proposed to run all Shatabdi and Rajdhani trains with high speed latest technology coaches during the Plan period. These coaches use better quality of steel, other modern materials for the interiors and incorporate state of the art features such as modular controlled discharge toilet, large size windows, wheel slide protection device and longer length of coaches for increased seating capacity. Since these coaches have a speed potential of 160 kmph, their provision would ensure running of trains at higher speed, enhanced comfort and convenience to passengers. Development of an environment friendly coach with a controlled toilet discharge system, which goes a long way in improving the cleanliness of the coaches, is a mission area.

Safety: It has been the endeavour of Indian Railways to minimize accidents to passenger trains. Even in the unfortunate event of a passenger train accident, the effort is to contain the incidence of injuries to travelling passengers by improving the design of coaches by enhancing safety features.

Performance Improvement

Punctuality: To monitor the punctuality of over 8500 passenger-carrying trains and manage a fleet of over 38,000 coaches on suburban and long-distance routes, a need was felt to replace the slow and complex manual monitoring system. Therefore, the computerized Coaching Operations Information System (COIS) is being developed with three main modules viz. Punctuality, Timetabling, and Coaching Stock Management.

Information Dissemination: To improve enquiry services, 23 Call Centres would be set up across the country, one in each telecom circle. These would provide easy access to enquiry services through Interactive Voice Response Systems (IVRS) and computer-assisted manual response. While the basic infrastructure will be provided by the railways, provision of other facilities, equipments and services would be through sponsorships/private partnerships with revenue sharing arrangements. Queries pertaining to train running position, reservation, status, seat availability, and other important information would be answered by these Call Centres. For easy recall, a universal 3 or 4 digit telephone number would be allotted to these Call Centres. This service will be provided by 2005-06.

The National Train Enquiry System (NTES) provides online train running information to the IVRS systems at different stations. The same information is also given through the Train Enquiry website. To eliminate manual input of information, seamless integration with computerized Control Charting system is also being planned. Divisional Control offices of Indian Railways will be computerized for this purpose. NTES information would be available to the Call Centres through direct integration. This system is targeted for commissioning in 2008-09.

Safety: Modern track-structure is to be adopted while cleaning the arrears as per norms and consistent with traffic requirements. On bridges, composite sleepers are to be laid in lieu of wooden sleepers. The state-of-the art high output track machines in being procured on Indian Railways and the level of Mechanization of track renewal and maintenance activities are being increased to achieve the desired track geometry enhance the safety environmental work sites, fewer speed restrictions, better quality, reduced manpower and faster execution of work.

It has been decided to make provision of Tract Circuits to improve safety in train operation by eliminating the human factor involved in physical verification of clearance of track section. ACDs will be installed to prevent Signal Passing at Danger Cases and avert train collision, thereby enhancing safety in train operations.

Provision of BPAC will be made to ensure the clearance of Block Section (portion of track between two Block Stations), thus, enhancing safety in train movement. It is to be provided on all routes other than those provided with Automatic Block Signaling (ABS).

Semi High Speed (150 kmph) Network

A high speed network is a quantum technology jump over traditional rail network. Indian Railways intends to speed up its first Shatabdi train to 150 Kmph between New Delhi-Agra this year. Introduction of such inter-city trains would reduce the travel time and provide fast, efficient and comfortable services to passengers, comparable with airlines. Two inter-city routes will be developed to run these 150 Kmph trains using latest technology high speed coaches. These two corridors would be Delhi-Patna-Howrah and Delhi-Chennai.

Freight Business

Customer needs in freight business:

Modernisation Needs at Booking

Modern Freight Terminals: Most of the terminals on Indian Railways other than those which are part of the industrial siding, suffer from capacity constraints in terms of inadequate infrastructure. The Modernisation of freight terminals is inescapable to provide quicker loading/unloading of rakes, improved turnaround and customer satisfaction. It is proposed to modernize 40 terminals during this Plan period. This would include full length rake handling facilities, engine on-load working, adequate shunting necks, illumination for round the clock working, weigh bridges, etc.

IT Enabled Information Office System: The major share of Railway revenue comes from Freight traffic. Freight revenue is collected at the Goods sheds/sidings at the time of loading/unloading of the wagons. Commercial aspects of the freight business and working of the Goods sheds and sidings are being computerized under the Terminal Management (TMS) module of the Freight Operations Information System (FOIS).

Heavy Haul Operations

In IR, running of longer trains on corridors with mixed trains is difficult. Advantage, therefore, lies in higher axle load and better pay load to tare ratio in wagons.

Indian Railways now manufactures new generation 4000 h.p. three phase, AC-AC diesel locomotives designed by M/s General Motors. These locomotives have a number of state-of-the-art features such as computer controlled brakes, AC-AC transmission, microprocessor-based control with self-diagnostic feature, 100 percent dynamic braking, creep control for better adhesion, etc. Passenger locomotives can haul longer passenger trains with 24 coaches and have a speed potential of 160 kmph.

Open wagons mainly operating in the coal circuits corrode on account of combined effect of corrosive acids and high abrasions due to mechanized loading/ unloading. Corrosion resistant stainless steel body for open wagons have been induced to minimize this adverse effect.

Corrosion takes place mainly in coal carrying open wagons due to the combined effect of corrosive acids and high abrasions caused by mechanical loading. Aluminium body wagon would improve availability and reliability of stock significantly through reduced corrosion. The biggest advantage will be the ability to carry an additional payload of four tonnes per wagon.

Capacity constraints on the certain routes necessitate introduction of double stack freight trains. The feasibility of running double stack container trains is being assessed. It is planned that double stack container trains is being assessed. It is planned that double stack container trains would be introduced on one of the identified routes connecting North India with Gujarat ports. The project would involve upgradation of fixed infrastructure and induction of specially designed modern wagons. The funding mechanism will be through involvement of stakeholders.

Higher Speed of Goods Trains

The growing challenges posed by the projected growth of freight traffic in core sectors necessitate that the speed potential of freight trains is increased to 100 Kmph. This involves upgradation of the existing fixed infrastructure. Indian Railways have recently inducted freight wagons fit for 100 Kmph. It is proposed to introduce running of freight trains at 100 Kmph on the high density Golden Quadrilateral and its diagonals connecting four metropolitan cities.

Throughput Enhancement Works

Besides the major throughput enhancement works included under National Rail Vikas Yojana (NRVY), completion of 68 ongoing sanctioned works at an approximate cost of Rs.2390 crore would result in immediate throughput enhancement and de-bottlenecking of saturated sections. In addition, seven other identified works at an approximate cost of Rs.2000 crore shall also be completed during this period. On completion of these works, a large number of existing capacity constraints shall be overcome.

On the Indian Railways, standard train load of 4700 tonnes are being run on Ghat Section by using 6 to 7 loco in consists of 3 to 4 in front, middle and on the rear. Communication between these two consists is almost impossible with the existing means of exchanging the signal through whistle and even with the walkie-talkie particularly in tunnels, endangering safety. Indian Railways has a number of graded sections such as Quelem-Castle Rock, Igatpuri-Kasara, Lonawala-Khandala, etc., which necessitate the provision of Locotrol for safe and efficient operation.

Other Modernisation Initiatives

Modernised Track Structure, Maintenance and Relaying Activity.

Modern track structure of heavier 52/60 kg Rails with higher Ultimate Tensile Strength (UTS) of 90 kg/mm2 and low hydrogen content (1.6 ppm), is to be adopted while clearing the arrears as per norms and consistent with traffic requirements. On bridges, composite sleepers are to be laid in lieu of wooden sleepers.

The state-of-the-art high output track machines are being procured on Indian Railways and the level of mechanization of track renewal and maintenance activities is being increased.

The objective is to achieve the desired track geometry, enhance the safety environment at work sites, fewer speed restrictions, better quality, reduced manpower and faster execution of work. This will reduce the requirement of corridor block and also facilitate maintenance of track etc., during night time.

Modern Bridge Management System

It is proposed to introduce a Bridge Management System (BMS) as a pilot project over South Eastern Railway followed by full scale adoption over Indian Railway System in the next five years. This computerized system will facilitate quick retrieval and analysis of data optimum resource allocations, network and project level management, planning based on "deteriorating models for bridges". The BMS will be Web-based to facilitate entry and access of data at field as well at headquarters level. Pilot project will be completed by 31 March, 2008.

Adoption of Modern Techniques for Inspection and Maintenance of Bridges

Several measures for modernizing the inspection, monitoring and health assessment of railway bridges with a view to ensuring safety and providing intervention in a need based manner have been initiated. Pilot projects in the following areas have been sanctioned.

- Adoption of State-of-the-Art Non Destructive Testing (NDT) equipments.
- Mapping of unknown foundations and integrity testing of foundations.
- Acoustic Emission Testing of Bridges.
- Fatigue testing and remaining life assessment of Steel Bridges.
- Strain gauging and load rating of bridges.
- Use of Mobile rail cum road Bridge testing laboratories.
- In situ Dynamic testing – Indo Austrian Programme.

It also proposed to undertake studies and develop projects in the following areas:

- Testing and Remote Monitoring of bridges using modern technologies – IIT/Mumbai.
- Vibration Signature Testing and Remote Monitoring of Bridges.
- Adopting Seismic Isolation Techniques and Earthquake Protection of Bridges in collaboration with IIT/Kanpur.
- Scour assessment, real time monitoring and protection of Bridges in collaboration with IIT/Kharagpur.

- Use of High Performance Concrete in Railway Bridges.
- Development and use of Advanced Corrosion Protection System for Bridges in collaboration with IIT/Mumbai.
- Under Water Inspection of Bridges.
- Inspection and maintenance of Railway Bridges by Mobile Bridge Inspection Units (16 Nos.)
- Residual Life estimation of Concrete Bridges in collaboration with IIT/Kanpur.
- Laying Long Welded Rails over Bridges taking Track Bridge interaction into account.
- Adopting modern Bridge Technologies for building bridges, rehabilitation of old bridges and use of Advanced composite materials in Bridges in collaboration with IIT/Mumbai.

Modern Disaster Management System

Indian Railways have a well-established system for providing rescue and relief services at the time of train accidents. However, with longer passenger trains and heavier freight trains running at faster speeds, there is a need to upgrade these services. Further, over the years there have been technological advancements in the field of rescue and relief, which need to be brought into the system to meet the current expectations of rail users.

In the above backdrop, the Ministry of Railways constituted a High-Level Committee to Review the Disaster Management System over Indian Railways. The committee have looked at all the issues and made certain recommendations.

The implementation of these recommendations will be done during the Plan period. Some of the important recommendations are as under:

- Self-Propelled Accident Relief Trains (SPART) with rescue and medical relief capability.
- Emergency Rail-cum-Road vehicles for accessing difficult areas.

- Setting up of an Institute of Rescue and Medical Relief at Bangalore.
- Emergency Rescue Vehicles for faster response by road.

Financial Strategy

Modernization necessarily encompasses many activities that are linked to day-to-day operations, those that have bearing on safety and investments for creating passenger amenities. Likewise, modernization could be in the form of creating new infrastructure and assets or replacement of existing assets with those using more advanced technologies. Accordingly, funding of the Integrated Railway Modernisation Plan would need to tap almost all sources of Railway financing n an appropriate mix. It will be the earnest endeavour of the Ministry of Railways to ensure that all the initiatives taken in the Integrated Railway Modernisation Plan are worked upon and targeted benefits are attained. The Modernisation Plan would provide broad guidelines and direction for future investments towards Modernisation of Indian Railway System within the next five years. Out of the total expenditure of Rs.24,000 crore, Rs.4000 crore is available under SRSF, Rs.3730 crore will be mobilized from internal generation, Rs.6000 crore from Market borrowings and the balance Rs.10,270 crore would be met through enhanced budgetry support.

(R K Singh is the Chairman, Railway Board.)

9

Indian Railways: IT Innovations in Passenger Services

Chinmoy Kumar

The article talks about the innovation strategies adopted by Indian Railways in the field of information technology to provide better services to passengers and also to take care of the comforts of passengers traveling by Indian Railways. The article also highlights the introduction of the internet reservation system, CONCERT, unreserved ticketing system, railway credit cards and mobile reservation, which were only some of the instances where upcoming technologies gave new dimensions.

"Seeing things from a customer angle can go a long way in improving Indian Railways and is, therefore, very vital. Seeing every problem from the customer's point of view can make Indian Railways a customer-driven, focussed organization."

– IIMS Rana, Former Chairman,
Indian Railway Board.

Source: The Icfai Journal of Services Marketing, March 2006.

"CRIS (Center for Railway Information Systems) is using information technology to take great strides towards remarkable social achievement in transportation."

– Daniel Morrow, Executive Director,
Computerworld Smithsonian Awards Program[1].

The Indian Railways operated in a highly complex environment that made it imperative for its operations to be continuously updated with timely and accurate information, to a variety of business concerns. Further, the optimum utilization of the available resources demanded deployment of a robust infrastructure through implementation of innovative and economical technologies.

This case provides the reader an insight into the various cost-saving innovations that were adopted by the Indian Railways (IR) in improving and advancing their passenger services. The progressive implementation of Information Technology (IT) served as a thrust towards better responsiveness to the rising passenger demands. The communication infrastructure that IR built up over the years not only helped it cater effectively to the ascending customer needs but also opened new avenues for revenue generation. It augmented its revenues and also helped it cut down surplus expenditures through better utilization of resources by way of improved demand analysis, better management of coaches and efficient utilization of railway tracks.

Background Note

The railway industry in India witnessed tremendous growth, both in terms of operational infrastructure and delivery of passenger services, ever since the first commercial engine rolled from Mumbai to Thane in 1853. Being the world's second largest organization[2] under the control of a single management, IR served more than 13 million passengers every year. By the end of the year 2004, IR boasted of 6853 stations, 63122 kilometers of track, 37840 passenger coaches and 222147 freight cars. There were more than 14,300 passenger trains providing transport services all through the length and breadth of the country. Over a

---

1 Computerworld Smithsonian Awards were presented to leading IT innovators instrumental in producing any remarkable social, economic and educational change. These innovators were nominated by a committee comprising CEOs of the United States' leading IT companies.

2 IR was the second largest organization after the Russian Railways.

period of more than one and a half century, IR had built up an extensive and far-reaching network of railroads that covered roughly 40% of the freight and 20% of the passenger traffic (refer Exhibit 1).

Despite the important socioeconomic role of the IR, the organization witnessed certain structural and operational challenges that served not only as impediments to growth, but also had a negative impact on the organization's finances. Being a medium of mass transport, the railways found it increasingly difficult to maintain stable fares to buffer the increasing expenses. There was an urgent need to look for ways to cut down expenses, increase efficiency, and search for additional sources of revenues. The continual increase in population, coupled with the liberalization policies of the government, significantly affected the operations of the railways. The growing passenger traffic and the competitive threats from alternative modes of transport like roadways put mounting pressure on the IR to revamp its operations and build up its capacity. The gradual liberalization of the economy boosted the transport industry that gained increased prominence due to the expansion of market. However, unlike the roadways that was dominated by profit-seeking private players, IR was a public-utility organization that played the dual function of a public utility service as well as a commercial organization. In order to meet its social commitments, IR compromised on its profitability. For instance, the IR ran many trains on unprofitable routes that hampered its services to the needier and more profitable ones. Besides, it also faced other problems like inefficiency in service delivery, overcrowding in trains, subsidized fares to certain categories of passengers, ticket-less travels, improper management of coaches, so on and so forth. These problems were not only functional in nature, but also had strong social and political underpinnings. Railways being a fully government-owned organization often became a soft target for political parties to further their own populist schemes. This not only dragged the IR off its limited resources, but also affected the organization in delivering transport services effectively and efficiently.

In order to remain profitable, the Railways started investing in cost-cutting technologies that helped the organization to economize on resources and also facilitated streamlining of its varied functional operations. However, the ticketing services of the IR received thrust only after the first passenger reservation system was implemented in 1985. The later two decades saw faster implementation of newer and more advanced technologies by the Indian Railways.

Pioneering the IT Wave

The Indian Railways was among the first organizations in the country to implement computerization on a large-scale. During the 1950s, the organization commissioned IBM mainframe computers for its zonal offices. The mid-1960s saw development of EDP centers that primarily dealt with payroll, inventory control and passenger accounting. Each application received data from different units once a month, and took five to ten days to complete the full processing cycle that involved record preparation, production and correction of error (exception) lists, program running and output printing. The payroll processing was the first application taken up by IR and was initially implemented at zonal headquarters with gradual extension to divisions, workshops and other units. The inventory control system took stock of more than 10000 items from stocking depots all over the zonal railways. The passenger accounting system eased the process of matching the monthly ticket sales with the receipts.

In 1985, the IR launched its first passenger reservation system IMPRESS (Integrated Multi-train Passenger Reservation System) as a pilot project in New Delhi. Developed by Computer Maintenance Corporation Pvt. Ltd. (CMC)[3], it was the first Online Transaction Processing (OLTP)[4] system of the IR. Subsequently, four more PRS (Passenger Reservation System) centres were opened at Secunderabad, Mumbai, Kolkata and Chennai. Despite its technical shortcomings (the initial PRS at five centers were discrete systems that functioned independently without any networking) it was instrumental in saving reservation costs, besides improving the overall service to customers. The major IT projects undertaken by the Indian Railways with their year of establishment is given in Exhibit 2.

CRIS – The Nucleus of Railways' IT Initiatives

The Center for Railway Information Systems (CRIS) was established in 1986 as an umbrella for all IT activities at IR. With its own in-house R&D efforts, CRIS

[3] CMC Limited (*http://www.cmcltd.com/about_us/corporate_profile.htm*) was an information technology solutions company providing services to a clientele of premier organizations in the government and private sectors.

[4] Online Transaction Processing (OLTP) systems are optimized for data entry operations involving capture, validation and storage of large amounts of relatively small database transactions.

was highly instrumental in the implementation and expansion of various IT projects undertaken by the organization. One noticeable achievement of CRIS was the development and implementation of CONCERT (Countrywide Network of Computerized Enhanced Reservation and Ticketing) based on a distributed computing architecture[5]. CONCERT was first implemented at the Secunderabad PRS in September 1994. The networking of the five PRS centers was complete by April 1999, when the PRS center at Chennai also came under the CONCERT platform. All the five sites were initially networked with a modest Internet speed of 64 kbps on leased communication lines from the Department of Telecommunications (DoT). By July 2004, IR had over 2500 terminals at nearly 1100 locations throughout the country. This covered more than 94% of the total reservation requirements of the IR. CRIS actively worked to expand its computerized reservation facilities so as to cover more stations, satellite locations, city booking offices and other non-rail head state capitals. A significant step in this direction was the extension of this facility even to state capitals not having direct rail links, e.g., Shillong, Itanagar, Kohima, Gangtok, Port Blair, etc.

The implementation of CONCERT yielded substantial benefits. The reservation procedure became less labor-intensive and more technology-based, and there was significant increase in the number of transactions handled per day. The new system also offered ease in computation of differential fare structures which hitherto took sizeable amount of time. CONCERT had provision for cluster booking, wherein a passenger could book tickets for onward journeys from a single window two months in advance. The new application could prepare charts that gave well-defined layout of passengers and their seating arrangements. These charts were posted outside the railway coaches and were also placed at respective platforms for the convenience of the passengers.

Going Online: Railways on the Web

The Indian Railways launched the online reservation system in August 2002, under the aegis of IRCTC (Indian Railway Catering and Tourism Corporation), the organization's marketing arm that handled the catering and tourism-related functions. The online reservation system was an extension of the PRS system and

[5] Distributed computing is a programming model in which processing occurs in many different places (or nodes) around a network. Processing can occur on a server, website, personal computer, hand-held device, or any other smart device.

served as an interface between the users and the PRS. With its Web-based interface, passengers could enquire information about trains, find out their reservation status and also book tickets online. The service was initially offered at Chennai, Delhi, Hyderabad, Kolkata and Mumbai and in the very first month the department sold 3343 tickets. By the end of December 2003, IRCTC sold more than 70,000 tickets and extended its services to more than 120 cities all over India.

The procedure of online reservation was simple. A user was required to register himself with the IRCTC website by furnishing his detailed personal information. He was subsequently provided with a login ID and a password through which he could enter as a registered user and perform online transactions. The IRCTC website worked in tandem with the PRS, calculated the fare and tallied the results with the PRS system. Upon successful approval from the PRS, the site displayed the fare (including the courier charges to the user). The user was finally directed for payment through a highly secure 128-bit SSL[6] payment gateway that offered the users the convenience to pay either through credit cards or debit cards. Once the payment was successfully made and booking confirmed, the user was provided a PNR number and an IRCTC transaction ID through which he could track the status of delivery of his ticket. The PRS and the payment gateway also provided authorization codes to the IRCTC website which was forwarded to the printing stations. An operator manually copied the authorization code from the IRCTC system to the PRS. Finally the printed tickets were despatched to the individual users through private courier service.

This facility was efficient, convenient and also economical for officially busy users who could not afford to personally go to a PRS center or who otherwise found the service charges of touts and agents exorbitantly high. While these agents charged service charges depending upon the number of passengers, the IRCTC had a flat rate for up to six passengers.

Difficulties in Implementation

The workload on the PRS was enormous. It handled more than 1.3 million queries on roughly 14,300 trains. Amitabh Pandey, Group General Manager, IT Services, IRCTC, once remarked, "The PRS had to handle close to the tune of

6 Secured Sockets Layer (SSL) is a protocol that transmits communications over the Internet in an encrypted form. On-line shopping sites frequently use SSL technology to safeguard credit card information.

600,000 reservations per day. Internet connectivity at that time was poor and the Web pages took a lot of time to load and sometimes the customers used to book a ticket multiple times since they kept clicking repeatedly."

To overcome these snags, their two payment gateways, ICICI Bank and Citibank, upgraded their services to a higher bandwidth. The department also reduced the response time by implementing Xeon and Pentium processors that powered the different application and database management modules through four separate four-way servers. As a sequel to these improvements, the IR website became a hub for a perpetually increasing number of online enquiries from varied categories of passengers.

Other Innovations

The IT strategies of IR did not remain confined to the implementation of the passenger reservation system or the online internet system. The organization kept on investing in several state-of-the-art technologies that, apart from being user friendly, also emerged as avenues for higher profits.

Integrated Voice Response System

Way back in 1994, the Integrated Voice Response System (IVRS) was introduced for the first time in New Delhi by AT&T[7] in alliance with CMC in the development of an interface with the PRS system. The system was gradually implemented in major cities and by August 2004, it found presence in 27 stations all over India. IVRS was a telephone-based, computerized railway enquiry system. IVRS brought immense benefits to the railway passengers as they could enquire about the reservation status of their seats or berths over phone without any hassle of personally going to a station.

Unreserved Ticketing System

Another important landmark in these progressive implementations of IT at the railways was the introduction of the Unreserved Ticketing Services (UTS). The service was initially launched in August 2002 as a pilot project at ten stations of Delhi area. Hitherto, the PRS offered services only for reserved tickets overlooking the concerns of a huge crowd of more than 550,000 passengers who could not avail advance tickets for commuting small distances on unreserved trains. Unreserved

---

7 AT&T was a leading networking company providing voice and data solutions for businesses worldwide.

tickets were earlier offered only two hours before the scheduled departure of trains. This not only caused inconvenience to passengers (as they had to wait in long queues to purchase their tickets) but it also affected the IR adversely in terms of loss in revenues, cumbersome reporting and poor demand analysis. While some of the trains ran overcrowded, the others went partially vacant.

CRIS took about nine months to develop UTS. The implementation eliminated the earlier lapses in ticketing and helped the IR to substantially control overcrowding. The system comprised a network of terminals wherefrom the passengers could buy unreserved tickets for any journey 30 days in advance.

The Unreserved Ticketing System allowed advance planning and rational analysis of passenger demands for unreserved coaches. It also helped the IR to effectively monitor sales of tickets on various trains and regulate the train capacities to the fluctuating demands of passengers. With an aggressive use of leading hardware, data management and network technology, IR could successfully address the needs of the passengers of unreserved trains.

National Train Enquiry System

The National Train Enquiry System (NTES) was introduced by the IR to provide passengers real-time information on the movement of trains. Designed and developed by CRIS, NTES was a robust, centralized information system that enabled the passengers to get up-to-date information concerning arrival or departure of passenger trains (including expected time), platform berthing, journey planning, available facilities at stations and railway rules. The information was collected from stations, control offices and other database administrators and fed into computers after every half an hour in 61 control offices across the country. All information was made available to the users through display boards, IVRS, public address system, face to face enquiry, online touch screen kiosks, close-circuit TVs, Passenger Operated Enquiry Terminals (POET) and Internet. Initially implemented at Secunderabad in 1999, NTES was later extended to 11 stations by July 2004.

Tele-Booking Services

This service was first launched by the Northern Railways in alliance with the Standard Chartered Bank. The facility was initially launched in Delhi, wherein passengers possessing the co-branded rail credit cards issued by the bank could book tickets over phone, 48 hours before the scheduled departure of the train.

Wireless Services

Railtel Corporation of India Limited, a 100% subsidiary of the IR, planned to introduce Wi-Fi-enabled Internet services on running trains. Technical trials were conducted on the Tughlakabad-Faridabad section. The department also had plans to offer the facility of making international long distance calls using VoIP (Voice over Internet Protocol).[8] Four pairs of Shatabdi trains were already provided with telecommunication facilities available on payment of normal charges.

Another grand feat for the IR was the introduction of railway reservation facility through mobile phones. The concept was executed by IRCTC in September 2004 and the service was initially offered through Hutchinson and Reliance cell phones. The facility was initially offered in the National Capital Region (NCR) as a pilot project and later more and more places were covered. By the end of 2004, the IR planned to extend the mobile reservation service to more than 120 cities all over India.

Leveraging on IT

To stay competitive, the IR had to improve its performance in terms of regularity and speed of carriage, the comfort of travel and overall safety of passengers. The optimum utilization of the available resources demanded deployment of a robust infrastructure which made it even more important for the IR to implement newer technologies and employ them as critical managerial tools for confronting and tackling various business challenges. The IR, being a multi-locational, multi-functional and multi-divisional organization, proved to be an ideal backdrop for investment in Information Technology.

Operational Challenges

Indian Railways faced challenges on many fronts. The growing traffic needs of the country made it difficult for the Railways to continue with the elaborate and well established manual information system. Earlier, most of the IR communications

[8] VoIP is a technology for transmitting ordinary telephone calls over the Internet, using packet-linked routes, instead of the normal Plain Switched Telephone Network (PSTN) line.

were carried out through dedicated voice communications network that collected and transmitted information from the remotest corners of the country to control centers at the highest level. The size and complexity of the operations, growing traffic and changing technologies placed a heavy burden on this manual information system. IR also faced competition from roadways that had gained significant popularity as a fast mode of transport. The success of the roadways in carrying 80% of the passenger traffic laid in the existence of predominantly private players who offered cheaper and point to point transport service. Moreover, roadways did not witness the common operational problems of IR, like overcrowding and delays. The cost of maintenance and expansion of the railway infrastructure was enormous. In order to reinforce the passenger services, the need for a technology-intensive infrastructure became an operational necessity.

The Most Economical Mode of Transport

Despite all operational constraints, railways remained an energy efficient mode of transport, ideally suited for long distance travel. The railways had always been ecologically safe and much less polluting to atmosphere, compared to aircrafts and motor vehicles. European ecologists had established that the energy required by the railways per kilometer of passenger carriage was 4-5 times less than that of airlines and 3-4 times less compared to that of airways; at the same time railways polluted the air 7-8 times and 4-6 times less, compared respectively. In proportion to traffic handled, railways used 2.5-3 times less land than highways. The same was true with airports. In proportion to the carriage of passengers they required more land compared to that of high speed trains.

Gaining Competitiveness through Technological Innovations

In order to carry out the broader social goal of providing affordable transport service to the country, IR made substantial investments in resource saving technologies. The progressive implementation of IT served as a thrust towards better responsiveness to the rising passenger demands. The communication infrastructure that IR built up over the years not only helped it cater effectively to the rising customer needs but also opened new avenues for revenue generation. The Internet reservation system, CONCERT, unreserved ticketing system, railway credit cards and mobile reservation were only some of the instances where upcoming technologies gave new dimensions to customer satisfaction. They augmented IR's revenues and also helped cut down surplus expenditures through better utilization of resources by way of improved demand analysis, better management of coaches and efficient utilization of railway tracks.

Exhibit 1: Rail Road Shares in Traffic

	Passenger Traffic		Freight Traffic	
Percentage Share	**Rail**	**Road**	**Rail**	**Road**
1950-51	80	20	89	11
1996-97	20	80	40	60

Exhibit 2: Major IT Milestones at Indian Railways

Year	Milestone
1985	Implementation of IMPRESS, the first passenger reservation system.
1986	Centre for Railway Information System (CRIS) established.
1994	CONCERT implemented at Secunderabad. IVRS also introduced at New Delhi.
1999	NTES (National Train Enquiry System) implemented at Secunderabad.
2002	Unreserved Ticketing Service (UTS) launched in New Delhi. The IRCTC website also launched in the same year. Internet Ticketing began.

M Ravindra, the former Chairman of the Indian Railway Board, observed at one place, "If the cost-profit center approach has to be brought in and zero-based budgeting made a must, there is no alternative to having wide-scale usage of information technology."

(Chinmoy Kumar is Associate Consultant, the Icfai Business School, Kolkata. He can be reached at chinmoyk@ibsindia.org).

References

1. Agrawal V K, "Indian Railways: A Profile Since Independence", *http://pib.nic.in/feature/feyr2000/fjan2000/f130120001.html*, January 28, 2005.
2. "Bombay to Goa?", *http://www.rediff.com/travel/tretc.htm*
3. "Indian Railways Runs State-of-the-art Passenger Reservation Systems on HP Open VMS Alpha Server Systems", *http://www.h71000.www7.hp.com/openvms/brochures/indiarr.*
4. "Indian Railways—Introduction", *http://www.asiatradehub.com/india/railways.asp*
5. "Indian Railways is 150!", *http://www.chennaionline.com/cityfeature/features/indianrail.asp*
6. "Indian Railways", *http://www.trainenquiry.com/StaticContent/Indian_Railways.aspx*
7. "Indian Railways to Receive Computerworld Honor", *http://news.indiainfo.com/2004/06/01/0106railways.html*

8. "IRCTC Opens Up A New Train of Thought", *http://www.expresscomputeronline.com/20040405/coverstory01.shtml*, April 5, 2004.
9. ibid
10. Mariam Joseph, "Sybase Powers Indian Railways and China Railways via Software", *http://www.domain-b.com/companies/companies_s/sybase_india/20030205_software.htm*, February 5, 2003.
11. Mathur S S, Director ME (C&IS), Ministry of Railways, "Steam-rolling with IT", *Dataquest Special Supplement*, March 31, 2004.
12. "Message to Stakeholders from Chairman, Railway Board", *http://www.irsuggestions.org/servicetopassengers.htm*
13. "On the Right Track", *http://www.rediff.com/netguide/2003/jul/29train.htm?zcc=rl*, July 29, 2003.
14. ibid
15. "Our Story", *http://www.210.212.218.5/web/history.htm*
16. Performance Evaluation of Coaching Services in the Indian Railways—A Case Study, *http://www.asosai.org/journal1985/performance_evaluation_of_ coaching_services.htm*
17. "Prospects for the Development of the Railway Transport in Russia", *http://www.analytics.ex.ru/cgibin/txtnscr.pl?node=21&txt=414&lang=2&sh=1*
18. "Railways Launch Reservation on Mobile", *http://www.sarkaritel.com/news_and_features/sep2004/9railways.htm*, September 9, 2004.
19. Ravindra M, "Reorganization, A Dire Need", *The Hindu* Survey of Indian Industry 2004.
20. "Telephone and Internet Facilities in Trains", *http://www.pib.nic.in/archieve/lreleng/lyr2003/rmar2003/18032003/r180320031.html*
21. "Top 10 IT Implementations of the Year", Maximum Social Impact, Online Rail Ticket Booking System, IRCTC, Indian Railways, *http://www.pcquest.com/content/implementation/2004/604061001.asp*, June 10, 2004.
22. "Unreserved Ticketing System", *https://www.secure.cwheroes.org/briefingroom_2004/pdf_frame/index.asp?id=5051*
23. *http://www.allahabad/netfirms.com/douknow.htm*, January 28, 2005.
24. *http://www.indianrail.gov.in*
25. *http://www.210.212.218.5/web/history.htm*
26. *http://www.cris.org.in/ntes.htm*
27. *http://www.indianrail.gov.in*
28. *https://www.secure.cwheroes.org/briefingroom_2004/pdf_frame/index.asp?id=5051*

10

Safety as Key Business Theme! – Indian Railways Perspective

P C Sharma and Amitabh

Since the railways are recognized as the safest mode of mass transportation, safety is recognized as the key issue and special attribute. Safety is basically the product of good practices at all levels of functioning i.e., design, manufacturing, maintenance and operations. It is the key performance index which the management needs to monitor along with productivity. Investment in safety improves productivity and is a good business proposition. This article covers the strategy and proper investment planning for safety with the pounding efforts of Indian railways, which has helped in strengthening the infrastructure and modernization of rail system by substantial improvement in safety performances.

1.0 Introduction

Railways have come to be recognized as the safest mode of mass transportation on account of inherent characteristics of the system. Railway managements have zealously guarded this image over the ages. Safety has thus come to be recognized as the key issue for the railways and one of its special attributes. No railway system can survive by ignoring this vital aspect as safe and timely transit is not only significant for passenger traffic but also for transportation of materials, in today's highly competitive environment. Safety ranks highest among the factors in selection of a mode of transportation – above the cost and transit time. Accidents hurt business not only in the immediate context but also in the long run and ultimately only those means of transport flourish which are perceived to be safe. It is, therefore, the key performance index which the top managements need to monitor along with productivity. The two cannot be divorced from each other and are, in fact, end products of the business activity in a transport organization which it needs to pursue to excellence.

2.0 Indian Railways – Building the Nation

The foremost task for the Indian Railways after independence in 1947 was to strengthen and modernize its infrastructure not only to support the economic development in the planned era but also to rid the system of obsolesce and poor maintenance. 1950s were primarily devoted to pulling up arrears in maintenance of track, signaling and rolling stock, besides providing small rail links to the heavy industries like steel plants that were being set up. The inputs given by the nation for renewals and restoration not only brought about an improvement in productivity, but also helped bring down the incidence of accidents on the Railways to a great extent. Number of accidents on Indian Railways came down from 8481 in 1950-51 to 2131 in 1960-61. Derailments which constituted bulk of the accidents came down from 7527 to 1415 over the same period. There was also appreciable reduction in the number of collisions, although there was increase in the categories of 'fire in trains' and level crossing accidents. The unrelenting efforts of Indian Railways in strengthening the infrastructure and modernizing it have led to substantial improvement in the safety performance in subsequent decades, which primarily forms the basis of this paper.

3.0 Indian Railways – Mega-Size Railway System

Indian Railways operate on continental and gigantic dimensions with nearly:

- 63112 route kms
- 39900 Passenger vehicles

- 7681 locomotives
- 215 thousand wagons
- 6850 block stations
- 1472 thousand work force
- 120 thousand bridges
- 16750 manned level crossings
- 20600 unmanned level crossings
- 97 loco sheds
- 50 workshops and production units
- 318 carriage and wagon maintenance depots
- Rs.520 million expenditure on staff per day
- Rs.1 billion revenue expenditure daily.

And daily transport output is approximately:

- 2 million train kms.
- 14 million passengers
- 1.5 million tonnes freight loading
- 8700 passenger trains run
- 5700 freight trains run

4.0 What is Safety?

Safety is basically the product of good practices at all levels of functioning i.e. design, manufacturing, maintenance and operations. Safety is compromised when the laid down standard practices are infringed. First symptoms of deterioration in the safety performance are evidenced by the increase in the number of failures. Overlooking these warning signals can be disastrous as each of these is an accident waiting to happen. Accidents and assets failures lead to hold ups, missing of schedules and disrepute amongst the customers, which affect the business adversely.

4.1 Although no technology is fail-proof, an error rate, howsoever small, being inherent in any man-machine system, reliability of the equipment is the most important factor in the efficiency and safety of a transport system. Objective of the various research organizations is to develop equipment and systems which have near zero level of failure rate. Side by side with the induction of advanced technology, it is imperative that the same is maintained properly and replacements, renewals made as and when needed. If the accidents have to be minimized, it is imperative that the equipment in use is always kept in fine fettle.

4.2 Over the last decade or so for which data is available, Indian Railways have laid special emphasis in improving health of the infrastructure and rolling stock. While steam traction, which was highly fault prone has been completely phased out from the main line operations, induction of modern technology and initiation of various measures have brought down the failures of diesel and electric locomotives on line to just about one-third. Four-wheeler freight wagons which were primarily equipped with screw couplings and vacuum brake system have been almost phased out. Small population of four-wheeler tank wagons that still exist are being moved in close circuits and under surveillance. All new rolling stock is being manufactured with more efficient air brake system and existing rolling stock with adequate residual life is being retrofitted to air brake in the workshops. These steps have also brought down cases of poor brake power, train partings and coach detachments very substantially. Failures of electric traction equipment have been contained despite substantial growth through induction of modern technologies. Failures of signaling and interlocking gear have been controlled substantially by accelerated replacement of mechanical signaling with improved systems of panel interlocking and route relay interlocking. Over the period, signaling and interlocking aids like track circuiting, block proving axle counters, and solid state technology have been inducted into the system to minimize incidence of accidents due to failures on the part of Station staff. Almost all high density routes have been provided with modern signaling equipment. Bulk of the failures in signaling gear are therefore, from the low density sections, which still have mechanical semaphore signaling systems. Number of failures of track have gone up, which is primarily attributable to substantial growth in the number of welds, more prone to failure, with progressive growth in long welded rails and aging effect on AT welds.

Table 4.2: Equipment Failure on Indian Railways

Year	Rail	Diesel Locomotives	Electric Locomotives	Wagons	Poor Brake Power	Train Parting	Coaches Detachments	OHE	Signals
91-92	7129	13609	8112	92798	3449	2142	573	1093	236289
92-93	6590	12753	7957	60983	4671	1989	579	778	206608
93-94	4184	11822	7047	71549	3314	1749	602	655	198445
94-95	2980	10220	6219	58415	3188	1583	604	382	161395
95-96	2810	8474	5891	44242	3458	1423	432	256	139730
96-97	2965	7625	4956	37150	3140	1313	361	169	125259
97-98	2672	7077	4686	23490	2367	1172	250	163	111014
98-99	3852	6347	4035	17631	1428	1135	200	144	100554
99-00	8416	5703	3806	13529	868	1034	169	166	118397
00-01	10660	5389	3685	8782	474	1081	230	503	132735
01-02	10678	4808	3211	7209	259	1013	194	309	121242
02-03	10374	4416	2976	5796	164	826	148	651	110640
03-04	8613	4301	2929	4586	60	688	156	475	117240

4.3 As a result of upgradation of the infrastructure, there has been consistent improvement in asset failures, despite steady growth in volumes of business both on freight as well as passenger segments resulting in high growth in revenue as can be seen from Graph 4.3:

Graph 4.3: Turnover Indices of IR

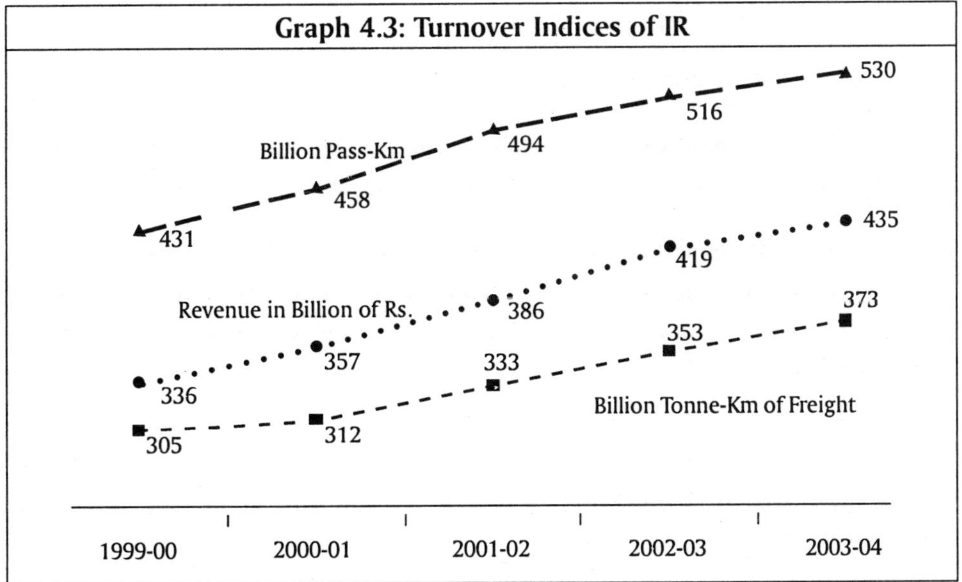

While freight in terms of billion tonne kms grew by 21.5 %, growth in the passenger traffic over the same period has been 18.4 %. Growth in the revenue has been of the order of 31.8 %.

5.0 Indian Railways – In Perennial Quest for Safety

5.1 With such a massive utilisation of assets, safety is of paramount importance not only for its sake, but also for operational efficiency. Hence, the highest priority is accorded to safety and the rail mode continues to be the safest means of transportation for public. Indian Railways have always considered safety as the key business objective at all levels of management. No compromise is tolerated in safety of Rail users and investment has been done in all possible areas which could enhance safety in working of Indian Railways. From time to time, Indian Railways has been periodically getting its safety preparedness reviewed by expert committees headed by eminent personalities, mostly retired Judges/Chief Justice of Supreme Court of India.

The following 4 Committees have scrutinised IR safety in the last four decades:

- Railway Accident Committee – 1962 (Kunzru Committee)
- Railway Accident Inquiry Committee – 1968 (Wanchoo Committee)
- Railway Accident Inquiry Committee – 1978 (Sikri Committee)
- Railway Safety Review Committee – 1998 (Khanna Committee)

Major recommendations of first three committees have been implemented and implementation of recommendations of Khanna committee is underway.

5.1.1 As result of regular review and initiatives undertaken, safety on IR has improved considerably by way of continuous reduction in train accidents despite manifold increase in traffic as can be seen from Graphs 5.1.1 and 5.1.2:

5.1.2 As can be seen from the graph 5.1.2, Accidents per million train Km., a composite index of safety, dropped sharply from 5.5 in 1960s to a figure of 0.39 in 2003-04. IR has thus taken long strides in improving safety of rail travel.

Graph 5.1.1: Trend of Train Accidents Per Year

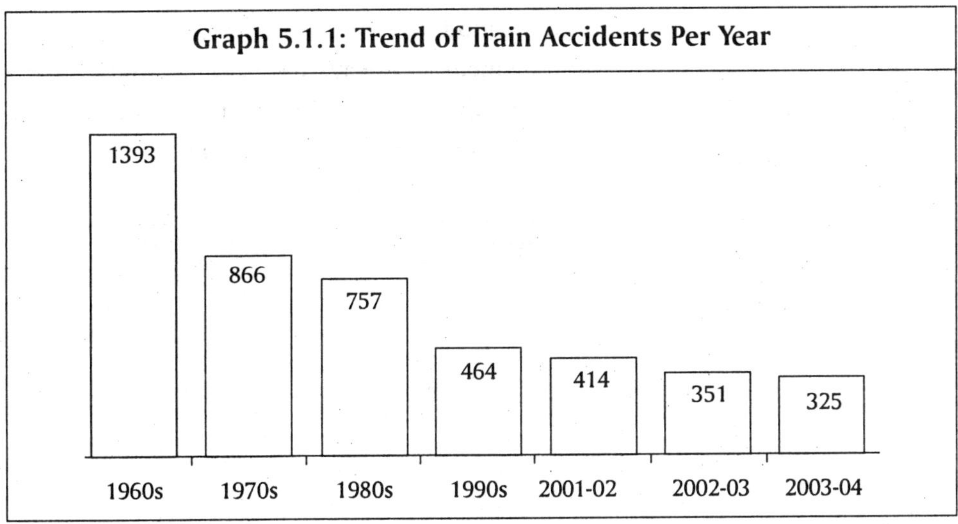

Graph 5.1.2: Trend of Accidents Per Million Train Kms

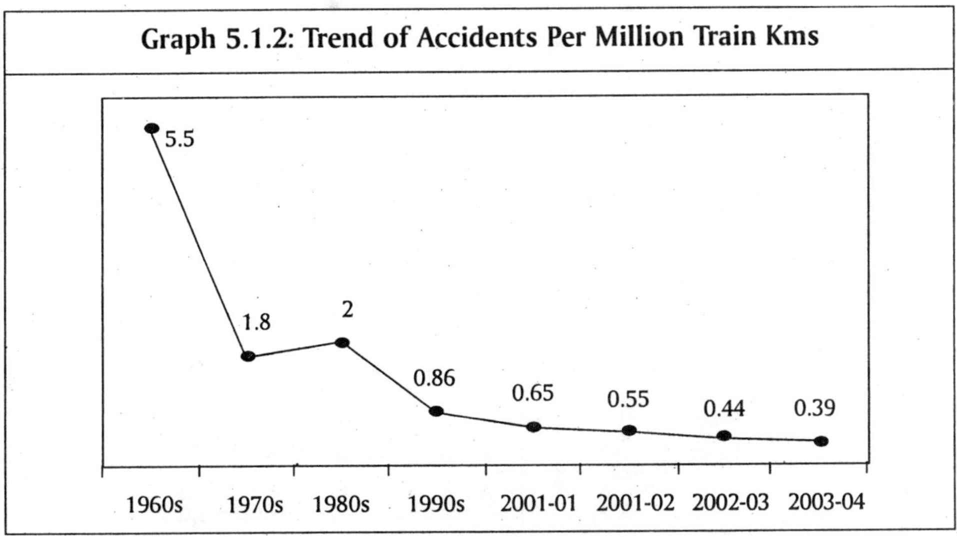

5.2 Category-wise share of consequential train accidents is important to comprehend potential hazards of different type of accidents and efforts made to contain each type separately. Looking at different categories of accidents in Graph No. 5.2 , derailments which form bulk of them, have come down from 1066 per year in the sixties to 202 in 2003-04, collisions which are the most serious type have come down from 83 per year in the sixties to 9 in 2003-04. Fires in trains have also registered substantial decline from 104 to 14 per year in the period under study. Level crossing accidents have not shown much improvement. Railways have no control over the road users, whose failures lead to almost all such accidents. Also, there has been phenomenal growth in the number of road vehicles in the period under study.

Graph 5.2: Type Wise Accidents on IR Since 1960 to 2004

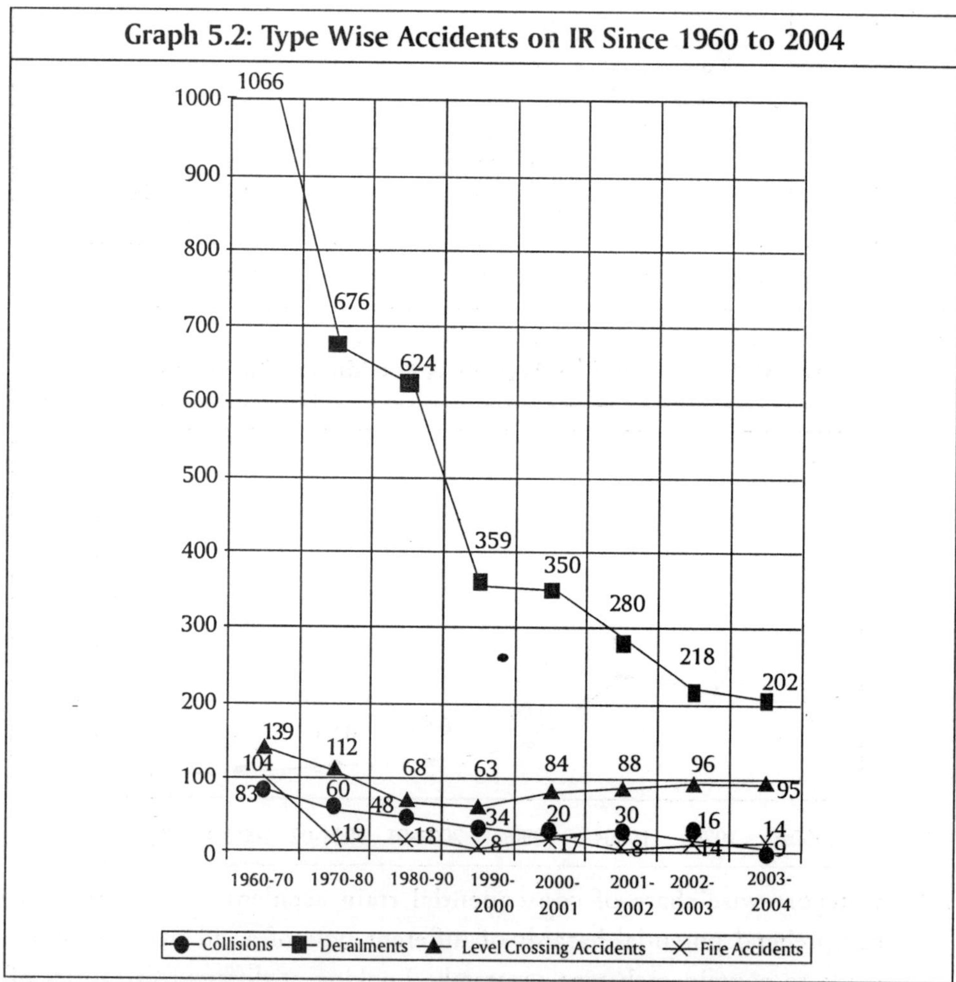

5.2.1 During the last decade (1993-94 to 2003-04) derailments were a major contributor (71%) in the total tally. These were followed by level crossing accidents (20%). Collisions and 'fire in trains' accounted for 6% and 2% respectively.

5.2.1: Type Wise Accidents Per Year (1994-95 to 2003-04)

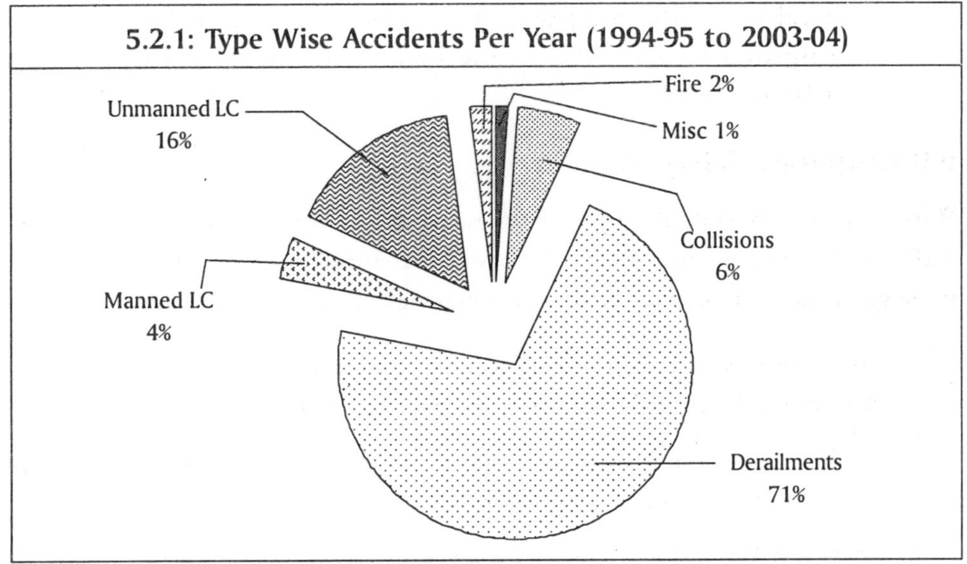

5.3 In any plan for prevention of accidents and minimising their impact, saving of human lives must merit the highest consideration. Collisions are the most dreaded accidents for any railwayman. On Indian Railways, collisions accounted for 6% of the accidents, of which only 4% involved passenger carrying trains, but these resulted in 32% of the total casualties. Accidents at level crossings accounting for 20% of the total

5.3: Casualties in Train Accidents (1994-95 to 2003-04)

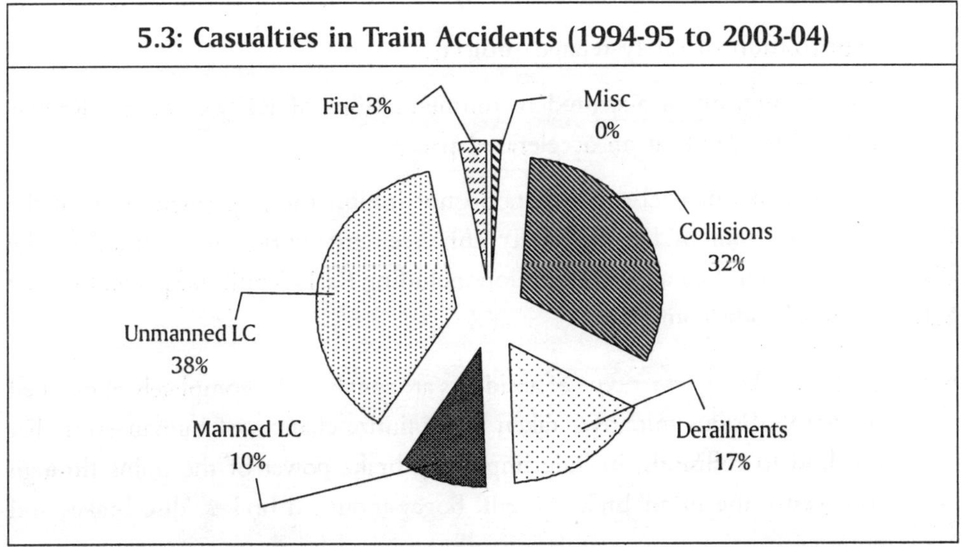

accidents on IR were responsible for 48% deaths. Derailments though constituted bulk (71%) of the train accidents, these accounted for 17% of the casualties.

6.0 Corporate Safety Plan

With view to accelerate the pace of the safety drive, Indian Railways formulated a 10-year Corporate Safety Plan, which was presented to the National Parliament in August, 2003. This plan envisages achieving following broad objectives:

a) To achieve reduction in rate of accidents per million train kilometers from the present level of 0.44 to 0.17 by the year 2013.

b) Implement measures to reduce chances of passenger fatalities substantially in consequential train accidents by 2013.

c) Focus on development of manpower through major improvements in working environment and training to reduce the accidents attributable to human failure by 40% by 2013.

d) Achieve safety culture on all fronts including maintenance depots, worksites, stations, controls etc.

e) Progressively achieve an environment of "Fail-proof" from the present "Failsafe" system of asset failures by upgrading the systems by 2013.

f) Prioritization of safety-related projects.

g) Implementation of accepted recommendations of Railway Safety Review Committee 1998 at an accelerated pace.

To ensure that financial constraints do not inhibit the implementation of the Plan, fund requirement for the safety enhancement works, as outlined in the Plan, has been identified as Rs.318 billion including Rs.170 billion Special Railway Safety Fund already committed.

6.1 Collisions, being worst type of accidents are sought to be completely eliminated by 2013. Various initiatives taken to minimize chances of human error that can lead to collisions, include improving brake power of the trains through progressive use of air brake system, bogey-mounted brakes, disc brakes and improvements in signalling infrastructure – 2500 of 4700 interlocked stations are fully track circuited. Auxiliary Warning System has also been installed over about 500 kms, including heavy urban area of Mumbai.

The biggest initiative underway in prevention of collisions is the introduction of Anti Collision Device (ACD) developed indigenously. Anti Collision Device (ACD) works on a satellite-based Global Positioning System (GPS) and Angular Deviation Count principle for identification of track lay out. It is an intelligent microprocessor based equipment, consisting of a central processing unit, a global positioning system and a digital modem for communication with other ACDs. There are two types of ACD equipments viz. 'mobile ACDs' for locomotives and brakevans and 'stationary ACDs' for Stations and level crossing gates. All the ACDs interact with each other and exchange information within their radio zones upto 3 kms and results of ACD interaction lead to a decision whether the loco ACD shall apply brakes or not.

6.2 There are about 38000 level crossings on Indian Railways, of which 16,750 are manned. All the accidents at un-manned level crossings take place on account of failure on the part of the road users, as evidenced the world over. While manning does bring down the accidents, it has other limitations of causing unduly long detentions to road users apart from problems of finding resources for the purpose, particularly when most of these level crossings exist in sparsely inhabited remote locations. Although massive inputs in providing grade separators (road-over-bridges/under passes), manning and interlocking with signals and telephones have been provided, the problem of negligence on the part of the road users is virtually beyond reasonable control. Since 1990-91, 203 grade separators have been provided, 1435 level crossing gates have been manned and 1747 level crossing gates have been interlocked. As most of these accidents lead to heavy casualties, involvement of government agencies and NGOs is being resorted to educate and counsel road users.

6.3 Derailments which though account for proportionately less casualties, have serious impact on operational efficiency and reliability. With the focused attention on human resource, technological upgradation and modern maintenance practices, the present level of human failures causing derailments is bound to improve substantially. With phasing out of derailment-prone and less reliable 4-wheeler tank wagons from the fleet, investments being made through SRSF/DRF into rehabilitation of track and rolling stock etc., and anticipated improvement in the skills and quality of manpower through enhancement of HRD, it is feasible to attain a substantial reduction in derailments.

6.4 Based on the above mentioned strategy the Corporate Safety Plan envisages reduction of accidents on Indian Railways by the year 2012-13 substantially. Collisions are targeted to be completely eliminated. Derailments will come down by 60% and Fire accidents by 80%. It has not been possible to project assured improvement in level crossing accidents, as there is no control over the circumstances that lead to such accidents.

7.0 Investment in Safety Improves Productivity

7.1 Indian Railways is placed in a peculiar situation in as much as it is not entirely free to revise fares and freight rates commensurate with the variations in cost of inputs. While rate of increase in cost is dictated by a multiplicity of factors beyond the control of the Railways, there is a strict parliamentary control over the fixation of tariff, which is generally done as an annual exercise with prior approval of Parliament. The compulsion of democratic

7.1: Expenditure on Safety

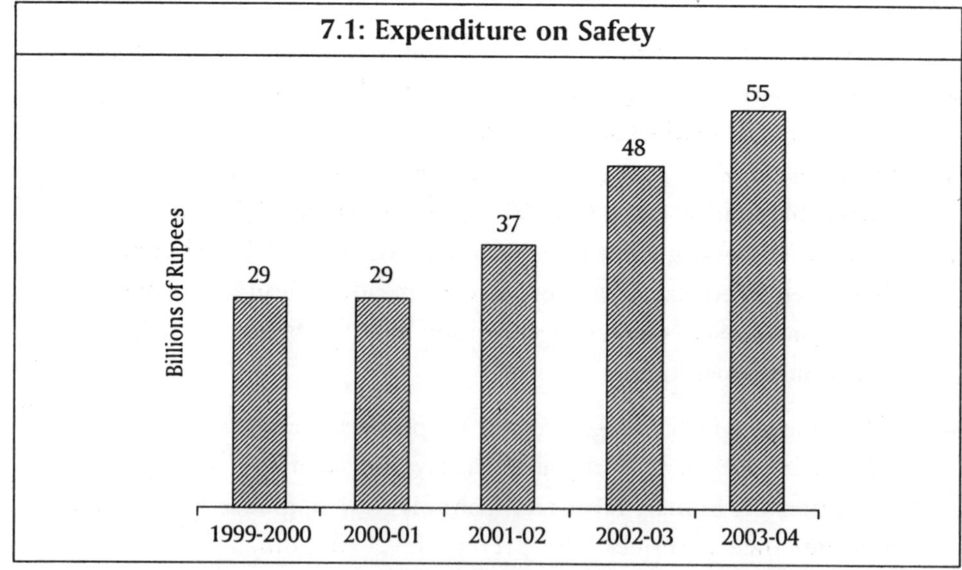

pulls and pressures compel the Railway management to carry certain sections of traffic far below the cost of carriage, resulting in the exercise of budget making a super balancing act. The special efforts have, therefore, to be made to ensure that adequate provision is made in the annual budget for replacement and renewals, highlighting this inadequacy. From time to time special expedients have, therefore, to be resorted to wipe out the arrears in renewals. One such effort has been in the recent past to create Special Railway Safety Fund of Rs.170 billion giving much needed impetus to the renewal of assets and technology inputs. The level of expenditure on safety related works including renewals of assets during the last five years has more than doubled as may be seen from Graph 7.1.

7.2 Safety-related inputs have been provided to Indian Railways steadily apart from inputs for capacity enhancement. While these have led to Indian Railways carry higher volume of traffic from year to year, there has been a gradual decline in the number of accidents as would be clear from the Graphs 7.2.1 and 7.2.2.

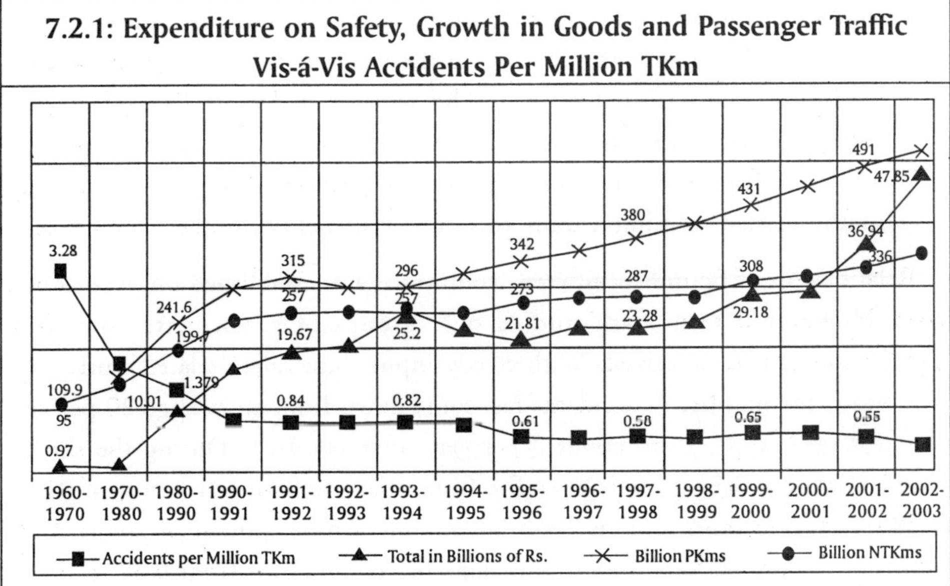

7.2.1: Expenditure on Safety, Growth in Goods and Passenger Traffic Vis-á-Vis Accidents Per Million TKm

7.2.2: IR Growth Vis-á-Vis Safety Performance

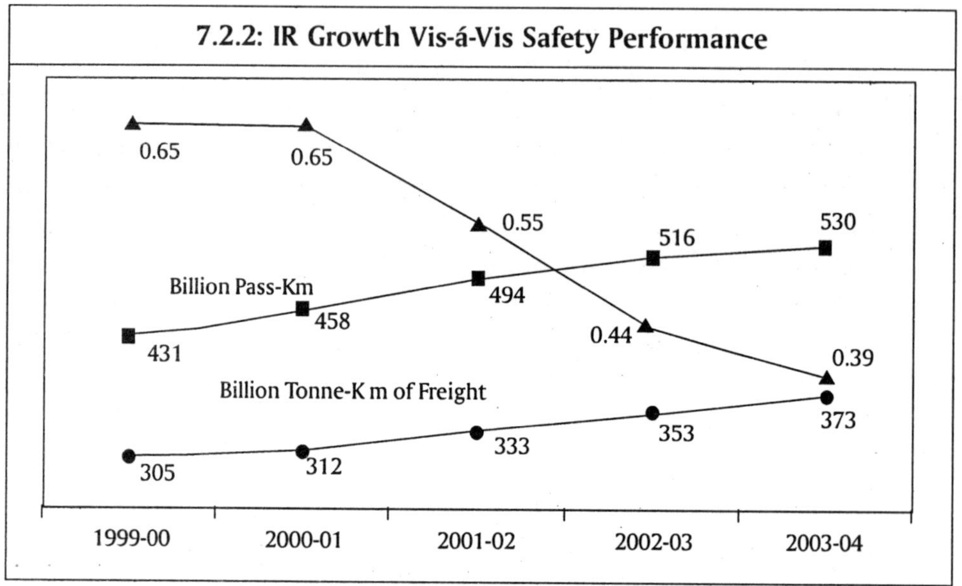

7.3 The efficacy of safety-related inputs can be illustrated from another example at micro level. Delhi-Mughalsarai is an important rail corridor on Indian Railways connecting coal mines, steel plants, and host of industrial units in the eastern part of the country to the economically rich northern India including the national capital. The section is double line, electrified equipped with modern signaling systems and deals with heavy passenger as well as freight traffic. Table 7.3 gives the year wise expenditure on safety, traffic carried in million train kms and accidents per million train kms.

Relationship of figures in different columns is not established on year to year basis. However if trends are studied over groups of years, better statistical appreciation can be perceived. With steady inputs into safety-related works over these years, the number of accidents has come down from an average 20 per year from 1991-92 to 94-95 to about 7 per year after 2000-01. During the subject period, there has been growth in traffic from 30.47 million train kms. in 91-92 to 38.04 million train kms in 2003-04, representing a growth of about 25%. Number of accidents per million train kms has come down from 0.39 to 0.13.

Table 7.3

Year	Expenditure on Safety in Crores of Rs.	Million TKm	No. of Accidents	Accidents per Million TKm
1991-92	83.5	30.47	12	0.39
1992-93	76.45	30.07	22	0.73
1993-94	50.73	28.98	22	0.76
1994-95	29.61	31.88	25	0.78
1995-96	37.7	31.27	11	0.35
1996-97	36.78	31.84	21	0.66
1997-98	31.39	33.16	10	0.30
1998-99	43.83	33.46	7	0.21
1999-2000	70.71	33.83	12	0.35
2000-01	91.68	33.85	6	0.18
2001-02	22.19	34.75	12	0.35
2002-03	18.32	36.67	6	0.16
2003-04	31.24	38.04	5	0.13

8.0 Conclusion

Investment in safety is a good business proposition. No service industry can hope to gain and sustain customers if it is not concerned, rather particular, about the safety of its customers. Inputs from upgradation and maintenance of operational infrastructure have been inducted into the system on IR over the last few decades with a fair degree of regularity. Not only had the safety performance of the system improved substantially but also the productivity. Barring just a few years when IR had to defer payment of dividend, which was also made up in subsequent years, the organization has declared profit, and paid dividend regularly on the capital employed despite discharging a number of social obligations imposed on it traditionally.

(P C Sharma is Adviser (Safety), Ministry of Railways, Government of India and Amitabh is Director (Safety), Ministry of Railways, Government of India.)

References

1. White Paper – Safety on Indian Railways, April 2003, Government of India, Ministry of Railways.
2. Indian Railways Corporate Safety Plan (2003-13), August 2003, Government of India, Ministry of Railways.
3. Indian Railways Year Books of relevant years, Government of India, Ministry of Railways.
4. Indian Railways – Safety Performance of relevant years, published by Safety Directorate of Ministry of Railways, Government of India.

Railways to Modernize and Upgrade Technology

Railways are now concentrating on the upgradation of technology which can help to improve their service as well as to minimize the cost of maintenance. Railways have been modernizing the coaches and the locomotives but there is a need to use modern technology for wagons and modern signaling equipment. As per the information provided by the Railway Minister Lalu Prasad Yadav in Lok Sabha, in the coming year, the prototypes of the new wagons with high capacity designed by the RDSO (Research and Development Organization) would be developed and trials were also expected to be done. Also as per the minister, it is expected to start the manufacturing of aluminum and stainless wagons in 2006-07. As announced by the minister, a new policy is expected to be framed considering the transfer of technology to build 25 tonne axle load wagons which can carry loads up to 80 tonne and to build special wagons capable to carry goods like motor vehicle, petrochemicals etc. He also announced that a new policy will be framed to increase safety, based on the report of the multidisciplinary team, which will be appointed to study advanced signaling and telecommunication options.

To enhance the utilization and maintenance of its rolling stock, Indian Railways decided to implement Information Technology. And the first step towards the usage of IT has been taken already as Indian Railways have launched a computerized Freight Operations Information System covering almost the entire network. It uses modern technology, which will help the freight customers to access the information regarding the status of their consignment in transit. This system is for managing and controlling the freight movement, thereby enabling the freight customers, better inventory and logistics management. FOIS consists of 16 modules of which two modules namely, Rake Management System and Terminal Management System has been implemented. Rake Management System is an operating module mainly for managing and controlling freight wagons and other freight operations. TMS is a commercial module which is pertaining to the commercial transactions responsible for providing information to the customers at the freight terminal counter and tracking the status of the train and its expected time of arrival. Integration of the planned modules would propel the Indian Railways with any other Railway system in the world. Information technology is also expected to be used for control charting, crew management and Coaching Operations Information System. Thus the use of such kind of state-of-the-art technology will enable Indian Railways to improve efficiency and earn profits both in freight as well as passenger sections.

(Compiled by Pooja Dave, Research Associate, Icfai Business School Research Centre, Ahmedabad.)

11

Radio Frequency ID in Railways
(A Feasibility Study)

R Senthil Kumar, I Jeyakumar, J S Bindra,
D Sunil, Siddharth Kati and Rajesh Kumar

In today's world, technology plays the main role in changes and innovation. Although railways have marched towards modernization, many new areas in railways require urgent combination of technology; out of which one is Radio frequency identification RFID, which is a broad term for technologies used for identifying objects and people with the help of radio waves. This project is carried out to study various alternatives available to tackle the issues and the viability of commenced RFID based technique in railways, which will certainly improve the efficiency of FOIS/COIS (Freight or Coaching Operations Information System) apart from cost saving aspects.

1.0 Introduction

After the age of efficiency in the 1950s and 1960s, quality in the 1970s and 1980s and flexibility in the 1980s and 1990s, we now live in the age of innovation and Information Technology.

Source: Abhivyakti Magazine, Volume 16, No.2 (From page 45 to page 50) April-June 2005. © Abhivyakti. Reprinted with permission.

In modern organizations, technology has become one of the main engines of change and innovation. Indian Railways (IR), the largest organization in the Globe under a single management has to respond and is responding rather slowly to the changing environment in business and technological development.

Technological development and implementation will either improve the efficiency and/or reduce the costs, thereby improving the finances, which is the bottom line of any organization.

Not that the railways has not looked towards modernization, but there are many more areas where infusion of technology is required urgently and is possible. One such area is use of Radio Frequency Identification Technology (RFID).

Indian Railways run thousands of coaching trains and freight trains every day. The amount of data required to be collected about various aspects of train running is enormous.

One such example is the number-taking of coaches and wagons being done by various departments at various nodal points. Many a time this activity is of repetitive nature and being done manually which is subject to inaccuracy and delays.

This duplication of number-taking, which is the basic function in train running, and monitoring can be dispensed with straightaway by introducing RFID based coach/wagon information system, which is comprehensive in nature and saves man-power.

With this objective in mind, the project team attempts to study the various alternatives available to address this issue and the feasibility of introducing RFID based technique of coach number-taking/information system with specific reference to TPJ division of Southern Railway.

2.0 Scope of the Project

a. To examine the present manual system of coach/wagon number-taking and the various reports generation.

b. To elucidate alternative technology/methods available to mechanise or streamline the coach/wagon number-taking process and the resultant information system.

c. To undertake a pilot study of the RFID technology introduction in MG system of TPJ division of Southern Railway.

d. To evaluate the Cost-benefit of the new technology and suggest the implementation strategy at a wider sphere.

3.1 The Present System

In the present manual system, immediately after the arrival of the train, the individual coach/wagon numbers are taken down by the TNCs (Trains Clerks) in a rough journal. After coming to his seat, the TNC then makes a fair copy of the numbers and hands it over to the YM or SM for further action. Apart from TNCs of Operating branch, the coach number-taking is being done at major junction points by various other agencies like Security (RPF) and Mechanical (C&W). Though the information is the same i.e., the coach number, the data is being collected manually by different departments for various purposes which could be combined by a common IT based information system, thereby saving considerable man-power.

The manual method is time-consuming and there is a chance that the wagon numbers will be read wrongly by the TNCs leading to inaccuracy in the information system. Though FOIS (Freight Operations Information System) and COIS (Coaching Operations Information system) have greatly improved the management of wagons and the coaches, the first and the basic input of data in the whole system of FOIS/COIS is still being done manually by TNCs and related staff. This is the weak link in the system. Introduction of IT based mechanized number-taking will provide value addition to the FOIS/COIS project.

3.2 Study of Alternatives

a. One of the technologies is bar coding, which uses optical signal to provide ID. However, this does not work if surface is dirty or if the weather is foggy or very sunny.

b. GPS based system is another method of tracking the moving objects, which is widely used in road and shipping sector. It is based on the principle of calculating the longitude and the latitude of the object from the signals received from the satellites. Since in railways the movement of rolling stock is on the defined path (track), use of GPS based systems will be superfluous and prohibitively costly.

c. Many countries are using Radio Frequency Identification (RFID) to provide more accurate in-transit information, enabling improved services, scheduling, tracking and reducing manual errors. It is a contact less and non-line of sight technology which can read at very high speeds to provide automatic identification of an item.

RFID technology can read through snow, fog, ice, paint, wood etc., and other visually/environmentally challenging conditions. Higher frequency can read at distance greater than 90 feet. They use RF signal in ranges of 30-500 khz, 850-950 MHz and 2.4-2.5 MHz.

3.3 RFID (Radio Frequency Identification) Technology

3.3.1 Components of RFID System

Following are the components of RFID system.

a. A RFID device (tag) that contains data about an item.

b. An antenna used to transmit the RF signals between the reader and the RFID device.

c. A Radio Frequency (RF) transceiver that generates the RF signals.

d. A reader that receives RF transmissions from an RFID device and passes the data to a host system for processing.

e. Application-specific software.

RFID Device-Tag

The RFID tag is programmed with data that identifies the item to which it is attached. Tags can be read only, read/write or write one/read many and can be either active or passive. Active tags contain their own power source, whereas the passive tags derive transmitting power from the radiation impinging on the tag and has battery only for retaining the memory of tag. Dynamic tags are also available which can give fuel level, water and oil pressure, temperature and other critical information. They are designed for long-range operations and can withstand exposure to harsh environmental conditions.

Antenna

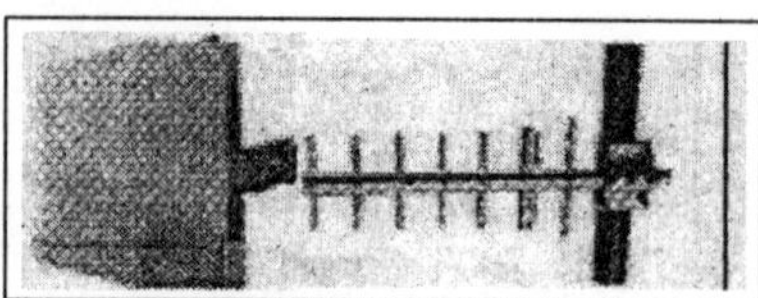

Antenna is used for transmitting and receiving RF signal. It could be either of Yagi type or log periodic type depending on the specific application.

RF Transceiver

The RF transceiver is the source of RF energy used to activate and power passive RFID. It is generally enclosed in the same cabinet as the reader. The RF output power of the transceiver ranges from 32 mw to 1W.

Reader

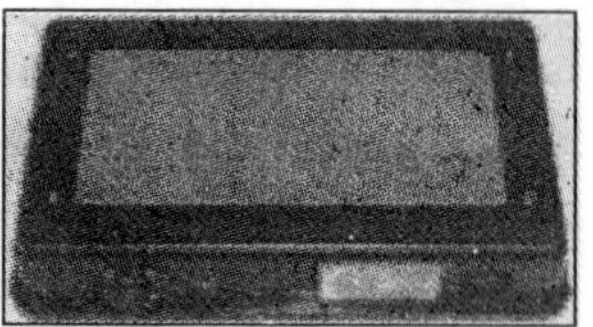

The reader directs RF transceiver to transmit RF signal, receive encoded signal, decode tag identification and transmit ID to host computer.

3.3.2 Application of RFID for Tracking Rolling Stock like Locos, Wagons, Passenger Coaches etc.

Each loco and wagon/coach is provided with tags. It can be mounted on both sides of engine/wagons with antenna placed besides the tracks. Tag on wagons/ locos could be read only, read/write or even dynamic tag.

Track readers will be provided at strategic points such as all entry points of a junction station, divisional interchange stations, entry and exit points of goods sheds and sidings, maintenance facilities such as Loco sheds, C&W depots, coaching depots and weigh bridges for automatic weighment in motion.

The readers provided at each junction station, can be connected through wireless or cable to a local host computer, which in turn is networked with central host computer to interface with existing FOIS servers.

Railways/RailTel are providing OFC system on all-important BG routes with 155 MBPS bandwidth dropped at each station with Ethernet connectivity.

Most of BG junction stations are already connected on OFC or work is in an advanced stage.

Whenever a freight train crosses such strategic point, the details of loco tags and IDs of wagons/coaches will be captured by trackside reader and it will relay the time, date or other programmed information to host computer.

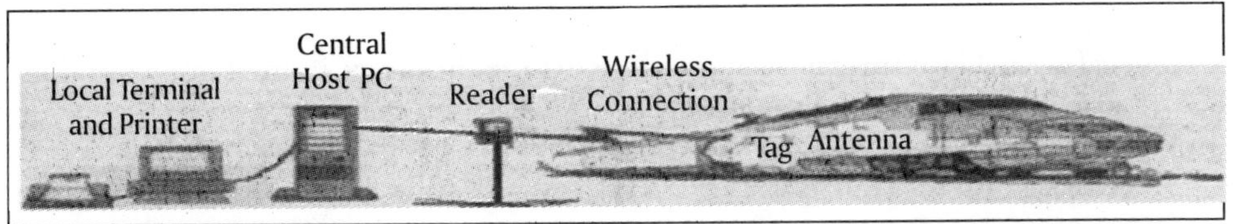

The above arrangement will provide automatic and accurate information for Yard and Goods shed management system and printing of RRs under implementation as Phase II of FOIS.

The MIS applications of rolling stock monitoring and maintenance modules can use online data for scheduling and the information from dynamic tags can be sent to loco controllers and sheds to decide on schedule maintenance, if any, required.

The location information of passenger trains can be used to provide accurate status of train to passengers and control display boards and announcement systems at stations. It can also update existing NTES or other server regarding train location. This can also be used to convey the approach of the train at a particular station to the passengers inside the train.

Every year-end, wagon census is carried out which wastes lot of man-power and other resources and still accurate information is not available. With this, there will be no need for such activity as information on census can be recovered at any moment.

3.3.3 RFID Technology in the Global Scenario

RFID is a generic system, which is being widely used for various applications. The following are a few examples.

1. **RFID in Supply Chain**: RFID tags are used to track the consignments on transit. Intelligent tags are used to monitor the condition of the consignment like pilferage, temperature etc.
2. **RFID in Containers:** Worldwide RFID technology is used for container security and tracking.
3. **RFID in Road Transport:** RFID system is used in automatic toll collection in many countries.
4. **RFID in Defence:** Countries like Denmark, the US and the UK are using RFID system for supply tracking. NASA is exploring ways to reduce costs and risk by using RFID to automatically identify and track hazardous materials.
5. **RFID in Railways:** Many foreign railways have gone in for RFID based system in a big way. The major users of RFID system are China and Vietnam. In these railways RFID system is used in areas of traffic and passenger information, operation and maintenance and positioning for onboard management.

4.0 RFID Trial

To study the practical applicability of RFID, Tiruchirappalli (TPJ) division of Southern Railway is chosen for studying the scheme of implementation of RFID technology.

For implementing RFID system in a particular section, all the moving objects should be provided with a RFID tag. The MG section in Southern Railway is limited to only TPJ, Madurai (MDU) and Chennai (MAS) divisions and is not having any interchange point with other Railways. As such all the MG rolling stock in this section belongs to Southern Railway only and this makes the implementation of RFID system simpler.

The RFID tags will be fixed on either side of all the MG coaches and locos such that all the coaches/locos will have a unique RFID number. The RFID readers will be fixed at the entry points of junction stations which will be connected through wireless or cable to the local host computer, which in turn is networked with central host computer interfaced with existing charting server.

The theoretical cost of Tags and readers and the resultant investment cost vis-à-vis the saving of man-power in terms of TNCs and RPF staff are studied in detail.

4.1 The Present System at TPJ

At TPJ division, the MG coaching stock number-taking is being done by the TNCs in the coaching depots/junctions viz. VM, MV and TVR. At each station one TNC per shift is being used for the number-taking and VG (vehicle guidance) preparation. The total number of TNCs in manual number-taking at the three junctions will be 12 (including RG/LR).

Apart from Operating branch, the number-taking is being done by Mechanical and security branches also for their own purposes.

4.2 Introduction of RFID

4.2.1 Based on the MG rake link, it is estimated that 200 MG coaches are in the circuit. Taking into consideration the spare coaches and for the MG diesel locos, the total requirement of RFID "tags" will be approximately 300 numbers.

4.2.2 Three RFID "Readers" per station will be fixed at the entry points of the three stations Villupuram (VM), Mayiladuthurai (MV) and Tiruvarur (TVR) respectively and the total requirement of "fixed readers" will be approximately 10.

4.2.3 For within the yard management i.e., preparation of final vehicle guidance for the use of GD, sick/POH marking by TXR and SSE (elec), "hand held reader/writer" are to be supplied. The total requirement of hand held readers for only two junctions would be 06 numbers.

4.2.4 Any sick/POH marking, attachment/detachment of coaches will be updated online by this system and the resultant coaching stock position gets updated which will be useful for Operating, Mechanical and Electrical branches.

4.3 Cost Benefit Analysis

4.3.1 Cost of RFID Trial

Sl.No.	Description	Qty	Unit Cost (Rs.)	Total Cost (in Lakhs Rs.)
1.	RFID Tag	600	1000	6.00
2.	RFID Fixed reader	10	30000	3.00
3.	RFID hand held reader/writer	06	50000	3.00
4.	Software	LS	50000	0.50
5.	Testing and commissioning	LS	150000	1.50
	Total cost			**14.00**

4.3.2 Man-Power Saving

Sl.No.	Department	Category	No. of Staff	Staff Cost/ Employee/Year (in Lakhs Rs.)	Total Cost (in Lakhs Rs.)
1.	Operating	TNC	12	1.10	13.20
2.	Mechanical	SSE	12	1.66	19.92
3.	Security	Constable	12	1.40	18.80
	Total Cost				**51.92**

In nutshell we can say that for an investment of Rs.20 lakhs on RFID, we will get a savings of Rs.51.92 lakhs in the same year which is worth investing and improve the efficiency of the system.

5.0 Benefits of RFID System for Railways

1. Apart from man-power saving, RFID based coach information will be faster and accurate.
2. By providing RFID readers at all enroute stations, the input from RFID based system can be integrated directly with the charting software so that the manual entry of Train arrival/departure details can be dispensed with.
3. Online monitoring of critical parameter, of rolling stock for safety and maintenance decisions.

4. Information of passenger trains to update existing servers for customer interface (NTES, Visual displays at stations, Web-based information etc.).

5. If all the rolling stock is fitted with RFID tags, wagon/coach census can be dispensed with.

6. RFID tags in wagons will furnish accurate information and the present method of manual entry of data in FOIS can be dispensed with.

6.0 Future Possibilities

6.1.1 **RFID as an alternative to Block proving axle counter:** If all the rolling stock are provided with RFID tags and all the stations are provided with RFID readers at the entry and exit points, then the information regarding the last vehicle clearing the block section can be obtained from this system. Thus, this can be an alternative to the present system of block proving through axle counters.

Assuming the average length of the block section as 10 kms, the cost of block proving axle counter system per block section will be approximately Rs.20 lakhs.

7.0 Conclusion

1. The use of RFID system will certainly improve the efficacy of FOIS/COIS apart from the costs saving aspect.

2. RFID based rolling stock information system will serve as a cost-effective alternative to the present block proving axle counters.

3. RFID system captures the rolling stock details at the point of origin and provides effective, faster and accurate information for multifarious purposes like Coach guidance system for station display, arrival/departure information for charting and NTES system as a replacement to station indication system inside the coaches, coach/wagon details for RPF (security aspects), and asset maintenance information of rolling stock etc.

(R Senthil Kumar, I Jeyakumar, J S Bindra, D Sunil, Siddharth Kati and Rajesh Kumar are participants in the MDP Course offered by Railway Staff College. Abhivyakti is a quarterly magazine of the Railway Staff College, Vadodara.)

12

Technology in Construction and Management of Konkan Railway

Prabha Shastri Ranade

Construction of Konkan Railway, a 760 km long new railway line was a major step towards infrastructure development on the western coast of India. It commenced operations since 26 January 1998. The latest available modern technologies were incorporated in the construction of this line. The Konkan Railway Corporation has invested heavily in the latest technology in areas of operation, communications and computerized working systems. This article gives a brief outline of some of these technological innovations. Konkan Railway project is a trend setter in the country in many ways. This is the first major infrastructure project in the country taken up on "Build, operate, transfer" (BOT) concept. Due to its engineering marvels, Konkan Railway itself has become a tourists' attraction. The longest bridge and tunnel, the tallest viaduct are found on this line. With new technology, it also brought new "work culture" in the organization. World Bank has appreciated KR for its cost-effective optimum utilization of resources and efficient management practices benchmarking it as a Model railway.

Introduction

Konkan Railway, a 760 km long railway line running almost parallel to the western coast of India, is the longest railway line ever constructed in one stretch in the country. Construction of Konkan Railway was a major step towards infrastructure development of the region. Konkan Railway is hailed as a gift to the nation in the 50th (Golden Jubilee) year of our Independence. Konkan Railway is unique in the world because of its magnitude, its location and the nature of terrain through which it has been constructed. Probably similar situation does not prevail in other parts of the world. Hence, the completion of Konkan Railway is described as the greatest event since Lord Parashuram created this region. The latest available modern technologies were incorporated in the construction of this line and in areas of operation, communications and working system. Keeping in view the technological developments in the field in the last 10 years, this article gives a brief outline of some of the technological innovations incorporated in the construction and management of Konkan Railway.

Profile of the Project

Figure 1: Konkan Railway Route

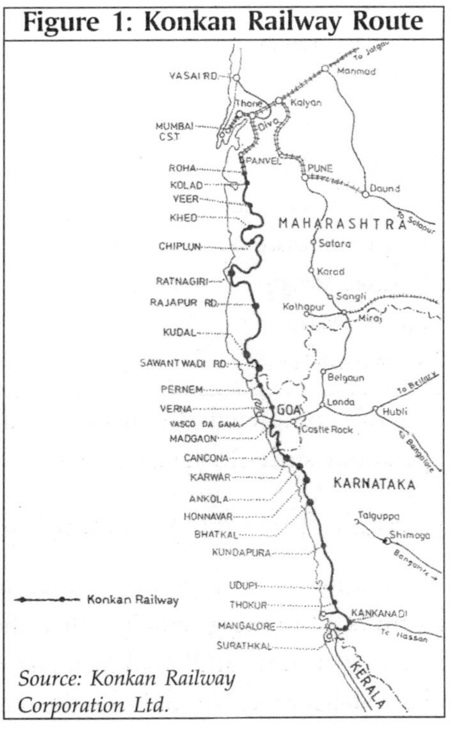

Source: Konkan Railway Corporation Ltd.

The Konkan Railway alignment is carved out of the Western Ghats. It passes through one of the most undulating and geologically unstable terrain in India. Laying of track across rugged terrain crisscrossing rivers and plunging valleys was a gigantic task. Though some sections were close to NH 17, most of the length was difficult to approach. Main reason why such a railway line could not be constructed earlier, was the enormous cost involved in bridging various rivers and valleys and boring tunnels through several hilly ranges. Due to its engineering marvels Konkan Railway itself has become a tourist attraction. The whole line was designed and constructed for a speed potential of 160 km per hour. The jurisdiction of Konkan Railway starts from the South of Roha under the Central Railway, in the Raigad district of Maharashtra State. From here it runs southwards in Ratnagiri and Sindhudurg districts, then enters Goa (North and South Goa districts) and southwards passes through Uttar (North) Kannada and Dakshina (South) Kannada districts of Karnataka and terminates at Thokur near Mangalore under the Southern Railway. Out of the total route length of 760 km, Maharashtra State has 382 km (fifty p.c.), Goa has 105 km (14 p.c.) and Karnataka has 273 km (36 p.c.). There are 63 stations on the Konkan Railway line to provide facility of goods and passenger transportation.

The project was opened up in phases from either ends progressively. Accordingly, Mangalore-Udupi sections in the South and Roha Veer in the North were completed first. The dates of opening of various sections for passenger traffic are as follows:

Section	Length in km	Date of Opening
Mangalore-Udupi	67	20-03-93
Roha-Veer	48	27-09-93
Udupi- Kundapura	33	05-04 95
Veer-Khed	52	25-09-95
Khed-Chiplun	30	23-02-96
Chiplun-Ratnagiri	77	16-11-96
Ratnagiri-Sawantwadi	161	20-01-97
Kundapura-Canacona	181	01-06-97
Canacona-Madgaon	32	05-08-97
Pernem-Madgaon	57	24-08-97
Sawantwadi-Pernem	22	26-01-98

KRC completed the project at a cost of Rs.3375 crores and commenced operations since 26 January 1998.

Konkan Railway: A Technological Marvel

The rail link is most preferable even in inhospitable terrain, in the sense that it is six times more energy efficient than the road transport. Over the years, technology in construction and management of railways has undergone changes at a phenomenal pace. Not only has the track structure improved, but also maintenance standard has improved considerably. Rail metallurgy has also improved. A lot of improvement has taken place in manufacturing process and quality assurance procedure in rail manufacturing. China has recently constructed a 1956 km long railway link at high altitudes to connect Lhasa (Tibet) with mainland China. A railway line is under construction to connect Kashmir valley to Jammu – the Jammu-Udhampur – Srinagar-Baramulla. The project involves tunneling through soft and medium fragile sedimentary rocky strata. The terrain is tough, approaches are difficult and overall unfavourable for working environment. Konkan Railway Corporation with its experience in tunneling is actively involved in the construction of this railway line, which will be a major achievement for Indian Railway, after the ambitious Konkan Railway. Experts moot Indo Nepal railway link between Birganj and Kathmandu through the majestic Himalayan mountains. These railway lines will have to employ more modern and upgraded technologies in their construction, compared to Konkan Railway. However, it needs to be appreciated that the designers of KR incorporated the latest available technology in the construction of Konkan Railway way back in 1990.

In the construction of bridges and tunnels, a number of technological innovations have been incorporated. Nearly 1500 streams had to be crossed. The bridges and tunnels were constructed at a cost of about Rs.2000 crores. Despite the formidable condition of the terrain through which the alignment passes, minimum radius of curvature of 1250 metres and a ruling grade of 1 in 150 compensated have been adopted in order to facilitate smooth movement of heavy-haul freight trains.

Bridges: The railway line has as many as 179 major bridges with a total linear waterway of 21.5 km and 1819 minor bridges with a total waterway of 5.73 km The longest bridge on Konkan Railway is 2.065 km long across river Sharavati near Honnavar in Karnataka state. There are a large number of viaducts, deep cuttings and high embankments. The bridges on Konkan Railway have been designed for 100 years return period flood based on the latest hydrological standards. Hence, the bridges on Konkan Railway are not vulnerable. The embankments on the Konkan Railway have been so designed that they do not exhibit any vulnerability.

Tunnels: The engineers faced their most difficult challenge in tunneling work. There are 92 tunnels with a total length of 84.6 km. Nine tunnels are longer than 2 km each. The longest tunnel is at Karbude near Ratnagiri which is 6.5 km in length. Keeping in view the possibilities of air pollution inside long tunnels due to diesel traction, forced ventilation has been provided in 5 long tunnels on KR route. Jet fan technology is used in 4 major tunnels and a centrifugal fan ventilation is provided in the Karbude tunnel. This ensures desirable environment inside the tunnels. Safety measures have also been taken to protect the life of passengers in the event of accidents inside tunnels. Fire extinguishers have been installed and sufficient lighting arrangement made in all tunnels. Its massive railway structures have become admired features. Panval viaduct in Ratnagiri district is the tallest viaduct in Asia. and has piers as high as 64 metres, taller than the Qutub Minar.

Konkan Railway: A Trend Setter

Konkan Railway project is a trend setter in the country in many ways specially in regard to innovative approach for financing. Historically the responsibility of providing transport infrastructure has been vested with the government. Konkan Railway project is a project well conceived and well executed through very novel and very imaginative funding. With the formation of the Konkan Railway Corporation Ltd (KRCL), India entered a new era of infrastructure planning and execution through private participation This is the first major infrastructure project in the country taken up on "Build, operate, transfer" (BOT) concept. If a project of this magnitude and dimension was to be completed through budgetary grants by the Indian Railways, it would have taken 25 to 30 years. A bold and unique financing scheme was therefore evolved. Konkan Railway Corporation Ltd. (KRCL) a separate statutory body was formed on 19th January 1990 under the Indian Companies Act, 1956 pursuant to the agreement between Government of India acting through the Ministry of Railways and the Governments of Maharashtra, Goa, Karnataka and Kerala as a joint venture with headquarters at CBD Belapur, Navi Mumbai. The beneficiary states became the partners in KRCL contributing 49 p.c. of equity capital – Maharashtra-22 p.c,. Goa-6 p.c. Karnataka-15 p.c. and Kerala-6 p.c. The Ministry of Railways contributed 51 p.c. Of the total estimated fund requirement of Rs.3350 crores (gross) inclusive of Rs.950 crores of financing costs, Rs.800 crores has been contributed by these five partners as equity and the balance has been raised by market borrowings mainly through tax-free bonds and external commercial borrowings to avoid time over run and cost over run. The common man, i.e. the consumer invested in Bonds issued by KRCL to raise funds for its construction. Though KR does not pass through Kerala, it shared part of the expenditure because it shares the benefits of KR arising out of better links with the coastal region and speedy transport. The BOT concept envisaged that the KRCL will construct the line and operate it for a period of 10 years after commissioning.

New Work Culture

With the adoption of modern technology, the requirements of manpower for KRC are much less than those of any equal length on the older system of Indian Railways. The manpower requirements are kept to the minimum workable level so as to minimize the recurring annual expenditure. As in the case of construction stage, during the operation stage as well, an entirely new work culture has been brought about by proper training and operation of the staff. The maintenance schedule and maintenance philosophy has also been completely recast – e.g. the permanent way maintenance is entirely machine-oriented, eliminating the concept of regular gangs, push trollying, etc. Mobile maintenance gangs with rail mounted fully equipped vans attend to non programmed maintenance, while two high speed tamping machines and one point and crossings tamping machine attend to programme maintenance. The result is that the requirement of permanent way maintenance staff is less than one person per track km (0.75). The concept of mobile squads has been introduced for signaling, telecommunication and electrical installations. The carriage and wagon maintenance is also based on a new philosophy, with the result that the total manpower requirement for KR for operation and maintenance is only 4.2 men per km for all departments put together as against the yardstick of 28-30 persons per km on Indian Railways. World Bank has appreciated KR for its cost-effective optimum utilization of resources and efficient management practices, benchmarking it as a Model railway. KR has received special certificate of appreciation for excellence in cost reduction. This award is instituted to encourage the Indian industry to adopt cost reduction measures to face the challenge of globalization of Indian economy. KR, a lean organization has one-third the number of employees in Indian Railways manning the same stretch of 760 track km. KR has achieved excellence in cost reduction through the extensive use of latest technologies and innovative design concepts and information technology systems. (Ministry of Railways, PIB Press Release, 10 March 2004). KRC has demonstrated that even a state sector organization, with dynamic management, extensive autonomy and latest technology can perform exceedingly well, and may even excel over the private sector. (Sreedharan, 1998)

Technological Innovations

The formation of an independent Konkan Railway corporation under the Railway Ministry for the first time in history, allowed an opportunity to try alternate model of railway working and the development of rail-based technologies. The pioneering spirit and the courage to experiment with new ideas was evident in the construction phase and this resulted in a very modern infrastructure. KR route is constructed to face earthquake at 6+Ritcher scale. KR route is without any joints or fish plates and track ballasts are not used anywhere on the track. A four-aspect colour light signaling system has been adopted for the first time.

Konkan Railway has developed technology solutions for conventional railways. It has also developed the following technologies: Track and civil Engineering, Boulder nets – special steel types, tunnels and cuttings – inspection and maintenance and self stabilizing tracks. KRC has invested heavily in the latest technology in areas of operation, communications and computerized working systems.

Use of Concrete Sleepers

Railway sleeper technology has changed completely over the years. Wooden and metal sleepers have been replaced with PSC (Pre Stressed Concrete) sleepers. These sleepers are provided 25 cm-30 cm ballast cushion and are maintained with the state-of-the-art track machines. Konkan Railway decided as an environment friendly measure, to utilize only concrete sleepers throughout its construction. Wooden sleepers were totally prohibited. This implied preservation of forests. KRCL avoided deforestation by use of cement concrete sleepers. Wooden sleepers were avoided even at traditionally common locations such as bridges, points and crossings, level crossings and switch expansion points. There is no trace of even a single wooden sleeper over a route length of 760 km. Concrete sleepers were used throughout. They were manufactured at four plants located along the track – in Chiplun and Kudal (Maharashtra) Margao (Goa) and Kaikini (Karnataka). The Chiplun plant also produced crossing sleeper sets for the entire project. The factories also produced special concrete sleepers required for switch expansion joints for bridges with extra holes for guard rails and for level crossings with extra holes for check rails. The sleepers were steam-cured till they attained a strength of 400kg/cm^2 and then placed in a water tank for 14 days. They were handled mechanically in the factory and even at the unloading site.

Anti Collision Device

Konkan Railway has designed and developed the Anti collision device (ACD) which is a self acting micro-processor-based data communication device. When installed on locomotives, the network of ACD systems prevent high speed collisions. The ACD uses both radio frequency and global positioning system through satellites, whereby a train is automatically brought to a halt if the track ahead is not clear. It does not depend on human action. KR has protected the entire 760 kms of its stretch with the ACD network. The ACDs are deployed and linked to 53 stations, 80 manned and 27 unmanned gates, 98 locomotives, 50 guard vans and 179 inclinometer protected cuttings. *(www.expresscomputeronline.com)* It is claimed that ACD network on KR route will prevent all types of collision-related accidents. Additionally, on the Konkan route it will work in tandem with inclinometers to give pre-warning of possible collapse of a soil/laterite cutting, and reduce the speed of an approaching train. ACDs will thus lead to safer travel. The North east Frontier railway is also fitted with ACDs. The same ACD will be deployed on the rest of the Indian Railways at an estimated cost of Rs.1600 crore for 64,000 km of rail routes by 2013-14. (*http://www.expresscomputeronline.com*) Pakistan has sought assistance from Indian Railways in ACDs that prevent train accidents. Inquiries have also come in from Indonesia and South Africa. *(http://www.business-standard.com)*

Telemedicine: KR has applied the advances in the digital revolution to the field of medicine by introducing Telemedicine where the human resources working in far off areas get specialized opinion from Bombay and other cities. KR has also helped North east Frontier railway to introduce telemedicine and to connect far off stations to Central hospital at Guwahati.

New Software Package: Railway Application Package is a comprehensive package of tightly integrated seventeen modules for day to day working of all departments of railway. It is a real time decision making system. KR commissioned a new software package in January 2006.

CCTVs at KR Stations

In view of the growing security concerns at the railway stations, Konkan Railway Corporation is in the final stages of approving the closed circuit TVs on major stations on the KRC route. The recent serial train bomb blasts in Mumbai had raised security concerns at the Margao railway station, as it is feared, could be a soft target for terrorists. Additional metal detectors are installed at the Margao station to plug all the entry and exit points of the station. (*http://oheraldo.in/node/17309*). Margao is identified as the "Developed model station" by the Indian Railways. (PIB Press Release, 8-5-06).

Automatic Train Washing System

This is listed as the new technology introduced by Indian Railways recently. It is meant for the improvement in the quality of exterior cleanliness of trains on Indian Railways. Two indigenous plants are commissioned, on Konkan Railway and Southern Railway. At the automatic coach washing plant, the coaches are washed sparkling clean.

Operational Safety Measures taken by KR

KR line has been constructed through difficult terrain and has to face all the vagaries of the nature. This coastal region normally receives very heavy rainfall in the monsoon season. The nature's fury affects the rail services also. Landslides and rock falls in cuttings are a regular feature, particularly during the monsoon. Tunnels keep on losing chunks of material due to water logging and the vibration of passing trains. KRCL has taken various measures to overcome these environmental problems. The Konkan Railway Corporation is taking all precautions to minimize the occurrence of accidents/possibility of disruptions. Konkan Railway had to devise new technological solutions to take care of safety on the route.

KRC has implemented safety technologies to make train journey safe on its entire track. These measures include installation of inclinometers, anti-collision devices and high strength steel nets. Safety measures have also been taken to protect the life of passengers in the event of accidents inside tunnels. All manmade structures on KR are designed to take care of seismic forces and rainfall intensity. KR is the only railway in India having a permanent Geologist for inspecting and monitoring cuttings and tunnels as well as supervising safety works. The system of KR is automated for quick responses in times of accidents and follow up action required to be taken. Due to the peculiarities of the terrain, KR has built up various safety features like boulder nets and geo-netting for increased safety of running trains and improved signaling. High strength steel nets have helped prevent some major accidents. A focused patrolling system has been designed for greater safety of goods and passengers. Intense short beat patrolling and portable field telephones using the optic fibre based communication system were introduced in the monsoon of 1998. KR has introduced special safety works as a strategic plan to reduce the probability of any mishap because of landslide or boulder fall. All vulnerable cuttings and embankment side slopes are stabilized by stone pitching, berming and increased use of ballast on the permanent way. The side slopes in the excavated cuttings are fenced to prevent rock falls and other collapses finishing up on the railway track. Sand bags are stacked at the mouth of tunnels to act as buffers. Permanent staff is maintained for inspecting and monitoring the various tunnels and cuttings. Intensive patrolling at the assessed vulnerable sections is done regularly. Workers are permanently posted at certain places to do 'running repairs' on the embankments to prevent them from sinking.

Raksha Dhaga, a predictive failure warning device, indigenously designed and developed by KR, sets off an alarm when a boulder or a branch of a tree falls on the chord. It gives advance information to the engine driver with warning light and hooter signal. (KR Press Release, 27th July 2003). All rock cuttings above 15 metres are provided with special KR designed high strength steel boulder nets. In all rock cuttings toe protection wall or pitching are provided. As per the requirement of the locations, 700,000 sq.metres of netting has been done with different design strengths for rock cuttings deeper than 12 metres. KR has installed indigenously developed "Inclinometers" which act as sensors and detect the movement of soil and any boulder falling on the tracks from a rock cutting.

About 30,000 inclinometers were installed in deep soil cuttings before the monsoon of 2004. Wherever full protection of steel nets are not provided, inclinometers are installed and they have prevented some serious accidents. Mini radio transmitters having electronic pendulums are linked to a radio modem. This in turn communicates with ACD technology based train control system and provides a predictive warning. This avoids the simultaneous failure of cutting and face to face collision of trains. Electronic rain gauges capable of measuring intensity of rainfall and coupled with ACD technology network through wireless connectivity is also being developed by KRCL for real time reaction to rainfall. *(www.konkanrailway.com)*

KR has constructed a seismic station at Ratnagiri to monitor seismic activity in the area and use the advance information to take preventive action. Flattening of steep slopes, construction of berms, micropiling, geo-matting, RCC walls, gabion walls, have been done on the entire route to make the route stable.

Engineering Projects

Due to its expertise in construction, KR is consulted by other railways in the country for executing similar type of work. It is involved in the construction of new Udhampur-Srinagar-Baramula railway line in Jammu and Kashmir, specially the tunneling and bridge construction. It was also awarded the work of construction of Mumbai-Pune Express highway and 14 road over bridges in Jharkhand state.

Environmental Conservation by KR

With the commencement of construction of KR, it was apprehended that KR may pose serious threat to the fragile eco system of the region. However, the construction was planned so as to fully preserve the ecology of the area and enhance the beauty of the environment. Extreme care was taken to avoid heritage, religious and community structures during the construction. KR has undertaken massive tree plantation programme along the railway line to make the route green and also in the premises of railway stations and staff colonies. An afforestation programme was taken up on embankments and acquired lands. As recommended by the MOEF, the most effective species to absorb the various elements of traffic related pollutants were planted. In addition, a variety of ornamental and fruit bearing trees and teakwood were planted. Use of wooden sleepers was totally avoided and concrete sleepers were used. Thus technological innovations and environmental conservation has been simultaneously achieved in Konkan Railway.

Efficient Management

The Railway Minister in the Budget speech on 24-02-06 announced that the railways will give utmost priority to technological upgradation, so that the reliability of services can be improved and operating and maintenance costs can be cut. Konkan Railway has been practicing this since its inception. Performance of Indian Railways in recent years have been quite commendable in all parameters of transport industry. A study by World bank has found IR's operating performance to be among the best in developing countries, when measured against yardstick such as track utilization, output per employee, equipment utilization, etc.In several areas it is comparable with railways in developed countries. Konkan Railway has been praised by the World bank for its efficient management practices, operational efficiency, IT-enabled services and use of innovative technologies to reduce the cost of asset maintenance while improving safety and reliability. Konkan Railway has also provided several innovative passenger amenities/services on its route and on its trains to make their journey comfortable. This includes providing UV treated drinking water at all taps on stations. It has constructed international standard waiting rooms and ecofriendly and aesthetic passenger shelters.

Future Climate Change and its Impact

The Konkan Railway could become vulnerable to increases in temperature and rainfall and changes in the sea level in the next 50 years, according to a study conducted by IIM Ahmedabad. The study "Climate change impacts on industry, energy and transport" conducted for a joint programme of the Union Environment and Forest Ministry and the UK Department of Environment said temperatures are projected to rise as much as 3 to 4 degrees Celsius, rainfall will increase and there will be more sea surges towards the end of the 21st century. (*The Telegraph*, September 13, 2005) The report observed that the region through which the Konkan Railway passes experiences moderate to heavy rainfall. Waterlogging results from continuous or excessive rainfall. The increase in rainfall can cause erosion of the coastal land. Changes in sea level are expected to lead to flooding. Konkan

Railway along the coast could be in trouble with rising sea level. The study predicted extreme climatic events increasingly disrupting the Konkan Railway services. (*The Times of India*, September 9, 2005) The report said temperature increases over the 21st century can directly affect the stability and strength of the building materials and indirectly increase the need for air conditioning on train. Therefore, more repairs and maintenance will be required. About one-fifth of its repairs and maintenance expenses of Konkan Railway are due to climatic factors like heavy rain. (*The Indian Express*, September 9, 2005) The Konkan Railway officials say the current design code takes into account the normal climate change variability. To conclude, technology in construction and management of Konkan Railway is capable to take care of future climate changes and the smooth operation of KP in the service of the nation.

(Dr. Prabha Shastri Ranade is a Consulting Editor at Icfai Business School Research Centre, Ahmedabad.)

References

1. Changing profile of Indias, West Coast, Konkan Railway, Publicity hand out of KRCL
2. Gokhale K K, Konkan Railway – A trail blazer, Indian Railways, April 2005, pp.147-149.
3. Gokhale K K, Railways and beyond, Indian Railways, April 2006, pp187-189
4. Jaruhar R R, Great turn round for Indian Railways – Role of civil engineers, Indian Railways, April, 2006, pp. 41-44.
5. PIB Press Releases, Ministry of Railways, Government of India, New Delhi.
6. Rajaram B, "Konkan Railway technologies for a paradigm shift in rail transport: Whither Engineers?" S B Joshi Memorial Lecture, 8 October 2004
7. Salelkar S V, (ed.) A Treatise on Konkan Railway , Konkan Railway Corporation Ltd. Navi Mumbai, 1999.
8. Shivdasani, Menka and Raju Kane, Konkan Railway, A dream come true. Konkan Railway Corporation Ltd. Navi Mumbai, 1998.
9. Sreedharan E, Success story of Konkan Railway, Indian Railways, April, 1997, p.67-72.
10. Sreedharan E, Konkan Railway: New frontiers in funding, technology and management. *Asian Transport Journal*, June 1998,p.83-91.
11. Website of Konkan Railway Corporation Ltd. *www. konkan railway.com*

Section III

Metro Rails in Indian Cities

13

Urban Mass Rapid Transit System: Current Status

One of the biggest demands of urbanization is a mass rapid transit system. MRTS is basically referred to be a hoist extension of the suburban network, not a metro system. But it can be considered as metro, as majority of its length is elevated and its services are special. But this system is applicable based on certain criteria, as urban planners have protested against MRTS requirements. This article takes a quick look at how modern MRTS projects have been planned in the cities of Mumbai, Delhi, Kochi, Hyderabad, Goa, Chennai, Bangalore, Visakhapatnam and Kolkata.

Indian urbanization levels have seen stupendous growth during the past three decades, resulting in crowding of existing metropolitan cities and the emerging of new mini metro cities. Urbanization rose steadily from 17.29 percent in 1951 to 23.34 percent in 1981 and further to 27.8 percent.

One of the biggest demands of urbanization is a mass rapid transit system (MRTS) – an area where India has just begun to take early steps. It is widely felt that mass rapid transportation is warranted once human traffic touches a peak level of 20,000 persons per direction per day. Today, several metro cities like Mumbai, Kolkata, Delhi, Hyderabad, etc., – qualify by this criterion.

Urbanization in India	
Year	**Percent**
1941	13.86
1951	17.29
1961	17.79
1971	19.91
1981	23.34
1991	25.71
2001	27.80

Urban transportation also influences proliferation of slums in urban centres. Since there are better employment opportunities in urban centres, there is a tendency of influx from city-peripheral areas into the main city. In the absence of an efficient transportation system, there is threat of slum proliferation in city centres.

India's Million-Plus Cities
(Municipal Corporations)

	Population			Population	
	Total (nos.)	**Slum* (%)**		**Total (nos.)**	**Slum* (%)**
Greater Mumbai	11,914,398	48.9	Bhopal	1,433,875	8.8
Delhi	9,817,439	18.9	Ludhiana	1,395,053	22.6
Kolkata	4,580,544	32.5	Patna	1,376,950	0.3
Bangalore	4,292,223	8.0	Vadodara	1,306,035	8.2
Chennai	4,216,268	25.6	Thane	1,261,517	33.3
Ahmedabad	3,515,361	12.5	Agra	1,259,979	9.7
Hyderabad	3,449,878	17.4	Kalyan-Dombivli	1,193,266	2.9
Pune	2,540,069	20.9	Varanasi	1,100,748	12.6
Kanpur	2,532,138	14.6	Nashik	1,076,967	13.2
Surat	2,433,787	16.7	Meerut	1,074,229	43.9
Jaipur	2,324,319	15.1	Faridabad	1,054,981	46.6
Nagpur	2,051,320	35.4	Haora	1,008,704	11.7
Indore	1,597,441	16.2	Pimprichinchwad	1,006,417	12.9
Total				**70,813,906**	**23.9**

Note: Values as of 1991. * Percent of Total Population.

Source: www.indiastat.com

Urban planners opine that an MRTS is necessitated once the population of a city (or urban centre) crosses 1 million. As population increases, augmentation of capacity is warranted. As of today, there are 26 cities (municipal corporations) having 1 million-plus population. However, modern MRT systems exist in only Kolkata and Delhi.

Over the past few years, initial positive steps are being noticed in creating modern MRTS in important cities including major metros.

In this special feature, *ProjectsToday* takes a quick look at modern MRTS projects proposed in the cities of Mumbai, Delhi, Kochi, Hyderabad, Goa, Chennai, Bangalore, Visakhapatnam and Kolkata.

Mass Rapid Transit System: Major Cities

City	Project	Current Status
Mumbai	Mumbai Metro (Phase I)	Bidders shortlisted, work to begin in April 2006
Delhi	Delhi Metro Rail (Phase II)	Phase I nearly commissioned, Phase II initiated
Kochi	Metro Rail Project	Formal nod awaited from Union urban development ministry
Hyderabad	Hyderabad Metro Rail (Phase I)	Six consortia shortlisted
Goa	Monorail Project	Skybus ruled out, EOIs invited for monorail
Chennai	Elevated Monorail MRTS	Bids invited in January 2006
Bangalore	Bangalore Metro Rail (Phase I)	Bids invited in April 2005, response awaited
Visakhapatnam	Mass Rapid Transit System	Bids invited for feasibility study
Kolkata	Mass Rapid Transit System	Techno-economic feasibility underway
Noida	Mass Rapid Transit System	Feasibility studies underway

Mumbai Metro Rail Project (Phase I-A)

The Mumbai Metro Rail is a colossal project aiming to alleviating the transportation problems faced by Mumbai – the financial capital of India – that currently houses over 12 million persons. The project, which is targeted to commission in phases till 2021, envisages creation of a mass rapid transit system covering 146.5 km of underground and elevated track connecting major regions within the city.

Mumbai Metropolitan Region Development Authority (MMRDA) is the nodal agency for this Rs.19,425 crore project (nominal prices) that would be implemented through private sector participation. The Mumbai Metro rail project will complement the ongoing urban infrastructure schemes of MMRDA like the Mumbai Urban Transportation Project (Phase II), the Mumbai Urban Infrastructure Project, the East-West Freeway Link project and the Mumbai Trans Harbour Link Project.

The existing transport infrastructure is heavily pressurized, thanks to the sheer population explosion in the metropolis. It is estimated that currently 61 lakh commuters travel by suburban trains that carry passenger loads three times their capacity. Around 45 lakh commuters ply on the 3,400-odd BEST buses and the 54,000-odd taxis in the city. The need for a mass rapid transit system is a burning exigency, given that Mumbai region's population is feared to cross 35 million by 2030.

Mumbai Metro Rail Project: Highlights

Line	Corridor	Corridor type (km)			PHPDT	Traffic
		UG	Elevated	Total		
		Phase I				
1.	Versova-Andheri-Ghatkopar	0.0	15.0	15.0	31,421	595,469
2.	Colaba-Mahim	9.9	26.1	36.0	43,356	1,322,294
3	Mahim-Mankhurd	2.1	10.7	12.8	28,022	472,368
		Phase II				
4.	Charkop-Dahisar	0.0	7.5	7.5	19,094	142,801
5.	Ghatkopar-Mulund	0.0	12.4	12.4	32,698	407,096
		Phase III				
6.	BKC-Kanjur Marg	8.5	11.0	19.5	21,441	539,973
7.	Andheri (E) – Dahisar (E)	0.0	18.0	18.0	25,504	443,135
8.	Hutatma Chowk-Ghatkopar	8.5	13.3	21.8	18,354	406,666
9.	Sewri-Prabhadevi	3.5	0.0	3.5	4,446	14,298

PHPDT= Peak hour per direction traffic.
Traffic = Total passenger km in peak hour.

The Mumbai Metro Rail project is being implemented in three phases, with full commissioning scheduled for 2021. Phase I will have three lines (see Tables), out of which pre-project activity has begun on the first line (hereinafter referred to as Phase I-A).

Phase I-A envisages a metro rail network connecting Versova to Ghatkopar, enroute Andheri. The 15-km track with 14 stations en route will be fully elevated. A special purpose vehicle, based on public-private partnership, will implement this Rs.1,500 crore project on BOOT basis. MMRDA, along with other government agencies, will have a minority stake of 26 percent with the private sector consortium holding 74 percent. Construction work on the project is likely to begin sometime in 2006 with completion targeted for 2013.

Mumbai Metro Rail Project: Phase-Wise Schedule

Phase	UG	Elevated (km)	Total	Cost (Rs.crore)	Completion Schedule
I	12.0	51.8	63.8	6,585	2006-13
II	0.0	19.9	19.9	3,585	2011-16
III	20.5	42.3	62.8	9,255	2016-21
Total	**32.5**	**114.0**	**146.5**	**19,425**	**2006-21**

Current developments: The final developer is likely to be selected by early February 2006, from the following three qualified consortia:

Consortium Leader	Other members
Reliance Energy	Gammon India, Siemens AG, Bharat Earth Movers
Larsen & Toubro	Connex (France), Metro Rail (Hong Kong)
IL&FS	Thai Developers (Italy), CTN, Unity Infra, Skanska

The winning consortia will form an SPV with MMRDA and develop the project on BOOT basis with a concession period of 30 years.

The Mumbai Metro project was approved by the planning Commission in May 2005, following the Maharashtra Government approval in April 2005. Delhi Metro Rail Corporation is the technical consultant for the project.

Meanwhile, preliminary work on Lines 2 and 3 of Phase I is also progressing. For Line 2, MMRDA has already submitted the project report to the Maharashtra government, while field survey is underway for Line 3.

Delhi Metro Rail Project (Phase II)

A pioneering effort of urban transportation system has been the Delhi Metro Rail Transit system. The Rs.10,000 crore project is being implemented jointly by the Union Government and the Government of the National Capital Region, through a special purpose vehicle called Delhi Metro Rail Corporation Ltd.

Phase I of the project involves the creation of a modern railway network 65 km in length, through a combination of underground, at grade and elevated railway, punctuated by 50-odd stations.

Delhi Metro Rail Transit System

Line		km	Completion
1.	**Shahdara-Tri Nagar-Rithala**	22.06	Apr-04
	Shahdara-Tis Hazari	(8.30)	Dec-02
	Tis Hazari-Inderlok	(4.50)	Oct-03
	Inderlok-Rithala	(8.90)	Apr-04
2.	**Vishwavidyala-Central Secretariat**	10.84	Jul-05
	Vishwavidyala-Kashmere Gate	(4.54)	Dec-04
	Kashmere Gate-Central Secretariat	(6.30)	Jul-05
3.	**Indraprastha-Dwarka-Dwarka Subcity**	31.67	Jun-06
	Indraprastha-Barakhamba*	(2.27)	Mar-06
	Barakhamba-Dwarka	(22.90)	Dec-05
	Dwarka-Dwarka Subcity*	(6.50)	Jun-06
Total		**64.57**	

* Under Execution

This project phase has been commissioned in stages with the first line – the 8.3 km Shahdara-Tis Hazari section – in December 2002. The last stretch to have got commissioned was the 22.90 km Barakhamba-Dwarka line which was opened to traffic in December 2005.

The entire project is complete except for two additional stretches, which were not part of the original plan. (See Table) The project in its revised form will be commissioned by June 2006.

Phase I of the project is expected to reduce road traffic by 21.8 lakh commuter trips per day. This would mean 2,500 less buses on the roads, increase in average speed of road buses from 10.5 km/h to 14 km/h, saving of 20 lakh man hours per day due to reduced journey time and saving in fuel cost worth Rs.500 crore per year.

(For latest developments on Phase II, see Section Urban Transportation under *Micro Review.*)

Kochi Metro Rail Project

The Kerala Government has planned to develop a mass rapid transit system in its capital city – Kochi.

In mid-January 2006, global expressions of interest were invited from potential concessionaires to develop the Rs.2,200 crore metro railway project.

The selected developer will be awarded the project on BOT basis with a concession period of 30 years from 2010, the expected date of commissioning. The project will be developed on design, procure, finance, build, operate, maintain and transfer basis.

The elevated two-way light metro rail will have a length of 25.253 km, with 21 intervening stations, connecting Alwaye (20 km north of Kochi) to Tripunithura (near Petta) in the south. Delhi Metro Rail Corporation is assisting the Kerala Government in the project.

The project will be financed through equity contribution from the State and Central Governments to the tune of Rs.895 crore (around 40 percent of the total cost). The concessionaire will bring in equity of Rs.340 crore and the remaining (around Rs.1,000 crore) would represent borrowings.

Hyderabad Metro Rail Project (Phase I)

The Andhra Pradesh Government has planned to develop an elevated Hyderabad Metro Rail Project at an estimated cost of Rs.4,300 crore. The project will come up on BOT basis, with private sector participation, with a concession period of 37 years.

In January 2006, a consortium comprising SREI Infrastructure Finance, Singapore-based SMRT Corporation, SembCorp Engineers and Essar Constructions was shortlisted. The BOT contractor is likely to be finalized in the coming weeks. Seven members were shortlisted in response to the Andhra Pradesh Government's expression of interest invited in August/September 2005. Other members in the fray include:

- Magna Allmore (Malaysia), Siemens AG (Germany), ETA (Dubai) and NCC (Hyderabad);
- Reliance Energy (Mumbai) and Bombardier (Canada);
- Metrail (Switzerland), Macquarie Bank (Australia and MMC Malaysia);
- GVK (Hyderabad), Gammon India (Mumbai), Alstom (France) and IDFC;
- Navabharat (Hyderabad), Maytas(Hyderabad), ItalThai (ITD-Thailand) and ITD Cem (Delhi);
- IVRCL (Hyderabad), Hitachi (Japan) and BHEL.

In Phase I of the project, work on which is expected to start in mid-2006, three sections would be developed totaling around 60 km, in the following scheme.

Hyderabad Metro Rail Project (Phase I)

Section	Route	km	Stations
1.	Miyapur-Chaitanyapuri	26.27	25
2.	Tarnaka-Panjagutta-Hitec City	20.00	na
3.	Secunderabad-Falaknuma	13.18	14

Meanwhile, technical consultants have also been sought who would assist in the bid process management, financial closure, etc. Six consultancy consortia are in the fray and the final selection is likely to take place by February 2006. The Hyderabad metro project envisages minimum carrying capacity of 25,000 pphpd, which would be scaled up to around 55,000 pphpd in the near future. The traffic forecast made by GoAP is 11.11 lakh passengers per day in 2008, rising to 12.21 lpd in 2011 and 18.81 lpd in 2021.

Goa Monorail Project

Goa has been the latest city to have proposed a mass transit system. In September 2005, the Goa Government invited expressions of interest to conduct feasibility studies for a monorail system connecting Margao and Mapusa via Panjim, aggregating 47 km.

The project will be executed on BOT basis with Central grant representing 20 percent of the total outlay. The cost of the project works out to Rs.2,500 crore (at Rs.60 crore per km.) The State Government will procure land required for the project.

In August 2005, the Goa Government gave up on the Konkan Railway Corporation's (KRC) skybus project, The Goa Government has given up on Konkan Railway Corporation's skybus project, following delays in getting Central clearance. (see Box – "Sky Bus Project: The Rise and Fall", at the end of this section.)

Chennai Elevated Monorail Project

The Tamil Nadu government has formulated plans for developing a mass rapid transit system for its capital – Chennai – which is today India's fourth largest city in terms of population.

In December 2005, Metropolitan Transport Corporation (Chennai) Ltd – a wholly-owned subsidiary of the Tamil Nadu Government – was appointed as the nodal agency for developing the MRTS in Chennai.

MTCL has identified 490 km of principal transit routes in Chennai city and surrounding areas. Out of this around 300 km have been earmarked for the proposed Chennai Elevated Monorail Mass Rapid Transit System Project.

In January 2006, MTCL invited bids from potential concessionaires for developing the project on a design, develop, construct, finance, own, operate, maintain and transfer (DBOOT) basis with a concession period of 40 years, including construction period. Bids close on 10 February 2006. Later in January 2006 itself, MTCL invited bids for selection of advisors who would assist in the selection of the concessionaires.

Bangalore Metro Rail Project

The Karnataka Government has proposed to develop a mass transit system in Bangalore of 36.5 km comprising elevated (29.15 km), at grade (0.65 km) and underground (6.70 km) sections, with 35 stations en route. The project cost has been estimated at Rs.5,065 crore with gestation period of five years.

In March 2005, Bangalore Mass Rapid Transit Ltd, the special purpose vehicle implementing the project, invited bids for general consultancy services. As of December 2005, no consultants were finalized. BMRTL in March 2005 had also invited bids for construction of elevated sections. The response to this tender notice is awaited. The following is a brief history of the project.

May 2003: Delhi Metro Rail Corporation, the project consultant submitted the detailed project report for Phase I of the project to the Karnataka Government.

February 2004: The Planning Commission accorded its "in-principle" approval to the project.

March 2005: The Karnataka State Cabinet approved the project on and gave its go-ahead to land acquisition, preliminary works like short listing of vendors/ contractors and identification and shifting of utilities.

Visakhapatnam MRTS

Besides Hyderabad, move is also afoot to develop a mass rapid transit system in Visakhapatnam – the second largest city in Andhra Pradesh with a geographical area of 505 sq km. Plans are yet in the nascent stage.

In December 2005, global expressions of interest were invited to carry out comprehensive traffic and transportation studies with special emphasis on the techno-economic feasibility of a mass rapid transit system.

Kolkata MRTS and Underground Metro

West Bengal Transport Infrastructure Development Corporation Ltd – a West Bengal Government enterprise – has initiated plans to develop a mass rapid transit system to connect various parts of the Kolkata Metropolitan area. In bids that closed in September 2004, WBTIDCL sought expressions of interest from manufacturers and developers for the proposed MRTS. The project details have not yet been defined. Options may include magnetic levitation, electric traction or any other proven technology. The MRTS would be, in whole or part, on grade or elevated. (No further developments to the EoI invitation are available.)

Kolkata already has the distinction of having the first underground metro railway in India. It extends over 16.45 km from Dum Dum (near the Kolkata airport) to Tollygunj in the south. There are 17 stations en route, roughly 1 km apart. The metro railway was constructed progressively from 1972 to 1995.

Work on expanding the metro railway by a further 8.70 km south of Tollygunj, up to Gharia, is underway. Sanctioned in 1999-00, the project comprising five elevated and one at-grade stations will connect the South 24 Parganas district to the Kolkata business district. The project, estimated to cost Rs.2,680 crore, is scheduled to commission by June 2007.

Sky Bus Project: The Rise and Fall

The indigenous Sky Bus mode of transport that was once considered as a path-breaking solution to modern transportation woes is today fading from public memory.

An innovation patented by Konkan Railway Corporation, the Sky Bus concept was at the zenith of its popularity during 2001-04. At one point, several large and mini metropolitan cities were enthusiastically factoring the Sky Bus in their urban transportation plans. In fact, the then Prime Minister, Mr Atal Bihari Vajpayee, in August 2001 cleared a massive programme to develop the Sky Bus in eight cities – Mumbai, Delhi, Kolkata, Chennai, Pune, Ahmedabad, Bangalore and Hyderabad – totaling 560 km. The project was even kept on Mission Mode. Other cities like Goa, Coimbatore and Kochi also viewed the Sky Bus with favour. The Sky Bus concept even traveled overseas and there were reports of countries like Iran and Singapore reacting positively to presentations made on this novel concept.

KRC spent Rs.50 crore in developing a 1.6 km test track at Goa and in September 2004 conducted trial runs to demonstrate the efficacy of this novel transportation mode. During these runs, there was a freak accident that resulted in some casualties, one fatal. This marked the beginning of the end of the Sky Bus project. To complicate matters, there was confusion about who would be the government agency to award safety certification. The technical aspects of the Sky Bus were out of the purview of the Indian Railways Act, and as such, the Indian Railways could not "interfere" in this matter. These adversities were compounded with the superannuation of Mr. B Rajaram, the then Managing Director of KRC who was the main proponent of the Sky Bus technology.

In August 2005, Goa decided against the Sky Bus project and opted for the elevated monorail. Other cities followed suit. Today, mass rapid transit system projects are under various stages of implementation in ten metropolitan cities – all of whom are staying clear of the Sky Bus.

Sky Bus Technology involved a two-way elevated track with suspended rail coaches. The elevation was to be 9.5 m, and trains could run at a maximum speed of 100 kmph. The cost was estimated to be Rs.35 crore per km, against Rs.200 crore for underground railway and Rs.90 crore for an elevated railway.

14

Interview with M D/ Delhi Metro Rail Corporation

Delhi Metro system ensures complete safety while running the trains as Automatic Train Protection and Automatic Train Operation has been employed. The article also covers various means that were adopted to bring metro awareness among the people of Delhi. As railways have been the safest mode of communication, metro is making traveling by trains all the more comfortable and safer.

"Railway background has helped me a lot..." says Dr. E Sreedharan, Managing Director, Delhi Metro Rail Corporation in his interaction with Editor, Indian Railways. Indian Railways magazine has been very fortunate on having a direct interaction with Dr. Sreedharan. Dr. Sreedharan took charge as the Corporation's first MD on 5th November, 1997. The target of commissioning the entire first phase by March 2006 was the biggest challenge lying before him to be met. Fifty years passed by, a dream was realized in the capital city on 25th December, 2002 when the first metro rail run was begun from Kashmere Gate to

* This is an interview with Dr. E Sreedharan, Managing Director, Delhi Metro Rail Corporation by the Editor of Indian Railways Magazine.

Seelampur. The dream came true for the commuters traveling between Shahdara and Tis Hazari on the inauguration of this section. Dr. Sreedharan is the receipient of many prestigious Awards, namely – Railway Minister's Award in 1963, Engineer of the Year – 1993, S B Joshi Memorial Award – 1995, Fie Foundation Award – 1995, ICI-Forsoc Award – 1996, Bharat Ratna Sir M Vishweshwarayya Award – 1996, Best Design Engineer Award – 1999, Padma Shri Award in 2001 for National Building, Jury's Award for Individual Leadership by CII, Award for Excellence in Infrastructure – 2002, AIMA for his Outstanding Management Style, Red and White Social Lifetime Achievement Award, Vocational Excellence Award, 2004 and Om Prakash Bhasin Award for the Excellent Contribution in the field of Engineering in 2002. The Excerpts of the Interview:

Sir, at last the Delhi Metro has arrived. Can you tell us how the story of Delhi Metro had begun?

35 studies were conducted for planning of a metro system in Delhi. However, none of these saw the light of the day and it was only in 1991 that RITES undertook a study for a MRTS system in Delhi at the behest of Delhi Government and the Urban Development Ministry. This study was completed by 1996 and the DMRC was formed. When I joined the DMRC in November 1997, there was not even a chair to sit on and the first task was to build up an Organisation quickly to implement the project. Initially, I brought in a lot of engineers and personnel from the Indian Railways on deputation as these people are extremely competent and well-versed with Railway technology. Subsequently, we have given them exposure through training and visits to Metros abroad to enhance their professional skills and ability.

What were your experiences, the good and the bitter, Sir, when the work began?

Delhi Metro is highly technical and a rail-based technology different from the existing system. We have to get the technology from outside and that was a great challenge. Secondly, constructing metro rail is a very difficult task in an urban environment. Since we are directly under the eyes of VVIPs, intense care was taken for minimizing the inconveniences. The third challenge was the period for completing the job. Compressing the period from 10 years to 7 years was very difficult. The disappointments – no, not many at all. A good job was done and the public has appreciated the DMRC, Ridership is building up and the metro functioning on operational profit lines. People have adopted the system and keep the metro neat, clean, with no littering and no graffiti. Of course, little regret – we wanted to bring the best modern metro in the world but the broad gauge was given to us. That is the only area we have a little regret.

What were the main reasons for taking so many years for the execution of Metro rail?

The project was initially supposed to have been completed in 10 years time but one of the first decisions we took was to reduce the implementation time to only 7 years. This was a historic decision and I am glad to say that we have implemented the same. In addition, the project when it was sanctioned initially constituted of only 55 kms but cover 65.1 kms today in Phase-1. In spite of the additional length, we continue to maintain the target date and are also finishing the project within the budget.

Since Delhi people are now becoming familiar with this transport, do you think Sir, it would out beat the road transport in future?

Metro cannot outbeat the road transport. Road transport is necessary. It is door-to-door service and it cannot be eliminated. Metro cannot go door-to-door because it has specific corridors. Instead, road and metro should complement each other and not compete.

Is there any similar project to come up in other cities like Delhi Metro?

DMRC has prepared detailed project reports for metros in Kochi, Ahmedabad, Mumbai, Bangalore, Hyderabad and a new east-west line in Kolkata. In addition, reports have been prepared for Gurgaon, Noida and Ghaziabad. A feasibility report has also been submitted for Chennai.

It has been seen that the world's most sophisticated and advanced safety measures have been implemented in all metro stations and trains. Please brief on this statement.

The trains at Delhi Metro system run with the help of Automatic Train Protection and Automatic Train Operation (ATO). This ensures a complete safety during train operations.

What are the various means by which you are bringing Metro awareness to the people of Delhi?

When we first launched the metro, a massive publicity campaign was undertaken to educate the users on how to use the metro system as there were a number of new features which the public was seeing for the first time such as escalators, automatic door closing system, automatic fare collection system etc. We have adopted unconventional method including Nukkad Nataks and Sahayaks (volunteers) to interact with the public to educate them in this regard. Our publicity has been extremely low budget but very effective.

Sir, your unforgettable moments when Shahdara-Tis Hazari section was commissioned.

Well, the first unforgettable moment was the First trial run of the train which was inaugurated by the then Deputy Prime Minister Shri L K Advani and then the commissioning of Shahdara-Tis Hazari section by the then Prime Minister Shri Atal Behari Vajpayee was the 2nd unforgettable moment. The response was very enormous – 8 to 10 lakhs people turned up in the first two to three days. A lot of confusion occurred but now everything is quite stable.

According to your opinion what are the gains of the metro to the Delhi city and to the nation?

Metro is a very reliable, safe and a comfortable mode of transport. It brought in a lot of glamour to the city which the city can boast of, social attitude of people is also changing. People are getting used to orderliness and are learning good social manners. At present, it runs 33 kms only carrying 2.7 lakh passengers a day which is equivalent to 800 buses lesser on the road. This means less pollution, less congestion and less accidents.

Now where does Delhi Metro stand with world metro countries?

We can be proud that our metro stands at par with other countries. In fact, our metro is much better than any metro in UK, USA or except for one or two lines in Europe, i.e. Paris line 14. Our metro is comparable to Hong Kong, Tokyo and Singapore metros.

A dream comes true. As Managing Director of Delhi Metro how do you feel Sir?

Well... really very satisfied and proud. I never thought I would achieve this.

Did your background as a railwayman help you in building the Delhi Metro?

Certainly. The Railway background has helped me a lot. The type of training, the type of background has really helped.

Do you think the technology inducted in the Metro is appropriate? Will this know-how be available to the Indian Railways?

Yes, we have adopted very advanced technology which is relevant to Indian Railways. Yes, Indian Railways can access this technology from us without any hesitation.

A number of railwaymen have acquired expertise in the latest technologies. How will their talent be utilized by the country?

Some stayed with Metro and some are going back to Indian Railways. The type of work culture and technology which they have gained here can be utilized when they are back to Indian Railways or any other railway.

What was the highlight of your career in Indian Railways?

Indian Railways career.... I would say that I rose from an Assistant Engineer to the highest post as Member Engineering.

How do you compare Delhi Metro with Kolkata Metro?

Kolkata Metro is an old technology built indigenously. It did not go for foreign inputs and technologically it is behind. It can be modernized and Delhi metro can help Kolkata metro in modernization.

Do you foresee any possibility of Delhi Metro's integration with Indian Railway System at any point of time?

No, physically it is not possible. There could be passenger integration but not system integration.

Thank you very much Sir.

Delhi Metro Moves Ahead

Delhi, capital of India has highly dense population. As per 2001 Census, population in Delhi was 13.8 million. Also it has a large number of registered vehicles which had reached to 4 million and commuter congestion was a problem. There was absence of a mass transit system as buses were the only mode of mass transit in Delhi. Also due to increasing congestion, pollution, fuel wastage and accident rates, a need to develop a mass transit system was realized. It was thought that the introduction of a rail based mass transit system which is a non-polluting mode would help to meet transport demand. On 1st October 1998, the Delhi Metro Rail Corporation commenced construction of Delhi Metro. Phase I of the Delhi Metro Project included construction of three lines and will cover 65 kms of the route length. The first section of Line 1 from Shahdara to Tis-Hazari was opened on 25th December 2002.

Delhi Metro consists of both underground as well as elevated corridors. It has Centralized Automatic Train Control which comprises Automatic Train Operation, Automatic Train Protection and Automatic Train Signaling systems. Automatic Train Protection System is responsible for detection of door opening and train protection. Automatic Train Signaling system takes care of the dwelling time of the trains, route setting and also keeps a watch on the train operations. Route maps and LCD displays are available in every coach and emergency communication between the driver and the passenger is also facilitated. There is a passenger alarm button near the doors of each car to be used in case of emergency like theft, fire. The train has high-tech, air-conditioned coaches. The trains are designed in a manner that makes them user-friendly as well as provide safety. Seating capacity of each coach is 60, while standing space for around 325 passengers exists. As a part of safety and security measure, CCTV cameras are fixed at stations. The speed limit of these trains is 80 kmp and they halt for 20 seconds at every station. Trains would run at a frequency of 3 minutes. Smart Card operated flap doors are used at entry and exit points of metro stations. Elevators as well as escalators are installed at every metro station for commuters' convenience. Tactile tiles are used to guide visually impaired and drop off points, ramps, lifts as well as specific places are earmarked in the coaches for physically challenged commuters. Public announcement systems are set in every station. Even each station is uniquely designed. Most of the stations on one of their lines conduct rainwater harvesting as an initiative for environmental protection.

The design of Delhi Metro is such that it can be integrated with other public transport in the city. Thus Delhi Metro has proved to be a role model and a convenient mode of mass transport.

(Compiled by Pooja Dave, Research Associate, Icfai Business School Research Centre, Ahmedabad.)

15

Understanding the Metro Rail Demand

Mukti Advani and Geetam Tiwari

Growing number of vehicular trips by cars and two wheelers which result in traffic congestion, air pollution and traffic accidents has become a major concern in urban areas. Investments in high capacity rail based mass transit systems are being promoted to arrest this trend. In the last two decades Kolkata, Chennai and Delhi have invested in MRTS/LRT systems. This paper analyses the methodology and arguments used to justify these systems. The paper presents evaluation of Delhi metro in terms of capacity, travel time and accessibility to the system and evaluation indices reflecting commuter's perspective.

Urban Transport

Transport situation in most Indian metropolitan cities is rapidly deteriorating because of the increasing travel demand and inadequate transportation system. Indian cities of all sizes are facing the crisis of urban transport. Despite investments in road infrastructure and plans for land use and transport development, all face the problem of congestion traffic accidents and air pollution and the problems continue to grow. Large cities are facing an unprecedented growth of personal vehicles (two wheelers and cars) and in medium and small cities different forms of intermediate public transport provided by informal sector are struggling to meet the mobility demands of city residents.

In Delhi, the number of two wheelers and cars continue to rise. Despite construction of flyovers and roads, the roads continue to face congestion at peak hours. In spite of the roads occupying 21 percent of the total city area, this large number of motor vehicles causes extreme congestion on roads, ever slowing speed, fuel wastage, environmental pollution and an unacceptable level of road accidents. Delhi metro has been planned to reduce congestion on Delhi roads and augment the current public transport, which is primarily buses.

Metro Rail in Indian Cities

Delhi Metro

RITES recommended a rail-based system, comprising a network of underground, elevated and surface corridors, aggregating to 256 km, to meet the traffic demand up to the year 2021. The whole project, estimated to cost 3350 million USD at the 1996 price level was expected to handle 12.6 million commuter trips per day in the year 2021, at the completion of full network of 256 km. (India Infoline, 2003). DMRC (2003) has attributed a number of benefits to metro. This includes time saving for commuters, reliable and safe journey, reduction in atmospheric pollution, reduction in accidents, reduced fuel consumption, reduced vehicle operating costs, increase in the average speed of road vehicles, etc. However, there has been no study which has documented the impact on travel time, pollution and accidents along the metro corridor after the introduction of the metro.

Expected ridership of Delhi metro has been modified several times since the commencement of the project DMRC (2005) lists expected ridership of metro rail for 2005 to be 1.5 million passengers trip per day (ppd). This has been further reduced to 0.7 million ppd by March 2006 (*The Hindu*, 2005). As shown in Table 1, ridership on line 1 of the phase I in April 2004 was 0.12 million ppd and in July 2005 it was 0.13 million ppd. Ridership of line 2 in July 2005 was 0.24 million ppd. This shows that after completion, of around 57% of phase I ridership was 0.37 million ppd, 20% of the estimated ridership.

Table 1: Estimated and Actual Ridership of Delhi Metro

Line	Length (Km)	Actual Ridership (Million ppd)				Estimated Ridership (Million ppd)	
		April 2004		July 2005		December 2005	
		Status	Ridership	Status	Ridership	Status	Ridership
1	22	Working	0.12	Working	0.13	Working	-
2	11	Not started	-	Working	0.24	Working	-
3	32.10	Not started	-	Not started	-	Not started	-
Total	65.10	-	0.12		0.37	-	1.5

Source: India Infoline (2003), Sreedharan (2004), DMRC (2003) DMRC (2004)

The total revenue generated during the year 2003-2004 was 10.30 million USD inclusive of income from operation, rentals from properties and consultancy. The total expenditure incurred for the same period was 7.1 million USD giving a profit before depreciation and interest amounting 3.25 million USD. The depreciation and interest charged was 8.43 million USD and 2.02 million USD respectively. Considering these two costs, the loss for the financial year 2003-2004 amounted to 7.21 million USD (DMRC, 2003-2004).

Chennai Metro

Vydhianathan, (2003) discusses India's first elevated rail transit system in Chennai. This system has escalators to platforms, lifts for the aged and the handicapped and modern stations. Chennai MRTS should be the most attractive travel option in a metro that has about 2 million vehicles on the road, endless hold-ups, rising pollution and a bad safety record. Yet, there are very few commuters in a three-car train and the stations are deserted – the city virtually denies its existence. Despite the huge investment of 60 million USD, there are no returns. Commuter patronage refuses to pick up, though the city buses are over crowded.

Simhan (2000) discusses that in the first phase, started in 1990, the Beach Station in north Chennai was connected to Chepauk in Central Chennai; this section was opened in November 1995. However, this stretch of the MRTS did not attract many passengers and most trains ran empty. The service was then extended to Thirumailai in October 1997, after which too the system has not got the anticipated patronage. The Southern Railway even extended a few services to far away places such as Gummudipoondi, at the other end, all to no avail.

According to the MRTS authorities (*Business Line*, 2000) it has a capacity to ferry some six hundred thousand commuters daily. However, the service has been attracting only around 25,000 passengers per day, that too most of them during peak hours. He points out that even people living near the MRTS railway stations prefer buses.

Kolkata Metro

The Kolkata metro railway is the first underground railway project implemented in India. Singh (2002) mentioned that according to Calcutta Mass Transit Study 1971, the average weekday transit trips estimated in 1971 were 4.6 million, which were projected to increase to 5.3, 6.7 and 8.3 million in 1976, 1983 and 1990 respectively. The expected traffic in 1978 after opening of the first phase was anticipated to be 469 million passengers per year and in 1990, 612.5 million passengers. The annual passenger volume was estimated to be 623.7 million by 2000. The number of originating passengers on the metro railway during 1999-2000 was only 55.8 million, which is approximately one-eleventh of the estimated traffic ten years ago in 1990. Low traffic is one of the main reasons for the metro railway being unviable. The system originally estimated to be constructed at a cost of 31 million USD, was completed at a cost of 355 million USD. (Singh, 2002)

Demand estimation procedure for all three systems needs to be analyzed in detail to explain the low ridership levels.

Overestimated Ridership and Underestimated Cost

Flyvbjerg (2006) studied the largest sample of its kind, covering 210 projects in 14 nations worth US$58 billion. The study shows with very high statistical significance that forecasters generally do a poor job of estimating the demand for transportation infrastructure projects. The result is substantial downside financial and economic risk. If techniques and skills for arriving at accurate demand forecasts have improved over time, as often claimed by forecasters, this does not show in the data. For nine out of ten rail projects, passenger forecasts are overestimated; average overestimation is 106%. For 72% of rail projects, forecasts are overestimated by more than two-thirds. For 50% of road projects, the difference between actual and forecasted traffic is more than ±20%; for 25% of road projects, the difference is larger than ±40%. Forecasts for roads are more accurate and more balanced than for rail, with no significant difference between the frequencies of inflated versus deflated forecasts. But for both rail and road projects, the risk is substantial that demands forecasts are incorrect by a large margin.

American Dream Coalition fact sheet presents that a myth is 'pay no attention to the high construction cost, because once rail lines are built they will last forever' and the reality is 'Rail lines must be rebuilt and equipment replaced every 20 to 30 years. Reconstruction often costs much as the original construction.'

The Washington, DC, metro rail system was built at a cost of $12.5 billion. Today, its managers say that over the next ten years they will need to spend another $12.5 billion renovating roadbed, replacing cars, and refurbishing stations. (americanderamcoalition.org). The federal transit administration calls these "capital costs" but really they are maintenance costs, and as such they make rail much costlier to maintain than buses. Total length of 198.5 km of metro rail will cost Rs.10751 crores (excluding taxes and duties) and metro has not mentioned anything about the maintenance cost. As mentioned above, maintenance cost of metro rail is as much as the original cost. It should have been considered in the cost evaluation, as it needs a large amount. Already 100% cost overrun is estimated for first phase of the metro (Rs.12000 crores instead of Rs.6000 crores estimated for first phase in 1996.)

Commuters' Perspective

Public transport service has to meet the needs of commuters. This includes accessible stations, minimum affordable time loss at interchanges, safer and reliable services. Limit of access to MRTS is based on the assumption of most comfortable walking distance as 0.5 km. When this distance increases passengers have to use feeder system, which requires a transfer. A transfer has a major impact on passenger journey. Generally simple long trip is preferred over short journeys involving transfers because each transfer implies added impedance in terms of time, cost, inconvenience and uncertainty but how much percentage of total trips are generally originated within this influence zone of 0.5 km is a matter to be analyzed.

To understand user's perspective of mode choice, all modes available to user and all elements of the current transportation system must be considered. Therefore, comparison of different choices available to users has to be evaluated considering total trip profile (full trip chain) from origin to final destination including access and egress trips. In addition to considering both access and egress, these components should not be treated in isolation from the total trip or line-haul time.

When DMRC expects that in 2021, 12.6 million commuter trips will be handled by metro, it means some passengers traveling by other modes at present will be shifted to metro. Who are these people? Are they car users? Or bus users? Or two-wheeler users or others?

Table 2: Modal Shift Possibility from Private to Public Mode of Bus or Metro

Issue	Bus	Metro	Remarks
Door to door service	Minimum walking distance to bus stop is 100 m. (maximum 500 m)	One can reach to the metro station by walk or by cycle rickshaw, auto rickshaw or by feeder bus	Probability of shifting the mode is very low
Transfer inconvenience	If destination does not lie in any bus route one has to shift in-between	If direct route is not available one has to get transferred in-between	Transfer type can be different for metro and bus
No need to follow timings	One has to follow the schedule of buses	One has to follow the metro schedules	If more frequencies are provided, then it can help to shift the two wheeler users to bus or metro
Work/shopping place is very near	In any case one will use two wheeler only	In any case one will use two wheeler only	As distance is short probability of shifting from two wheeler to bus or metro is negligible
Travel timings	If only in-vehicle time is considered it takes more time than metro	If only in-vehicle time is compared, Metro takes less time	User will compare a total profile, i.e. total access time of trip it includes transfer-waiting time, availability of connecting bus/rail, convenience to reach at stop/ station

Table 2 compares modal shift possibilities from private to public mode of transport. Again in public mode options, preference between metro and bus choice is compared.

Full Trip Profile Comparison

To compare different modes, full trip profile characteristics including access and egress trips have to be compared. Table 3 shows the time taken for access and egress trip for different modes.

Table 3: Access and Egress Trip Time for Different Modes

Mode	Access Time	Egress Time	Average Speed at Line Haul
2-wh	Time for taking out vehicle from garage = 2 minutes	Time spent for parking vehicle and reaching the destination = 2 minutes	20 km/hr
3-wh	Time spent in walking from home to 3-wh stand = 5 minutes (average distance of 350 m)	Time spent in getting off from 3-wh and to reach the destination = 2 minutes	18 km/hr
Car	Time for taking out vehicle from garage = 5 minutes	Time spent for parking vehicle and reaching the destination = 3 minutes	25 km/hr
Taxi	Time spent in walking from home to taxi stop = 7 minutes (average distance of 500 m)	Time spent in getting off from taxi and reach the destination = 2 minutes	25 km/hr
Bus	Time spent in walking from home to bus stop = 7 minutes (average distance of 500 m)	Time spent in walking to reach the destination from bus stop = 7 minutes	18 km/hr
Metro	Total time spent in walking from home to metro station (avg. distance of 500 m) and time spent inside the metro station for getting ticket and to reach the platform= 8 minutes	Time spent in walking to reach destination from metro station = 8 minutes	33 km/hr

Figures 1(A), 1(B) and 1(C) show the total trip profile including access, egress and main haul line time for 5 km, 10 km and 15 km trip length respectively, for all private and public mode options.

Figure 1(A): Total Time by Different Modes for 5 Km Distance

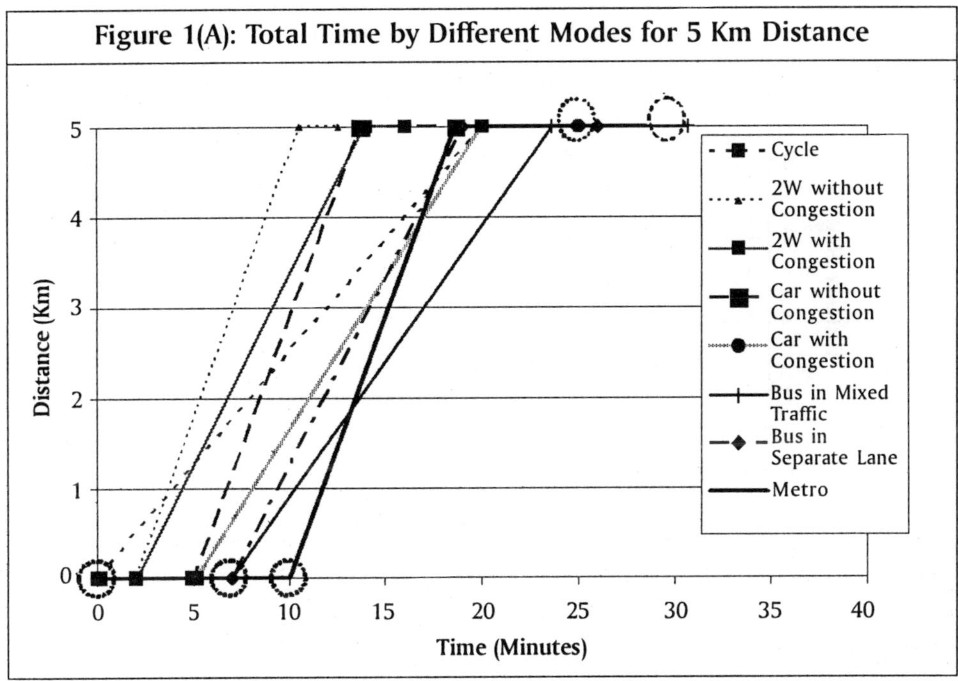

Figure A shows that metro is not first preferred mode for trip length of 5 km or below. Figure B says that for distance of 10 km, metro and BRT will be equally

Figure 1(B): Total Time by Different Modes for 10 Km Distance

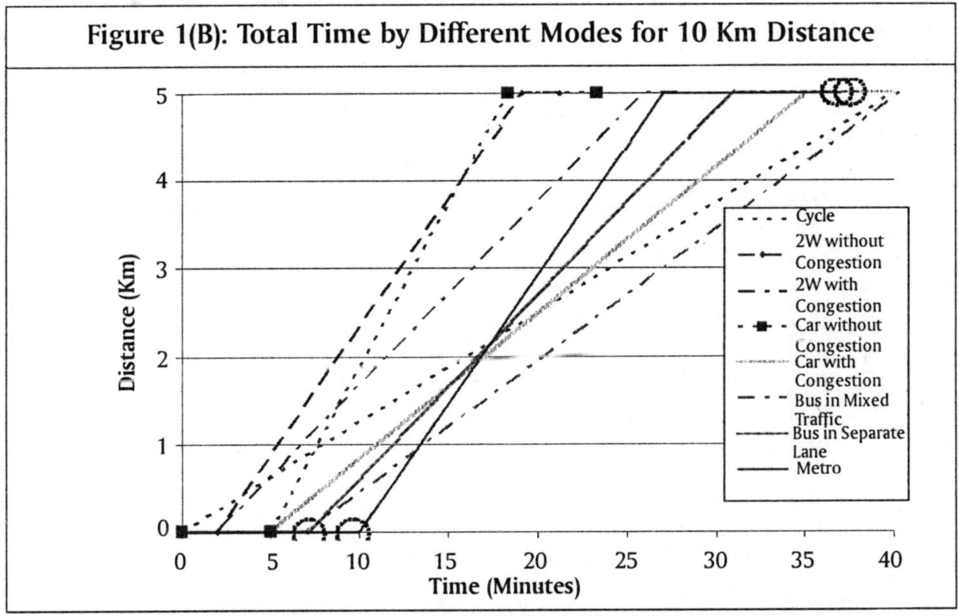

Figure 1(C): Total Time by Different Modes for 15 Km Distance

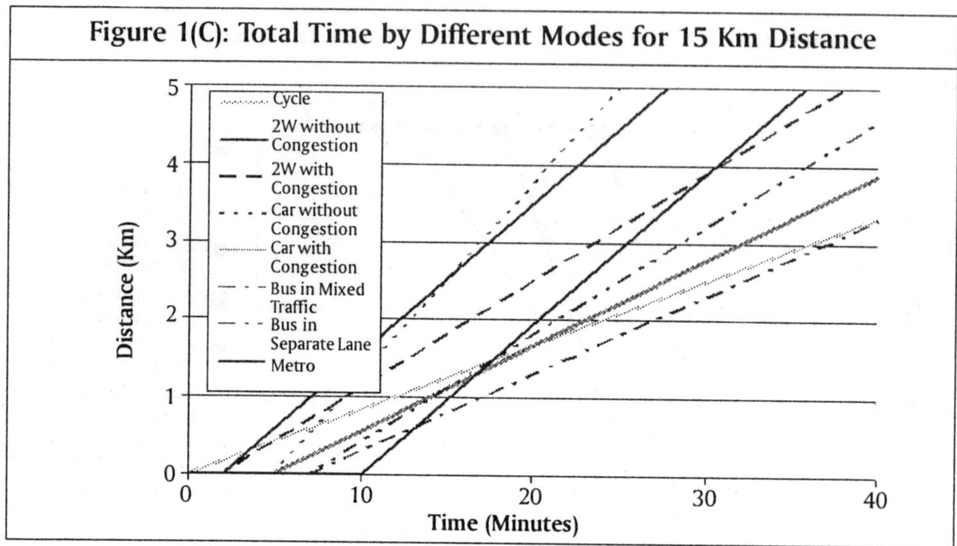

preferred mode of transport and Figure C indicates that for distance of 15 km or higher, metro is the preferred mode to make a trip. Figure 2 shows that in Delhi, around 25% of trips are of this or higher length.

Therefore, demand estimation for the metro needs a careful analysis including access and egress time factors. According to Siemiatycki (2006), it is still an open question that whether the Delhi metro will actually achieve its stated objectives,

Figure 2: Share of Trips Versus Trip Length

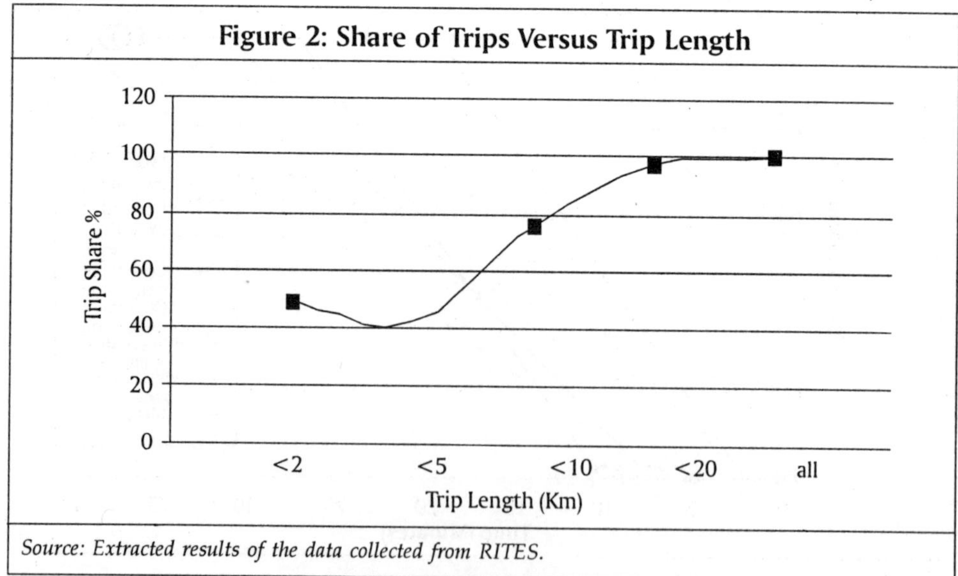

Source: Extracted results of the data collected from RITES.

although to date even a positive image has not been able to attract the predicted number of riders to the system.

Conclusion

Metro systems planned in India shows cost overrunning and under utilization of capacity. Methodology and arguments used to justify these systems need careful analysis. High capacity system does not necessarily generate high demand. Estimation of passenger demand for transit services should consider complete journey of commuters including access and egress time.

(Mukti Advani is a Research Scholar and Geetam Tiwari is an Associate Professor, Transportation Research and Injury Prevention Programme, Indian Institute of Technology, Delhi.)

References

American Dream Coalition Fact Sheet # 1, "Myths & Facts about Rail Transit" *americanderamcoalition.org.*

Business Line (2000) 'Chennai's MRTS: Not on fast track, yet' an article dated 29th May 2000 by *The Hindu* group of publications, India.

DMRC (2003) 'The Need' - Delhi MRTS project, an article by Delhi Metro Rail Corporation. *http://delhigovt.nic.in/dmrc.asp.*

DMRC (2004) 'Annual Report 2003 - 2004', Delhi Metro Rail Corporation, Delhi India.

DMRC (2005) Delhi Metro Rail Corporation we site. *http://www.delhi metro rail.com*

Flyvbjerg, (2006) 'Inaccuracy in Traffic Forecasts'. Transport Reviews, Volume 26 (1), pp.1-24

India Infoline, (2003) 'Metro rail...2500less buses on roads!' An article on *http://www.indiainfoline.com*

Simhan T, (2000) 'Chennai's MRTS: Not on fast track', *Business Line* - A news letter by *The Hindu* dated 29th May 2000. *http://www.blonnet.com/businessline/ 2000/05/29/ stories/ 092971rs.htm*

Singh, Y P (2002). 'Performance of the Kolkata Metro Railway: A case study'. Cooperation for urban mobility in the developing world - Codatu - X, Pp. 337-342

Sreedharan, (2004) 'Mobility in major cities', Good Governance of India Volume 1, No. 4

The Hindu, (2005) A newspaper article dated 26th November 2005, New Delhi, India.

Vydhianathan, S., (2003) 'On the wrong track?' a newspaper article. *The Hindu* dated 28th September 2003.

16

Mumbai Urban Transport Project: Development and Challenges

P Nair and Deepak Kumar

The Suburban Railway system in Mumbai is perhaps the most complex, densely loaded and intensively utilized system in the world. Due to the magnitude of the project and the need for continuous assistance and involvement of the Government of Maharashtra, a separate corporation, the Mumbai Railway Vikas Corporation (MRVC) was set up jointly between the Ministry of Railways and the Government of Maharashtra. MRVC has made substantial improvements in the Mumbai suburban railway system since its inception, but it has to go a long way. This article discusses the developments and the challenges of MRVC. A brief description of suburban systems of different Indian metro cities has also been presented.

About Mumbai Urban Transport Project

Over 88 percent of the commuters in Mumbai travel by suburban trains or Bombay Electric Supply and Transport Undertaking (BEST) buses. In other words,

Source: The Icfai Journal of Infrastructure, March 2005.

Mumbai's Suburban Rail System carries about 64 lakh (6.4 million) passengers per day. On the other hand, about 4700 passengers travel in a 9-car rake during peak hours, with a rated carrying capacity of only 1,710[1] (Details in Box 1).

This has resulted in, what is known as, super dense crush load of 14-16 standing passengers per square metre of floor space![2] . Like other poor migrants in Mumbai, the people living in the railway slums could not find affordable housing when they came to the city and consequently were forced to make their homes wherever they could find space. Over the years, many of those who managed to find space to settle on government or privately owned land have gradually obtained informal tenure security as well as some basic services such as water, electricity and sanitation from the State Government. This has resulted in the expansion of the city boundaries.The fast expansion of the city has increased the need for quick, safer and reliable transportation-means running across the city.

Thus, the suburban railway system forms the backbone and is key to the development of Mumbai, the commercial capital of India. As a sequel to the Bombay Urban Transport Project (BUTP), which was completed in the year 1984, at a cost of about Rs.390 million, the MMRDA (Mumbai Metropolitan Region Development Authority) has formulated a multi-modal project viz. Mumbai Urban Transport Project (MUTP) to bring about improvement in traffic and transportation situation in the MMR with the World Bank assistance[3]. Mumbai Rail Vikas Corporation (MRVC), a joint venture of Indian railway and the Government of the Maharashtra, is set up for implementation of rail projects under MUTP.

Key Features

- It is one of the largest ongoing urban transportation projects in the country.
- Perhaps the most complex, densely loaded and intensively utilized system in the world, which has spread over 302 route kms and operates on 1500 Volt DC power supply.

---

1 *http://www.mrvc.co.in/intr.htm*

2 Ibid

3 *www.mmrdamumbai.org/projects_mutp.htm*

- Two Zonal Railways, the Western Railway and Central Railway, operate the Mumbai Suburban Railway system.
- It covers three areas i.e., railways, roadways and rehabilitation. The major part of the money has been invested in spreading the railway network. Till now, about 20,000 families have been relocated, which shows that the project also takes care of socio-infrastructure issues.

Partners and Funding of the Project

The project includes the partnership of the Government of Maharashtra (GOM), Indian Railways (IR), Mumbai Metropolitan Region Development Authority (MMRDA), Mumbai Railway Vikas Corporation Ltd. (MRVC Ltd.), Municipal Corporation of Greater Mumbai (MCGM) and Bombay Electric Supply and Transport Undertaking (BEST).

On June 18, 2002, the World Bank sanctioned a loan of Rs.26,020 million (US$542 mn) i.e., 57 percent of the total cost while the total estimated cost of the project is Rs.45,260 million (US$943 mn)[4]. In addition, MRVC plans to raise revenue from commercial development of railway and advertising space for financing future projects. The funding for the MUTP will come from the Government of Maharashtra, the Union Government, the railways and the World Bank.

The Ministry of Railways (MOR) incorporated MRVC Ltd., a public sector unit of the Government of India under Companies Act, 1956, on July 12, 1999. This was especially for the implementation of rail projects under MUTP. Under this project, the Ministry of Railways and Government of Maharashtra have shared an equity capital of Rs.25 crore in the ratio of 51:49 to implement the Rail Component of an integrated rail-cum-road urban transport project called MUTP[5], headquartered at Churchgate Station Annexe, Mumbai.

The entire cost of the Rail Component of the project is to be shared equally by the Ministry of Railways and the Government of Maharashtra. The purpose of the corporation is not only executing the projects identified so far, but is also involved in the planning and development of Mumbai Suburban Rail System.

---

4 Mumbai Metropolitan Region Development Authority

5 *http://www.all-science-fair-projects.com/science_fair_projects_encyclopedia/Mumbai_suburban_railway*

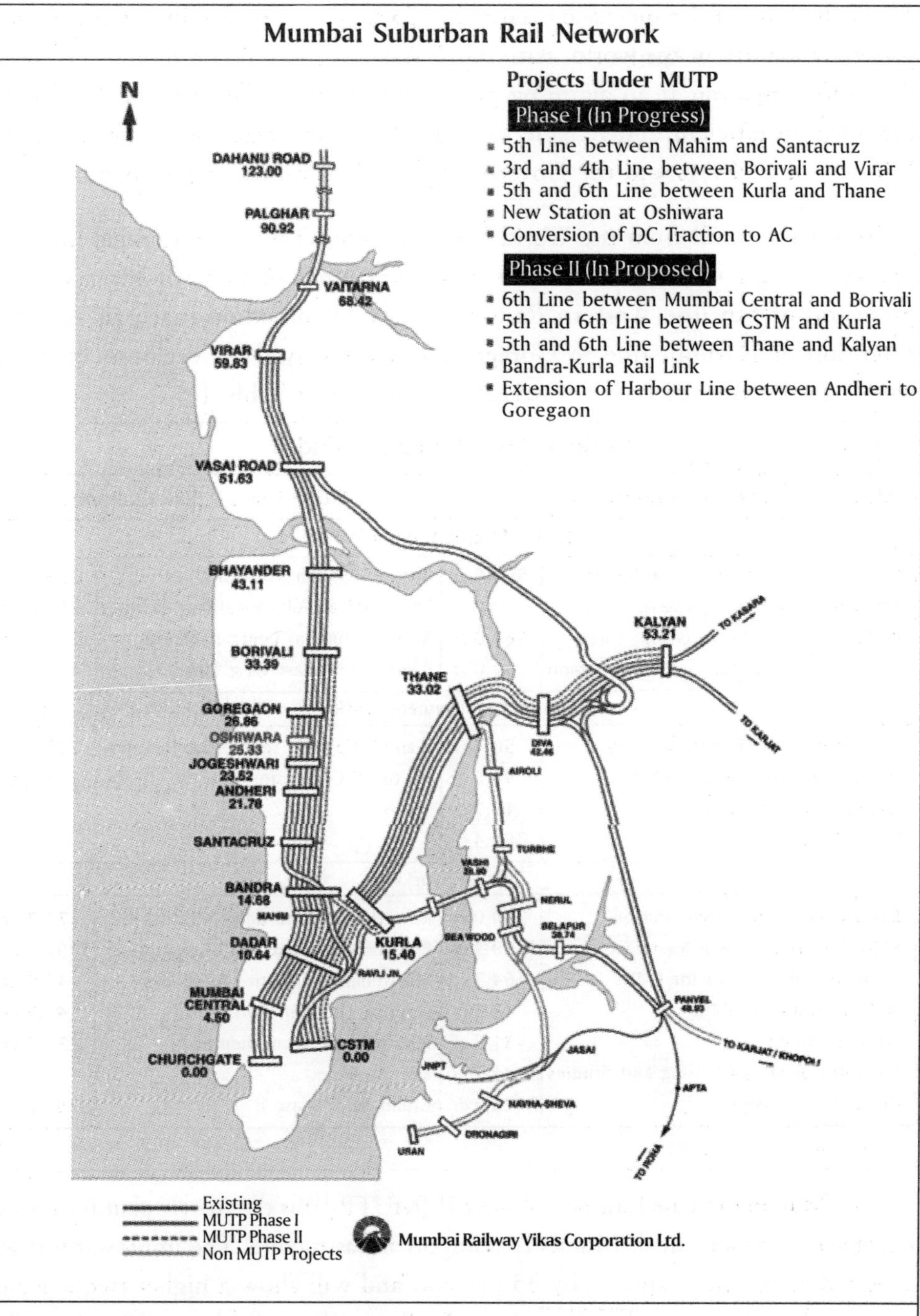

Source: http://www.mrvc.co.in/overview.htm

This is because of the increasing traffic in MSRS which no doubt has the highest passenger density in the world, with more than 6.1 million commuters.The tariff has been increasing at an alarming proportion, but despite this, the MSRS has provided an efficient and reliable service. This is the basic reason that led the Ministry of Railways and the Government of Maharashtra to join hands.

To get the funds from the World Bank, the project has been divided into two phases. Phase I included the works of Quadrupling of Borivali-Virar section, provision of 5th line Western Railway, Kurla-Thane additional pair of lines, extension of Harbour line to Goregaon and some system development works with a total estimated cost of Rs.3125.20 crore (refer Table 1).

Table 1: MUTP Phases I and II

MUTP Phase I (Rail Component)		MUTP Phase II (Rail Component)	
Capacity Augmentation Works			
Quadrupling of Borivali-Virar section	509.0 cr	Kurla-CSTM 5th and 6th Lines	229.0 cr
Provision of 5th Line Western Railway	59.0 cr	Thane-Kalyan Additional Pair of Lines	280.0 cr
Kurla Thane Additional Pair of Lines	166.0 cr	Borivali-Mumbai Central 6th Line	294.0 cr
Extension of Harbour Line to Goregaon	59.0 cr	Bandra-Kurla East West Link	480.0 cr
System Improvement Works			
Optimization of Western Railway	50.1 cr	S and T Upgrade to improve Headway	240.0 cr
Optimization of Central Railway	99.5 cr	DC to AC Conversion	147.0 cr
Optimization of Harbour Line	19.7 cr		
DC to AC Conversion	380.4 cr		
Other Works			
Resettlement and Rehabilitation	290.0 cr	Resettlement and Rehabilitation	71.0 cr
EMU Procurement and Manufacture	1359.2 cr	EMU Procurement and Manufacture	1967.0 cr
Maintenance Facilities for EMUs	64.3 cr	Maintenance Facilities for EMUs	42.0 cr
Stabling Lines for EMUs	48.5 cr	Stabling Lines for EMUs	42.0 cr
Track Machines	31.3 cr	Institutional Strengthening and Studies	30.0 cr
Institutional Strengthening and Studies	48.2 cr		
Grand Total Phase I	3125.2 cr	Grand Total Phase II	3881.0 cr

Source: www.mrvc.org.in

The Mumbai Urban Transport Project II (MUTP-II) is the master plan for further integrated development of Mumbai's transport infrastructure. The improvements are expected to increase capacity by 35 percent, and will allow a higher frequency of train services during peak hours. AC-DC Electronic multiple units have already been introduced as part of the optimization plan, and eventually all of the Mumbai suburban system will switch from the 1.5 KV DC traction system, to the 25 KV AC traction system which offers greater economies and efficiencies of operation[6]. By the way, the plan has been named 'MUTP-II', as it is a predecessor of MUTP-I, which was completed in 1984 and provided several improvements to the suburban services. Society for the Promotion of Area Resource Centres, (SPARC) has received the contract for preparing the Baseline Socio-Economic Survey (BSES) and the Resettlement Action Plans (RAPs) for the Project Affected Persons (PAPs) living along the railway track. SPARC has been assigned to carry out the work of 13 rails and one road sub-project under the Mumbai Urban Transport Project II.

Challenges Found

- Major projects like the MUTP II have been delayed since the State and the Central Governments have not been able to come to an agreement on the sharing of costs.
- **Constraints in Funding and Designing the Revenue Model:** The World Bank and other multilateral agencies have clearly indicated that funding would be available for viable and properly planned schemes. They want a portion of the funds to come from own sources, to ensure commitment from the local authorities. It would be unrealistic to expect all the repayments to be made through running revenue. The ideal situation would be to earn revenues so that at least the running expenses, plus interest, are met. For financing future projects, another challenge before MRVC will be – how to raise revenue from commercial development of railway land and air space.
- **Rehabilitation:** Apart from funding and designing the revenue model, there are various problems and challenges in implementing such a system. One of the foremost is slum clearance and relocation. Many of the central lines in particular have slum dwellers right on the tracks, which result in a number of deaths of slum dwellers per day. This considerably slows down the speed of the trains. The Railways argued that they are not responsible to shift the slum dwellers and it was considered to be the job of the

---

6 *http://irfca.org/faq/faq-metro.html*

authorities like the Municipal Corporation or the State Government Slum Clearance Board. But, till 1987, no significant result was seen. In 1988, however, Maharashtra's Housing Department suggested that the railways, the Mumbai State Government and SPARC should undertake a joint survey to assess the number of households encroaching on Railway-land and resettlement of the encroached households[7].

- **Future Financing:** The light rail system is a method by which a huge number of people can be transported, with a reasonable degree of comfort, at the lowest cost per rupee of investment and running expenditure. But the initial investments are huge, and have to be planned very carefully. There is also a need for a proper backup transport system to bring people from their homes to the nearest station. There are ample opportunities for earning revenue from this system, through passenger fares, advertising, provision of ancillary facilities etc. Such opportunities will reduce the burden on an already overburdened public exchequer.
- **Future Challenge:** In future, the implementation of switchable technologies and magnetic rails will be a challenge to the light rail transit systems of the Indian cities.

Accomplishments

- Conversion from DC to AC system of power for suburban trains saves a huge saving in energy losses, which has lowered the cost of operation and the longer trains have attained greater pulling power.
- Modern information system with proper displays and safer halting technologies have been established.
- The passengers get both tangible and intangible benefits because of the introduction of longer train lengths and new design coaches. With the introduction of longer train lengths, the overcrowding has been reduced and the carrying capacity of the passengers has been increased by almost 35 percent during peak hour. Moreover, the transit time has been reduced by 5-15 percent and has improved the punctuality of trains. This is really a win-win situation for MUTP and the passengers. With the introduction

7 *www.unescap.org/tctd/pubs/files/bulletin69_d.pdf*

of new design coaches, better riding quality can be felt because of better lighting, ventilation and air circulation and these have also facilitated the smooth and easy passenger flow inside the coach.

A list of the accomplishments of MUTP, given by the World Bank, is as follows:

	Benefits/Accomplishment	Beneficiaries
1.	Enhanced rail system capacity, improved efficiency and service quality.	Rail commuters and other travelers in MMR currently representing over 80% of the public traveling over 80% of the transport.
2.	Reduced congestion, travel time and delays for road traffic on project.	All road users but in particular: Commercial corridors/area vehicles on enhanced east-west, and roads over rail bridges (ROB), and bus users.
3.	Provision of title to house with improved basic amenities and opportunities for economic rehabilitation.	Families that will have to relocate or will be affected through displacement or through change in their economic status due to involuntary resettlement.
4.	Reduced emission from buses and other intensively used road vehicles.	Entire population of MMR but in particular, pedestrians and those living on or near to main traffic routes.
5.	Enhanced institutional capacity to plan, operate, manage and maintain the transport transport system.	All involved institutions in the sector; benefits should flow through to all users through better services.

Source: http://wbln1018.worldbank.org/sar/sa.nsf00f6d051364efafc485256ba70058c8a2 OpenDocument

Conclusion

There is no doubt that India needs such large integrated projects in order to ease the life of daily commuters. While there is no doubt that India lives in its villages, still the major engines of growth will continue to be through its major metros and mini-metros. This is particularly true as regards the growth of the service sector. It could be expected therefore that:

- The mini-metros such as Hyderabad, Ahmedabad, Pune and Jaipur would swell rapidly in size and population.

- Townships would develop on the outskirts of the 5 major metros and a rapid mass transit system would be needed to transport people to their places of work.

Cities such as Delhi, Kolkata, Hyderabad and Chennai already use trains for mass transit purposes and it is only a question of upgrading the existing systems (see Box 2). Other major cities are yet to get started, although there is much talk of the same. There is also a need to gradually ensure that such enterprises are run by management professionals with core expertise in the sector to ensure better maintenance and efficiency. The days of entrusting it to the municipality are over. Thus MRVC has a long way to go, in order to provide better services to its commuters.

(P Nair, Consulting Editor, The Icfai Journal of Infrastructure and a member of New Initiative Group, Icfai University. He can be reached at paddynair@icfai.org. Deepak Kumar was associated as Associate Consultant with the Icfai University Press, Hyderabad.)

Glossary

BSES – Baseline Socio-Economic Survey.

BEST – Bombay Electric Supply and Transport Undertaking.

BUTP – Bombay Urban Transport Project.

MMR – Mumbai Metropolitan Region.

MMRDA – Mumbai Metropolitan Region Development Authority.

MRVC – Mumbai Railway Vikas Corporation.

PAPs – Project Affected Persons.

RAPs – Resettlement Action Plans.

SPARC – Society for the Promotion of Area Resource Centres.

9-car rake – A Train containing 9 coaches.

12-car rake – A Train containing 12 coaches.

References

1. *www.mrvc.org.in*
2. *http://www.mrvc.co.in/intr.htm*

3. *Ibid*
4. *www.mmrdamumbai.org/projects_mutp.htm*
5. Mumbai Metropolitan Region Development Authority.
6. *http://www.all-science-fair-projects.com/science_fair_projects_encyclopedia/ Mumbai_suburban_railway*
7. *http://irfca.org/faq/faq-metro.html*

Box 1: The Lifeline of Mumbai City – Mumbai Local Railway

Mumbai is served by two zonal railways, the Western Railway (WR) and the Central Railway (CR). The railway suburban services, which are in fact metropolitan services in view of the frequency and short distances between stations, carry close to six million passengers per day on some 2000 daily EMU services. Mumbai metropolitan region is a continuous and united urban area and yet the two zonal railways, WR and CR, operate within the area as independent agencies with separate lines, separate policies and no service integration.

The suburban railway system in Mumbai is spread over 302 route Kms and it operates on 1500 Volt DC power supply from overhead catenary. The suburban services are run by Electric Multiple Units (EMUs). 181 rakes (train sets) of mainly 9-car (coach) and some 12-car composition are utilised to run 1942 train services to carry 6.04 million passengers per day.

Two corridors (one slow and the other fast) on WR run northwards from Churchgate terminus parallel to the west coast upto Virar (60 Kms). Two corridors on CR run from Chhatrapati Shivaji Terminus (CST) to Kalyan (54 Kms), from where it bifurcates in Kalyan-Kasara (67 Kms) in the northeast and Kalyan-Karjat-Khapoli (61 Kms) in southeast. The 5th corridor on CR runs as the harbour line starting from CST to Raoli Junction (11 Kms) from where the line splits. One line goes northwest to join WR at Bandra and goes upto Andheri (11 Kms) and the other goes eastward to terminate at Panvel (39 Kms) via New Mumbai.

Believe it or not, the rakes which ferry over 60 lakh commuters on one of the world's densest suburban railway networks were designed way back in the 1950s. Some of the rakes used on the Western and Central lines are three decades old and use an overhead 1500 V DC system of 1927 vintage. The aging rakes, which suffer from periodic faults, are incapable of handling the explosive passenger growth in the next century. Transport conditions for travellers are intolerable. Average peak hour loading of trains is in excess of 4500 passengers per train compared to a "design capacity" of about 1800 per train and "crush load capacity" of 2600 per train. Buses also tend to be overcrowded. There is, therefore, an urgent need to improve travelling conditions for public transport users to avoid encouraging a shift to private transport.

Source: http://www.geocities.com/mumbairail/railway.html

Box 2: Suburban Railway System in the Indian Metros

1. **Kolkata Metro and Suburban Railway:** The Kolkata Metro is the only underground railway system in India and currently more than 70 trains are being run every day carrying over 2 lakh passengers. It is a great relief to the daily passengers, as the road transport facility is really pathetic out there. However, the Kolkata metro needs further extension to cover the other untouched areas.

Kolkata suburban has a very well developed electronic motive utility system serving the suburbs of the metropolitan area. The headquarters of the Kolkata metro are at Metro Rail Bhawan, Jawahar Lal Nehru Road, Kolkata. The construction was begun in 1972 and finished in 1995. The metro line runs from Tollygunge to Dum Dum, about 16.5 km with 17 intermediate stations, in addition to two terminals. The extension is expected to be an elevated line and will bring the total route length to about 24.5 km. The termini are on the surface while the rest of the stations are underground. The Kolkata Metro uses a 5'6" gauge, and traction is via a third rail, using 750 V DC.

2. **Madras Rapid Transit System (MRTS)**

- MRTS is a partially elevated double track suburban railway in Chennai (Madras).
- The first phase of MRTS, from Beach to Thirumayilai, was opened on October 19, 1997. It consists of eight stations covering nine km long distance.
- MRTS Phase II is an extension of MRTS Phase I, which will extend from Thiruvanmiyur to Velachery, would cover 11 km and is still under construction and was scheduled for opening in the late 2005.
- MRTS Phase III an extension from Velachery to St. Thomas Mount station would cover 5.8 kms. The construction of phase III was expected to begin from 2004.

3. **Delhi Metro:** The project is a joint venture of the Government of India (Ministry of Urban Affairs) and the Delhi government. The need of Delhi metro was felt because of traffic burden and increase in pollution. The frequency of trains here is also optimum and subsequent improvement has been made in due course of time. There are 51 stations and unlike Kolkata, most part of this metro is opened. The ridership has been increased, as it has been considered more convenient transport mode in the fast moving life of Delhi and saves the time of the daily passengers. The ridership has been expected to increase at around 2.2 million passengers per day by 2006. This means that 2,600 less buses will run on the roads, which will increase the average speed of road buses from 10.5 km/h to 14 km/hour, which in turn will benefit in saving the time of 2 million man hours and saving of fuel cost worth Rs.5 billion per year. This will also reduce the accident rates and will improve the quality of life. Metro will reduce journey time by 50 to 75 percent. Thus, a rail network on the lines of the Delhi Metro is seen as commercially viable.

4. **Hyderabad Multi Model Urban Transport System:** The State Government has entered into a Memorandum of Understanding with Indian Railways for Multi Model Suburban Railway Services in the city of Hyderabad and its suburbs. The Falaknuma–Secunderabad, Secunderabad–Bollaram, Secunderabad– Lingampally, and Secunderabad–Nampally links are being taken up on priority basis. The State Government and the Indian Railways are sharing the expenditure on 50:50 basis. The first phase of the project is estimated to cost Rs.69 crore.

Contd...

Contd...

Just like the light rail systems in many states, a separate urban local body needs to be formed to raise resources and implement the various light rail projects in the state. This body could be wholly or partly government owned, depending on the socio-political framework. The recent report by TOI reveals that the State and Central Governments will bear the cost needed to put SPV on its feet for the phase II. The phase II route will include Secunderabad-Medchal-Mourhiradabad (43 Km), Falaknuma-Umdanagar-(20 km), and Secunderabad-Ghatkeskar (46 km). The Central Government will contribute 178.5 cr (i.e. approximately 50% of the total cost). With the completion of phase II, the traffic flow is being expected to increase to 1 lakh per day from 25,000 passengers per day and the income to be increased to 5 lakhs from 1 lakh at present. The new focus areas are – to increase the frequencies, aggressive advertisement of its services and to enhance the rail and bus connectivity.

17

Technology in Indian Metro Rail – A Boon to Commuters

Ajab Gandhi

India has been facing enormous difficulties in managing the congestion and traffic jams all over the country. The country faced this problem earlier with its major cities like Mumbai, Delhi, Kolkata, Chennai and Bangalore but now it seems that the problem has crossed tolerance limits and needs immediate attention as well as solutions.

The Kolkata metro which started operations in 1984 adopted various advanced technologies for the first time in India. Since then the metro has been successful in providing a range of benefits to commuters and plans for further expansion to enhance the services provided and to increase its reach further. Metro rail is a boon to commuters as they need not to travel by bus or personal transport. Also there would be no traffic jams and less travel time along with safety.

The successful completion of first phase of Delhi metro has opened avenues for development of metros in other cities. Various companies have provided support and service for the development of this metro in the Delhi, which has in turn

blessed the commuters with a safer and comfortable ride without any hassle. The prospects for development of the metros and the advancement of technology which can be accomplished are in store for us in the near future.

Introduction

India has been facing enormous difficulties to manage the congestion and traffic jams all over the country. The country faced this problem earlier with its major cities like Mumbai, Delhi, Kolkata, Chennai and Bangalore but now it seems that the problem has crossed tolerance limits and needs immediate attention as well as solutions. The various modes of public transports systems in the major cities have been overworking its capacity and are under immense pressure. To decongest the traffic in urban cities and provide faster and smoother travel to the commuters, various projects have been proposed incorporating elevated railway and underground railway apart from surface railway and city bus system. The Kolkata metro has been providing transport facilities since 1984, but the growing population has created avenues for its expansion. The successful completion of the first phase of Delhi metro has opened avenues for further development of the metros in other cities of India.

The Kolkata Metro – Technology First Timers in India

In 1969 the government took a decision to construct an underground railway system. This not only opened a new dimension in Indian Railways, but also gave a new dream to the people of Kolkata who were under deep trouble due to over population resulting in an acute transport problem. To meet the requirements and come up with a permanent solution, the government of India and the then Chief Minister of West Bengal, Dr. B. C. Roy, set up the Metropolitan Transport Project (MTP) (Railways) in 1969. Five rapid transit lines were predicted to be constructed as per the master plan prepared by the MTP (Railways) in 1971. These were[1]:

- Dum Dum to Tollygunge,

[1] Dr. Nilay Kumar Saha, "The Management Accountant"- Volume 40 No., "An Analytical Survey of Indian Metro Railway from 1995 to 2000", *http://myicwai.com/manacc/Dec05.pdf*, December 12, 2005.

- Sealdah to Howrah,
- Tollygunge to Garia,
- Sealdah to Salt Lake Town and
- Howrah to Howrah Maidan

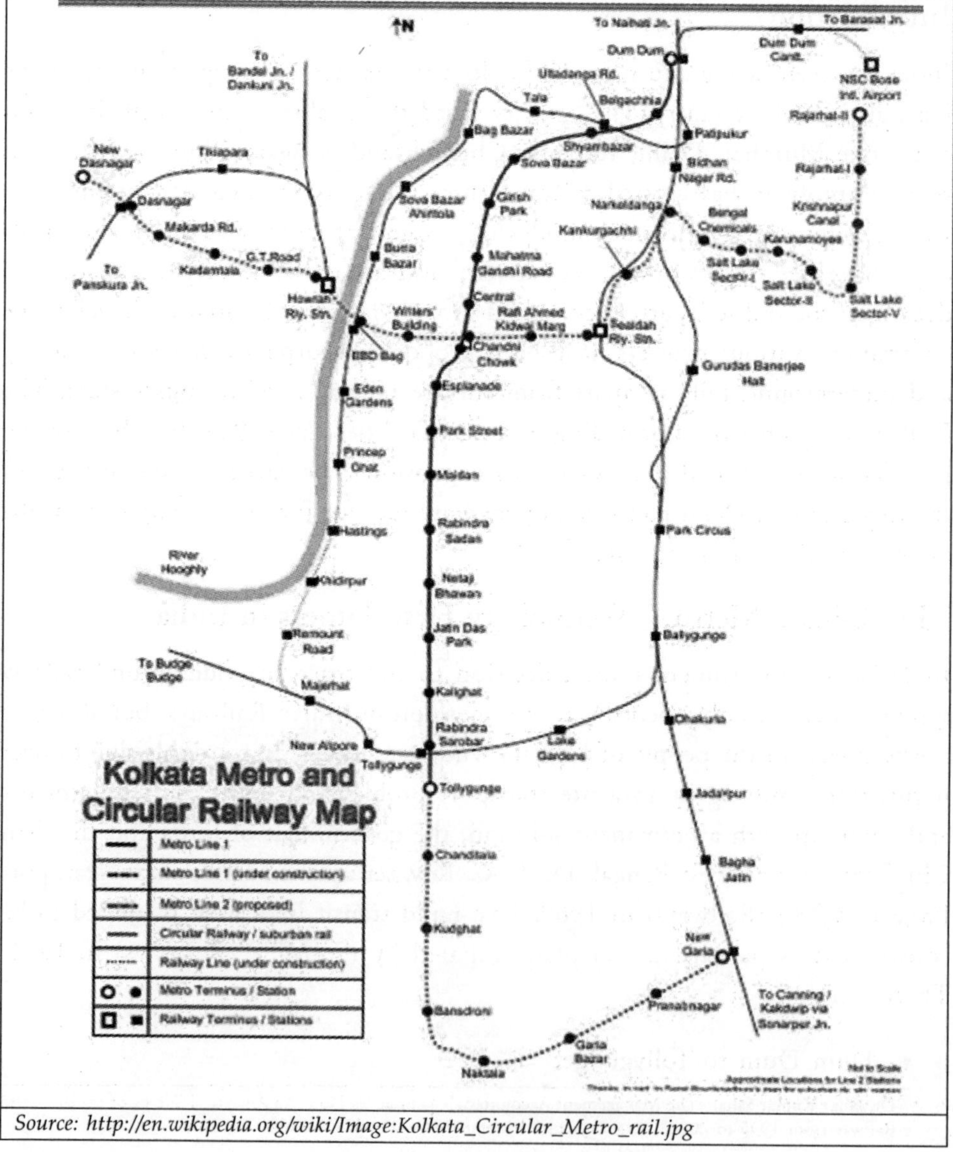

Source: http://en.wikipedia.org/wiki/Image:Kolkata_Circular_Metro_rail.jpg

Total route covered by all these lines would come to 97.5 kilometers.[2] The construction of the first line between Dum Dum and Tollygunge of 16.4 kms[3] in length should be given a very high priority was recommended by the team of five specialists and one technical secretary from USSR which was sent to India on 14th November 1970[4] to provide technical assistance to the Indian specialists. The construction of a metro rail is multipart which needs mode of applying various new technologies like civil, electrical, signaling and telecommunication engineering into it. For the first time Indian engineers were adopting advanced technologies in various fields with the help of their experience adjunct by foreign studies. This included certain criteria like:[5]

1. Using diaphragm walls and sheet piles by cut and cover method.
2. Using extensive decking to avoid traffic during construction in progress.
3. Using compressed air and airlocks in Shield tunneling.
4. Using elastic fastening, rubber pads, epoxy mortar and nylon inserts through ballastless track.
5. Using air-conditioning and ventilation system on stations and tunnels.
6. Proper current collection tracking system.
7. Application of dry type transformers and SF-6 circuit breakers on underground substations.
8. Application of VHF- radio communication system in subway.
9. Applying train control system based on micro-processor and supervisory remote control system.
10. Applying reflex mode of transaction and inspection system.

---

2 Dr. Nilay Kumar Saha, "The Management Accountant"- Volume 40 No., "An Analytical Survey of Indian Metro Railway from 1995 to 2000", *http://myicwai.com/manacc/Dec05.pdf*, December 12, 2005.

3 Ibid.

4 Ibid

5 *http://www.kolmetro.com/features/technical.html*

Moving People and Saving Time

Every technology has two sides of the coin. Many pervasive economic and social impacts were found to be experienced by the society too, in Metro rail project. How this project can be related to the society, can be seen by the following[6]:

1. It provides a source of income for the country which can be leveraged to increase productivity
2. It provides employment opportunities
3. It can attract assets from external sources
4. It provides a cheaper mode of transport decreasing travel time
5. It reduces pollution and is a very safe mode of transport

Despite of the above mentioned advantages, metro rail has been facing problem of not recovering the operating expenses. Not only that, the MTP (Railways) had to go through some situations uncalled-for because of lack of proper planning and unambiguity in authority's vision about the future outlook. This is evident from the fact that it took 22 years to complete the project. In addition to this, the report also stated that the construction of the axis starting from Dum Dum till Tollygunge was expected to be completed in 6 years i.e. by 1978 without any break. However it took many intervals in the course of completion of the project. The fastest means of transport MTP (Railways) of 16.45 kms[7] was thus completed in phases (1).

Kolkata Metro has been a pioneer in the real sense. It has not only been the first metro in the country, but has also proved the possibility of a metro rail system in a highly congested city. The efficiency and cleanliness that the metro rail has maintained in its functioning has prompted even *The Independent* of London to observe, *"Calcutta's Metro is cleaner than the underground in London or Paris. It runs better too"*.[8] The southern most point in Tollygunge was to be extended

---

6 Dr. Nilay Kumar Saha, "The Management Accountant"- Volume 40 No., "An Analytical Survey of Indian Metro Railway from 1995 to 2000", *http://myicwai.com/manacc/Dec05.pdf,* December 12, 2005.

7 Ibid.

8 Suhrid Sankar Chattopadhyay, "Metro Matters," Frontline Volume 22 - Issue 25, December 03 - 16, 2005, *http://www.flonnet.com/fl2225/stories/20051216003209400.htm*

by 8.7 km connecting New Garia covering six new stations as a part of second phase of the extension project sanctioned in 1999-2000 (3).

Over the past 20 years, metro rails performance has being proved to be helpful to the people of Kolkata but still its purpose is not served completely. *"The Metro was designed to decongest the city's roads. I am afraid it has not been able to do that, through no fault of its own, though, A. Chaturvedi, Chief Operations Manager, Kolkata Metro Railway"*[9], observed (3).

New Horizons – Plans Ahead

Tollygunge to Garia

The extension of the metro line from Tollygunge to Garia totaling 8.70kms is an ongoing project in Kolkata city. The project was sanctioned in 1999-2000 with an estimated cost of approximately Rs. 907 crores. The corridor has been planned on an elevated structure which will connect Eastern Railway at Garia. This section will also bring Kolkata's Central Business District close to the South 24-Parganas.

Princeghat to Majerhat

The extension from Princeghat to Majerhat runs 5.8kms in length with an estimated total project cost of Rs. 115 Crores. Out of the total stretch of 5.8kms, 3.2kms will be on elevated structure. This extension will benefit the people of South Kolkata immensely, as the completion of this extension will cover the periphery of entire Kolkata.

Dum Dum Cantonment to N S B Airport

The extension from Dum Dum Cantonment to N.S.B. Airport covers 4kms with total project cost of Rs. 62 Crores.

Kolkata's Underwater Metro Project

The Central Government cleared an underwater metro line project worth Rs. 4000 crores[10] connecting Kolkata with Howrah in November 2006. In 1984 when the first metro of India was inaugurated in Kolkata, the underwater metro

---

9 Suhrid Sankar Chattopadhyay, "Metro Matters," *Frontline* Volume 22 - Issue 25, December 03 - 16, 2005, *http://www.flonnet.com/fl2225/stories/20051216003209400.htm*

10 "Underwater metro in Kolkata gets central nod," *Hindustan Times*, 18 November, 2006, *http://www.hindustantimes.com/news/181_1847058,000600010003.htm*

plan had been thought by former Prime Minister Indira Gandhi. This metro will travel a distance of 19 kilometer covering 18 stations and plans to go under the Ganga River through a tunnel stretching 9 kilometers underwater from Ramrajatala in Howrah to Salt Lake. The plans are to design the corridor for a high density metro which would carry 60,000 to 75,000 people per hour in peak hours. This passage will link Dum Dum near the Netaji Subhash Chandra Bose International Airport to Tollygunge in South Kolkata covering 16.45kms. The West Bengal government has been permitted by the Centre to discuss the project details with Japan Bank of International Cooperation (JBIC). The government is exploring the feasibility for collaboration from private parties and the probability of Kolkata Metro Railways to bag this project seems to be high because of their experience of running a metro since decades.

The Delhi Metro – The Technology Behind it

Delhi based city-rail transportation has become an unavoidable compulsion as the road accident rate in Delhi is about 40 times[11] in excess of UK Delhi is facing rising population i.e. 57 lakh in 1981 to 138 lakh in 2001[12] but still short of a well-organized mass transportation system. Delhi is the only city in the world having public transportation system wholly road-based where roads have occupied 21 percent of the total city region[13] and the number of motor vehicles has increased from 5.4 lakh in 1981 to about 38 lakh in 2001[14], causing high risk of environmental pollution and road accidents (6).

Delhi's Transport

In 1989, the practical study for introducing MRTS for the first time in Delhi was done through (RITES) Rail India Technical and Economic Services by NCT and Central Government, for systematizing the traffic demand in future. For this project recommendation was made to have a rail-based system which would include a connection of elevated, underground and surface corridors totaling 198.5kms[15]. The NCT Government of Delhi has decided to execute the project

---

11 E Sreedharan, "Metro Rail in Delh", PIB Press Release, *http://pib.nic.in/feature/feyr2003/fjan2003/f020120031.html*, January 2, 2003.

12 Ibid

13 Ibid

14 Ibid

15 Ibid

in phases due to high cost, which involved an estimated cost to be Rs. 15,000 crore[16] at 1996 price level (6). As per the source: www.ircfa.org, the first phase comprises of three lines –

> *"**Line I**- Shahdara to Tis Hazari (8.3 km) - December 2002, Tis Hazari to Trinagar (4.8 km) - September 2003, Trinagar to Rithala (8.8 km) - March 2004, Rithala to Barwala (6.1 km) - March 2005.*
>
> ***Line II**- Delhi University to ISBT (4 km) - December 2004, ISBT to Central Secretariat (7 km) - September 2005.*
>
> ***Line III**- Connaught Place to W Patel Nagar (7 km) - September 2005, W Patel Nagar to Dwarka (16.5 km) - September 2005."*[17]

The Companies Behind the Scene

In May 1995 DMRC company was registered to support implementation and functioning of Delhi MRTS, in ownership of government, having equal sharing by the Central and state government. The completion period of the project was 10 years from April 1, 1995 to March 31, 2005 but it had interlude for 3 years, which actually started from April 1, 1998 adhering to the original completion target of 2005.

Financing

The completion cost without taxes and duties has been estimated at Rs.10, 570 crores.[18] This does not include the cost of line 3 extensions into Dwarka Subcity funded by DDA. In the project both the Centre and Delhi Government have equity of 30% while 56%[19] of the finance would be provided by Japan Bank of International Cooperation in the form of soft loan with the 30 years repayment period. Around 8%[20] of the project will be financed in the form of interest free

---

16 E Sreedharan, "Metro Rail in Delh", PIB Press Release, http://pib.nic.in/feature/feyr2003/fjan2003/f020120031.html, January 2, 2003.

17 "First phase of Delhi Metro inaugurated (NDTV)", *http://www.irfca.org/users/delhimetro/news/dec24.txt*, December 24, 2002.

18 E Sreedharan, "Metro Rail in Delhi", PIB Press Release, *http://pib.nic.in/feature/feyr2003/fjan2003/f020120031.html*, January 2, 2003.

19 Ibid

20 Ibid

loan as agreed to be given by the two governments to meet the cost of land acquisition. Remaining 6%[21] is to be sourced through property development.

Benefits[22]

- It is projected that the MRTS phase I network would be able to provide transit to 21.8 lakh passengers per day in 2005[23]. Three minutes of frequency have been planned for during peak hours the surface as well as underground corridors along with the system capacity to provide transportation facility to 60,000 – 75,000 passengers per hour each way.[24]
- Air-conditioning and ventilation system has being designed in tunnels and coaches to meet the climatic conditions of Delhi, especially in the month of July and October where humidity levels are high.
- Smart card ticketing through automatic mode are provided to metro passengers. It is read through laser and no bodily access is needed, whereas it can be used for single or multiple journeys based on the value of the card. Multiple journeys can be done by purchasing a ticket of higher amount once and its value gets reduced by readers installed at the MTRS stations.
- The control centre of the DMRC has an optic fibre communication channel which monitors the entire fare collection system whereas the mechanical entrance flap gates through which 45 to 60 passengers can pass are used to control all entry points of the stations.
- The idea of DMRC's integration of metro ticket with DTC and other services in the capital would be novel and revolutionary idea under consideration. This integration would make the same ticket valid for buses and trains.
- The pressure on DMRC stations gets reduced through proper outsourcing planning, by handing over the task of selling the stored value cards to nominated vendor in different parts of the city.

---

21 E Sreedharan, "Metro Rail in Delhi", PIB Press Release, *http://pib.nic.in/feature/feyr2003/fjan2003/f020120031.html,* January 2, 2003

22 Ibid

23 Ibid

24 Ibid

- DMRC power requirement is three percent of total peak hour needed by Delhi area which is very minimal. Considering the present power system design, all other synchronization system consisting of trains, lifts, air-conditioning, escalators etc would need 75 MW[25].
- In MRTS system designing will be taken utmost care as power supply will be sourced from three different centers which will provide a support to each other. In case of power failure, emergency lighting facility has been provided in tunnel and MRT stations with the help of generators.

Conclusion

The future prospects are an inter–relation between the needs of Indian Railways and the requirement for modernization of mass transit in urban cities. The emphasis is heavily laid on the safety and comfort of the passengers along with the interest of various cities in the long term. The plans for further expansion and initiation of metros in other cities like Mumbai and Bangalore pose a huge potential and a boom in the infrastructure segment.

(Ajab Gandhi, Research Associate at Icfai Business School Research Center, Ahmedabad).

References

1. Dr. Nilay Kumar Saha, "The Management Accountant"– Volume 40 No., "An Analytical Survey of Indian Metro Railway from 1995 to 2000", *http://myicwai.com/manacc/Dec05.pdf*
2. *http://www.kolmetro.com/features/technical.html*
3. Suhrid Sankar Chattopadhyay, "Metro Matters," *Frontline* Volume 22 – Issue 25, December 03 - 16, 2005, http://www.flonnet.com/fl2225/stories/20051216003209400.htm
4. "Underwater metro in Kolkata gets central nod," *Hindustan Times*, 18 November, 2006, *http://www.hindustantimes.com/news/181_1847058,000600010003.htm*
5. *http://www.indiainfoline.com/infr/spfe/delh.htmld*
6. E Sreedharan, "Metro Rail in Delhi", PIB Press Release, *http://pib.nic.in/feature/feyr2003/fjan2003/f020120031.html*, January 2, 2003.
7. *http://en.wikipedia.org/wiki/Kolkata_Metro*
8. "First phase of Delhi Metro inaugurated (NDTV)", *http://www.irfca.org/users/delhimetro/news/dec24.txt*, December 24, 2002.

[25] E. Sreedharan, "Metro Rail in Delhi", PIB Press Release, *http://pib.nic.in/feature/feyr2003/fjan2003/f020120031.html*, January 2, 2003.

18

Sky Bus: A Technological Innovation of India

Ajab Gandhi

India has been facing problems related to urban congestion and traffic jams for many years in its major cities and persistent efforts to transform its urban transportation system have met with roadblocks in the form of bureaucracy and red tapism. The alternatives to Sky Bus like elevated railways and underground railways which would help the surface railways in reducing the urban congestion fail because of elevated railways being evasive and underground railways posing risks of fire and evacuation. The 'Sky Bus' for urban public transportation is an innovation of Indian Railways which took more than 20 years for development and was certified by TUV Inter Traffic GmbH of Germany for its safety. Sky Bus would work better in Indian cities because this technology would not disturb the city plan and would still be effective. The various benefits of Sky Bus are zero percent possibility of derailment and death on rail track, a workable solution to ease urban congestion and reduce pollution levels in the cities. After an accident during a trial run in 2004, the project did not receive a clearance from the

Central Government. This incident raised apprehensions about passenger safety and the project got delayed. The cause of the accident and the related findings are highlighted in this article, summarizing the way forward for the restart of the project. An outline of some of the proposed Sky Bus projects for Mumbai, Mangalore and Hyderabad are given in the end.

Introduction

Anyone residing in any of the major cities of India would agree that the need of the hour for our congested cities is an efficient, safe and reliable public transport system. Such a system would create solutions for transport of people and goods through use of rail-based coaches. The reason why only rail-based solution is preferable is no road-based solution or rubber-tyred solution would work for mass transit of people in the city. Only rail-based solution, railway technology is needed. However, the inadequate infrastructure prevalent in various cities does not complement the technology required for a railway system which impedes the use of such a transport system. Moreover, past incidents of derailments limits the scope of such a system as people may fear the trains from the overhead bridge structure.

"Sky Bus" is the right answer to these problems. Using a connection between the railway tracks and the coaches, in such a way that no derailment takes place, as well as no capsizing occurs, Sky Bus provides a safer and more reliable mode of transport. It further improves the already proven railway technology.[1]

The Transport System in India and its Challenges

With over 1.1 billion people, urban congestion and traffic jams have emerged as serious concerns in India. The public transportation in major metro cities of India has been overloaded. The elevated railway or underground railway systems are the alternatives to be considered, as they can help in decreasing traffic load on existing surface railway and city bus system but both pose risks of fires and evacuations respectively. The requirement of the country is a system which would

---

1 Er B Rajaram, "Sky Bus Metro System," 13 April 2005. *http://www.atrilab.com/Sky Bus/SkyBusMetroimprovesrailway.pdf*

not disturb the existing city infrastructure but at the same time provide efficient, reliable and safe transport to its residents. To address this problem, an innovative solution – 'Sky Bus' has been introduced for urban public transportation. The patent for this innovation has been acquired worldwide during 2001and 2004. In the safety point of view, it took in excess of 20 years to develop and obtain certification by TUV Inter Traffic GmbH of Germany. The existing Indian Railways have bad history of accidents with more than 2000 deaths[2] each year on rail tracks, as per records. On the other hand, there is technically zero per cent possibility of derailment and death on rail track in case of Sky Bus, which is a great transformation. The technology of Sky Bus will also help in reducing pollution levels in the cities (M Gulawani,n.d)(2).

For this project technical collaboration has been provided by the Austrian Company Elin EBG Traction. Although various government and non-government organizations are providing support, Sky Bus project has been going at a slow pace (M Gulawani,n.d) (2).

Sky Bus Metro System

The "Sky Bus Metro" system is the brainchild of B. Rajaram (Former MD/Konkan Railway Corporation) with the objective to address the problem of transportation of people. His invention was patented by the US and he also tested his invention on a test track in Goa.

2 Makarand Gulawani, "Sky Bus Of India: 21st Century Innovation In Urban Public Transportation," *http://www.ifz.tugraz.at/index_en.php/filemanager/download/300/Gulawani_SA%202004.pdf*

The following specifications are required for the Sky Bus technology:[3]

a) 52 to 60 kg/m heavy rails placed at standard gauge

b) 8 meters X 2 meters box enclosure

c) Supporting columns of diameter 1 meter at a distance of 15 meters and at a height of 8 meters above the road surface.

These specifications provide support and guidance for powered bogies to run at 100 km/hr, thus carrying passengers comfortably without disturbing the existing road traffic. The design of the fixed structure required for the smooth functioning of the Sky Bus at 8 meter height above road level does not pose any threat to the road users. This unique mass transit system does not have any signaling as well as crossing making it safer than the existing rail-based systems. The Sky Bus metro operates along existing roadways and within municipal limits, hence falls under

Parameter	**Sky Bus offers**
Performance	• Scalability up to 20000 passengers/hr • Cargo handling ability • Speeds up to 110 km/hr
Safety	• Sky Bus is collision protected • Like existing metro rail system it can never get separated from the tracks – so there is no hazard of accident
Protection to existing city infrastructure	• It does not require new land but makes use of space above the existing structure of Bus system • Can go where a bus goes with short stations of 50 m length
Costs	• On an average the capital cost of double line route is Rs.50 cr per km, including all rolling-stock and train control as compared to Delhi which spent Rs.120 cr on elevated metro. • Due to maintenance-free tracks and coach bodies, the maintenance costs are very less in the Sky Bus

Contd...

[3] "Sky Bus (The Urban Transport Technology for the New Millennium)", *http://www.konkanrailway.com/website/ehtml/sky_bus.htm*

Contd...	
Construction	• The routine life of city would not disturb much because it uses pre-fabricated technologies during construction
	• Construction of Sky Bus can be done in much less time as compared to other metro rails construction
Charges for travel	• The charges are very affordable to regular city passengers, they can travel 500 km per month at just Rs.250.
Financial viability	• Sky Bus Metro can give a 15% to 20% return through fare-box collections and commercial usage of the extra urban space. Also, if about 60% to 70% debt is used, then the capital can be recovered within 7 to 10 years.

the tramway category, under Art 366(20) of the Constitution of India and is excluded from Indian Railways Act.

The "Sky Bus" has several advantages over the traditional transport systems like the monorail or light/heavy metro rail.[4]

Advantages of Sky Bus

Sky Bus needs smaller stations as compared to conventional mass transit systems, waiting time for passengers is almost nil as it can give service in every 30 seconds or 1 minute. Sky Bus is fully automated with air condition coaches and automatic doors requiring no drivers or guards and entry points are monitored through electronic prepaid cards. Stations provide only access facility and do not serve as a place facilitating passenger holding. Sky Bus is considered to be the best alternative for Indian Railways to meet the needs of the urban public transportation system. It is the best way out which will lead to the following advantages:[5]

4 Er B Rajaram "Sky Bus Metro System," 13 April 2005, *http://www.atrilab.com/Skybus/SkybusMetroimprovesrailway.pdf*

5 Makarand Gulawani, "Sky Bus Of India: 21st Century Innovation In Urban Public Transportation," *http://www.ifz.tugraz.at/index_en.php/filemanager/download/300/Gulawani_SA%202004.pdf*

1. No extra land is needed to be acquired apart from access to be provided on existing roadways and land of approximately 2000 to 4000 square meters at terminal points.
2. No disturbance to existing structures and gardens.
3. It is safer as the track is not susceptible to disturbing elements engaged into vandalism.
4. Quick and easy exit in a situation of fire.
5. As derailment or capsizing is not possible in the case of Sky Bus, it is safer than other modes of rail transport.
6. Financially viable because of lower capital cost than elevated and underground metro system.
7. It involves very less amount of running cost as the tracks are maintenance free and it requires no points or crossings due to the latest technology used in it.
8. As the train consists of coaches with fully automated door system, no death will occur due to falling off from train unlike in normal metro system leading to 2 to 3 deaths.
9. As the Sky Bus uses the present busy roads unlike normal railways, it helps in reducing the congestion on the roads and providing wide reach.
10. The time requirement for construction is relatively very less than other metro systems.
11. It is protected against flood and rain hazards, and other obstacles of the track.
12. One single authority at state level can handle and implement the whole project, because it runs on the tracks in the sky, which is different from the existing railway system.
13. Its construction is not at a barrier as it can be constructed on roads with fly over.
14. It does not obstruct the road traffic and requires no under or over bridges.
15. Sky Bus is free from noise and air pollution.

Test Run of the Sky Bus in Goa

Sky Bus's inventor – Rajaram had to put lot of efforts to negotiate with ministers and urban planners and ultimately the railway ministry authorized KRCL to utilize Rs.50 crore[6] out of its own funds to put up the test track. The land was allotted by the state government of Goa; the prototypes of bogies were created by IIT-Mumbai and local company, Kineco, while raw material was provided at discount rate by private companies like L&T, Tata Steel and ACC. It took eight months for the completion of a 1.6-km test track in Goa. Two coaches with overhead tracks on the underside of a concrete structure hung at a height of about eight meters from the ground. Even on the day of the test ride the rails were greased and oiled and the final touches were given to the paint [3].

The Sky Bus is a fully automated system requiring no drivers or guards but still it can be operated by 'sky man' manually. The air-conditioned travel in the Sky Bus, with its wide windows, and gliding comfort, could be superior to any other mode of city travel. However, the Sky Bus can provide seating arrangement for only 15 people in each coach, while others have to stand. The reason behind this arrangement is that the traveler will use Sky Bus to travel short distances of 4-5 kms, which could be covered within 7 minutes, therefore requiring no elaborate seating arrangement. Alternatively, around 150[7] people can stand comfortably in the additional space provided in every coach. Sky Bus had just successfully completed its first run and for KR Engineers team, this was the first move. Once the technology in Sky Bus is proved, it is to be marketed to private parties. For this, Konkan Railway jointly with PricewaterhouseCoopers (PwC) has invited bids for technology licensing of the skybus from private parties. Interested party, having a minimum networth of Rs. 150 crore[8], can select a 10 km Sky Bus route in the city as per their choice and bid for the project. In order to use this technology they will be required to pay 10% of construction costs[9] in the form of royalty to the KRCL [3].

---

6 Supriya Kurane, "A Ride in the Sky," *Businessworld*, 4 October 2004, *http://www.businessworld.in/oct0404/invogue01.asp*

7 Ibid.

8 Ibid.

9 Ibid.

Accident during Trial Run – Findings and Way Forward[10]

B Rajaram had identified the cause of the accident that took place during the trial run of the Sky Bus on 25th September 2004. He mentioned in the report available on the website *www.konkanrailway.com* that, the accident took place due to severe skidding of the Sky Bus system but 'skid marks' were not observed on the rail.

According to the report, Sky Bus seemed to have skidded while changing the direction on the entry of curve due to the presence of water and grease on top of the rail which caused the swerving. This is similar to the heavy vehicles skidding on the road because of the presence of a mixture of oil and water on the road. The coach should not have hit the column because the design of the Sky Bus even at the speed of 50 km/hr but it did hit the column, which was unfortunate. There is no other explanation or reason for the mishap that happened on 25th September 2004.

In the first run of the system, there were no problems with grease etc., because there was no drizzle during that time. But in the second run drizzle caused addition of water to grease which lead to the swerve of the bogie. The entire rail top was cleaned 10 days before, and the presence of grease on rail top is a great matter of concern.

Before the project restarts, the following are to be ensured[11]:

1. There should be a provision of mechanical braking systems with additional redundancy.
2. Any emergency mechanical brakes should be applied only after applying electrical brakes for control.
3. Just manual mode running should be executed. Auto driving devices are to be used in background as these are helpful in implementing brakes rather than driving, thereby acting as an Anti Collision Device (ACD).
4. In the first phase trials, signaled train control system to be implemented and the driverless system will be adopted later on, after six months of successful running according to the original plans.

---

10 *http://www.konkanrailway.com/website/skybusmetro/Test_Track/skybus_accident_report.pdf*

11 Ibid

Extending the Sky Bus Technology to Other Cities

Following the successful trial of the Sky Bus in Goa, the Kanada Chamber of Commerce and Industry (KCCI) proposed to the Konkan Railway Corporation to implement Sky Bus in Mangalore city. A top Malaysian company is also gearing up to begin negotiations with Indian authorities for the construction of 'Sky Bus Metro' in Hyderabad, after a techno-feasibility study.[12]

These two cities are just the beginning for the introduction of Sky Bus transport in India. Moving on, the city of Mumbai (famous for its local train network), is also preparing to introduce the Sky Bus transport system in the city.[13] In 2002, the Mumbai suburban railway system registered a death every 2.5 hours due to a railway accident, the highest in the world. With the highest density of vehicles per kilometer, Sky Bus is the best alternate mode of transport which can decrease the traffic load on the existing railway system. It is the best option for the highly populated metro cities of India, where availability of extra land to construct a new transport system is less likely.

Conclusion

Sky Bus is an excellent way for Indian Railways to meet the requirements of urban public transportation. It not only provides a cheaper mode of transport but also ensures safety and reliability.

(Ajab Gandhi, Research Associate at Icfai Business School Research Center, Ahmedabad).

References

1. Er B Rajaram, "Sky Bus Metro System," 13 April 2005, ***http://www.atrilab.com/Skybus/SkybusMetroimprovesrailway.pdf***
2. Makarand Gulawani, "Sky Bus of India: 21st Century Innovation in Urban Public Transportation," ***http://www.ifz.tugraz.at/index_en.php/filemanager/download/300/Gulawani_SA%202004.pdf***

---

12 "Hyderabad to get Sky Bus Metro by 08" 10 October 2005, ***http://www.rediff.com/money/2005/oct/10sky.htm***

13 Jaya Goyal, "Sky Bus vs Metro: Mumbai Deserves the Best", August 26, 2006, ***http://www.atrilab.com/files/JayaGoyalin_ORF.pdf***

3. Supriya Kurane, "A Ride in the Sky," *Businesworld*, 4 October 2004, *http://www.businessworld.in/oct0404/invogue01.asp*
4. "Hyderabad to get Sky Bus Metro by '08," *http://www.rediff.com/money/2005/oct/10sky.htm*
5. Jaya Goyal, "Sky Bus vs. Metro: Mumbai Deserves the Best," 26 August 2006, *http://www.atrilab.com/files/JayaGoyalin_ORF.pdf*
6. *http://www.konkanrailway.com/website/skybusmetro/Test_Track/skybus_accident_report.pdf*
7. "Sky Bus (The Urban Transport Technology for the New Millennium)", *http://www.konkanrailway.com/website/ehtm/sky_bus.htm*

Index

D

E

J

K

L

Y